The Politics of
Public Space

The Politics of Public Space

Edited by

Setha Low
and
Neil Smith

Routledge
Taylor & Francis Group
New York   London

Published in 2006 by
Routledge
Taylor & Francis Group
270 Madison Avenue
New York, NY 10016

Published in Great Britain by
Routledge
Taylor & Francis Group
2 Park Square
Milton Park, Abingdon
Oxon OX14 4RN

© 2006 by Taylor & Francis Group, LLC
Routledge is an imprint of Taylor & Francis Group

Printed in the United States of America on acid-free paper
10 9 8 7 6 5 4 3 2 1

International Standard Book Number-10: 0-415-95138-0 (Hardcover) 0-415-95139-9 (Softcover)
International Standard Book Number-13: 978-0-415-95138-8 (Hardcover) 978-0-415-95139-5 (Softcover)
Library of Congress Card Number 2005008804

Library of Congress Cataloging-in-Publication Data

The politics of public space / edited by Setha Low and Neil Smith.
    p. cm.
    "This volume grew out of a conference held at the CUNY Graduate Center ... co-sponsored by the CUNY Public Space Research Group and the Center for Place, Culture, and Politics located at the Graduate Center, and by the Alen Institute"--Pref.
   Includes bibliographical references and index.
   ISBN 0-415-95138-0 (hb : alk. paper) -- ISBN 0-415-95139-9 (pb : alk. paper)
   1. Public spaces--Political aspects--Congresses. 2. Public spaces--Government policy--Congresses. 3. Democracy--Congresses. 4. Social control--Congresses. I. Low, Setha M. II. Smith, Neil.

HT153.P654 2005
304.2'3--dc22
                                         2005008804

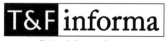

Taylor & Francis Group
is the Academic Division of T&F Informa plc.

Visit the Taylor & Francis Web site at
http://www.taylorandfrancis.com

and the Routledge Web site at
http://www.routledge-ny.com

Contents

Preface

This volume grew out of a conference held at the City University of New York (CUNY) Graduate Center entitled "The Politics of Public Space." It was cosponsored by the CUNY Public Space Research Group and the Center for Place, Culture and Politics located at the Graduate Center, and by the Van Alen Institute. The cornerstone of the conference was the recognition that public spaces are no longer, if they ever were, democratic places where a diversity of peoples and activities are embraced and tolerated. Instead, they have become centers of commerce and consumption, as well as places of political surveillance. The connections between public space and political and cultural economy deserve closer scrutiny because public spaces are simultaneously an expression of social power and a force themselves that help shape social relations.

We are grateful to the Graduate Center for a Faculty Development grant in association with the conference, and to President Frances Degen Horowitz and Provost Bill Kelly for introducing the event. In addition to the authors represented in this volume, a number of other scholars also participated in the event and we would like to thank them for their contributions: Rosemarie Bletter, Michelle Fine, Nancy Fraser, Raymond Gastil, William Kornblum, Jerome Krase, Victoria Pitts, Leanne Rivlin, Ida Susser, Elin Waring, Maurya Wickstrom, Cindy Wong, and Sharon Zukin. We are also indebted to Mike Lamb and Megan Schauer at the Center for Place, Culture and Politics for helping to make the conference such a successful event.

Our editor, Dave McBride, and the editorial staff at Routledge, guided this multi-authored volume through the many stages of production with speed and good humor. One editorial issue did arise when we found that the historians and social scientists use quite different bibliographic formats. We decided to retain these stylistic differences as part of this interdisciplinary endeavor.

CHAPTER 1

Introduction: The Imperative of Public Space

NEIL SMITH AND SETHA LOW

This is a pivotal moment for examining the politics of public space. The broad decay of twentieth-century American liberalism provides the crucial context for the restructuring of what counts as public space today, and this in turn was sparked by a range of social shifts and transformations: reactions against the liberatory maelstrom of 1960s politics; the implosion of official communism after 1989; and the consequent neoliberal onslaught after the 1980s. Together these developments brought a trenchant reregulation and redaction of public space. A creeping encroachment in previous years has in the last two decades become an epoch-making shift culminating in multiple closures, erasures, inundations, and transfigurations of public space at the behest of state and corporate strategies. In part, these are the result of supposedly antiterrorist policies initiated after the events of September 11, 2001, especially the far-reaching effects of the U.S. Patriot Act and related legislation, which produced a wholly unprecedented circumscription of popular uses of public space. From city parks to public streets, cable and network news shows to Internet blog sites, the clampdown on public space, in the name of enforcing public safety and homeland security, has been dramatic. Public behavior once seen simply as eccentric, or even protected by First Amendment rights, is now routinely treated as a potential terrorist threat.

The clampdown on public space, however, is not simply due to a heightened fear of terrorism after 2001, and it has many local- as well as national-scale inspirations. Many public uses of space are increasingly outlawed and policed in ways unimaginable a few years previously, but these rights were already under concerted attack well before 2001. The assertion of neoliberalism since the 1980s harkens back not to the somewhat progressive appeal of a twentieth-century American social liberalism but to the more conservative doctrines of seventeenth- and eighteenth-century liberalism. The latter were certainly progressive for their time. Adam Smith's modern political economy and John Locke's legal enlightenment (borne forth by revolutions from France to Haiti to the United States) dispatched the aristocratic elitism of the feudal era to the dustbin of history, opening up the market and the voting booth to anyone with the political standing (and socioeconomic collateral) to participate. While their doctrines liberated the emerging bourgeoisie from monarchical tutelage, they also enshrined universal private property (for those with the requisite military or economic wherewithal) at the expense of the long tradition of common land. The profitable use of space, Locke argued, justifies a certain kind of "natural rights"–based privatization of the commons against those who would occupy space merely for purposes of subsistence. The subsequent global land grab by the European bourgeoisie established private property immediately, undercutting land claims based on the logic of "special interests," such as dispossessed peasants, workers, and the poor. When property owners and participants in the market vote in their own interests, according to the new Enlightenment doctrine, the collective commonweal is ensured: property owners and consumers in the marketplace are the new citizens. As this principle is rediscovered at the beginning of the twenty-first century, we should understand that "neoliberalism" is a very precise definition of the conservatism overtaking us. Thomas Hobbes was also a child of the Enlightenment, and his deification of the state as the necessary prophylactic against social unrest has increasingly clear echoes today. Certainly by the 1990s, many urban citizens came to feel that daily life had become a *bellum omnium contra omnes*—a war of all against all, as Hobbes put it with such dour finality. With revanchist panache, this notion was implicitly mobilized by New York Mayor Rudy Giuliani, and public space was made the central target of that battle. The document that launched New York's zero-tolerance policy, a policy now globalized in cities around the world, was subtitled "Reclaiming the Public Spaces of New York" (Giuliani and Bratton, 1994; Smith, 2001).

The point of this volume is to highlight the historical and geographical specificity of repoliticized public space precisely in order to raise the possibility of a different politics of public space. It comes on the heels of several decades of critical social theory concerning space, much of it launched from within the discipline of geography but having a far broader influence. For many, the utterly quixotic notion of the "production of space," coined by Henri Lefebvre more than three decades ago, has become common sense. As well, it broadens and especially deepens our sense of public space inherited from twentieth-century American liberalism. In that latter tradition, a fairly straightforward opposition pertains between public and private space. However, in this book we attempt to wedge open a more multifaceted politics of public space that draws as much on the produced nature of space as on any necessary opposition either to private space or to the abstractness of space that was Lefebvre's principal target. This involves historical and political economic analyses of public space, but it also involves analyses that take the geography of the public sphere—public space—seriously. Equally and connected, it involves a spirited polemical engagement with the people and processes that are remaking the politics of public space.

A multiplicity of divergent meanings attaches to "public," "public space," and the "public sphere." By "public space" we mean the range of social locations offered by the street, the park, the media, the Internet, the shopping mall, the United Nations, national governments, and local neighborhoods. "Public space" envelops the palpable tension between place, experienced at all scales in daily life, and the seeming spacelessness of the Internet, popular opinion, and global institutions and economy. It is also not a homogenous arena: The dimensions and extent of its publicness are highly differentiated from instance to instance. Legally as well as culturally, the suburban mall is a very different place from the national park or the interior of a transcontinental airliner. Clearly then, the term has a broad definition. Stretching back to Greek antiquity onward, public space is almost by definition urban space, and in many current treatments of public space the urban remains the privileged scale of analysis and cities the privileged site. Far more rare are analyses that take rural space or global space, for example, as public, and while we retain here a focus on the urban we also broaden our purview. Public space includes very recognizable geographies of daily movement, which may be local, regional, or global, but they also include electronic and institutional "spaces" that are every bit as palpable, if experienced quite differently, in daily life.

Public space is traditionally differentiated from private space in terms of the rules of access, the source and nature of control over entry to a space, individual and collective behavior sanctioned in specific spaces, and rules of use. Whereas private space is demarcated and protected by state-regulated rules of private property use, public space, while far from free of regulation, is generally conceived as open to greater or lesser public participation. "Public space" has very different meanings in different societies, places, and times, and as all of this suggests, its meaning today is very much bound up with the contrast between public and private space. It is impossible to conceive of public space today outside the social generalization of private space and its full development as a product of modern capitalist society.

In this respect, the ancient Greek polis and agora, often and reasonably heralded as significant prototypes of the public sphere and public space, respectively, are rather different from today's public space. The agora was not defined against the ubiquity of private, capitalized space but vis-à-vis far more collective uses of space. Rights in the polis were highly restricted to a very narrow and privileged social class recognized as free citizens, and many others were excluded—women, slaves, and the throng of common people. Likewise, the publicness of the agora was also circumscribed (albeit in different fashion) and stratified as an expression of prevailing social relations and inequalities. The narrow definition of public space that pertained in ancient Greece may therefore be an unintentionally appropriate inspiration for the present, yet the most cursory scrutiny suggests that it also represents the converse of what we take to be the ideal public space. In practice, in both the Greece of old and the Western world today, truly public space is the exception not the rule.

Public space, in fact, only comes into its own with the differentiation of a nominally representative state on the one side and civil society and the market on the other. Implicated in this transition is the simultaneous pupation of the household as a privatized sphere of social reproduction. Prior to the emergence of the representative bourgeois state, any public sphere was far more partial, fragmented, and local; and with such a partial public sphere the publicness of space in the broad geographical sense can be considered formal, at best, rather than real. Public space comes about as a specific expression of civil society but does not remain contained within it; rather it emerges, according to Habermas's (2001: xi) account of the public sphere, "between civil society and the state."

This raises a crucial issue, namely the relationship between public space and the public sphere. In recent years, philosophers and political theorists, and literary and legal scholars have developed a considerable literature concerning the public sphere (see, for example, Fraser, 1990; Cheah and Robbins, 1998; Habermas, 2001). This literature emphasizes the ideas, media, institutions, and practices that all contribute to the generation of something that we can call the public, publics or public opinion, and this work is generally nested both in a larger historical framework concerning the state and the transformation of bourgeois social relations and in a normative search for political and moral effectiveness. Laments about the end of the public sphere or at least its political circumscription are met by reassertions of an ideal public sphere at the heart of liberal democracy and by an insistence on the multiplicity of public spheres. So viewed, the public sphere is rarely if ever spatialized. In Habermas's account, for example, the ideal public sphere is deemed universal and thereby, in any meaningful sense, spatially undifferentiated. If Fraser's critique opens some room for spatializing public sphere theory, and her more recent call that we consider the transnationality of the public sphere reiterates the invitation, the opportunity has not been taken up.

At the same time, architects, geographers, planners, anthropologists, urbanists, and others have delved into discussions of public space. This work is explicitly spatial, seeking to comprehend the ways in which social and political, and economic and cultural processes and relations make specific public places and landscapes, and the ways in which, in turn, these geographies reaffirm, contradict, or alter their constituent social and political relations. This volume pulls together interdisciplinary contributions from some of the central scholars working in this area.

These public space and public sphere literatures can certainly overlap but more often than not they occupy quite separate domains. The public sphere remains essentially ungrounded while public space discussions insufficiently connect to meditations on the public sphere (but see Mitchell, 2003). Yet the experience of public space belies such an abrupt distinction between public and private spheres and spaces. It is important to recognize that many constituents of public space are privately owned, managed, and regulated elements of the public sphere: the preponderance of media outlets, access to the Internet, many rights of way in the city and countryside alike, travel on railways, planes and buses, public houses, and so forth. Access to the global, even more than the local, requires private payment for Internet, television, or physical access. By the same token, there is considerable public (as in state) regulation over many aspects and uses of private space, from zoning laws to laws governing sexuality and social reproduction, the policing of national borders, state surveillance of personal activities, the right to congregate in public space, and so forth. The state is not by any means coterminous with the public sphere, but rather the product of specific power relations in any society—power relations that can exclude as many parts of the public as they include—yet many of the state's actions do indeed mold and frame what specific societies take to be the public.

It would be regrettable and self-defeating if the distinction between these literatures was summarily reduced to one of materialist versus idealist approaches; both literatures are far too internally diverse to be characterized usefully in this way. Yet they have not really come together, however complementary they appear: Where the weakness of the public space literature perhaps lies in the practical means of translation from theories of political and cultural economy to the materiality of public space, the public sphere literature offers an historically embedded discussion of the continual making and remaking of the public vis-à-vis the state and related institutions, and ideologies and modes of communication and power. By corollary, the weakness of the public sphere literature may lie in the distance that it maintains from the places and spaces of publicness, whereas it is precisely the insight of the public space literature that produced public spaces naturalize the very assumptions interrogated by public sphere theorists and provide an extraordinary palimpsest for detailed scrutiny. If the public sphere can be described as "the sphere of private people coming together as a public" (Habermas, 2001: 27), its emergence clearly has a history, as we have seen, but it has an equally clear geography. Once recognized, that spatiality of the public sphere potentially transforms our understanding of the politics of the public. An understanding of public space is an imperative for understanding the public sphere.

It may be no accident that public sphere and public space literatures have coalesced somewhat in isolation over the last few decades. The twentieth century witnessed what we might call a "lost geography" (Smith, 2003: 1–28). In the nineteenth century and certainly up until World War I, spatiality and geography were well understood as a crucial language of political power, but for various reasons having to do both with new modes of economic expansion and a new politics of global power, the public sense of the connection between geography and power eroded quickly—mid-century geopolitics, the revival of the linkage in World War II, and the banal geographical binaries of the Cold War notwithstanding. By the 1960s, the language of space was moribund and even as a curious Michel Foucault (1980: 77) famously mused about the causes of this (finding improbable answers in the influence of philosophy) a broad-based theoretical reintroduction of a spatial grammar was already afoot in social and cultural theory. Yet such compensation for a lost geography—the new spatial vocabulary of social theory—has had a very limited effect on discussions of the public sphere, and this is especially surprising given the centrality of Kant for recent retheorizations of the public sphere, especially in the literature considering a new cosmopolitanism which in turn tempts the possibility that universal liberal (or postliberal) norms may be assumed to undergird the public sphere. It was Kant after all who argued that time and space provided the two *a prioris* of conceptual knowledge, and that history and geography therefore rightly shared the expanse of descriptive and classificatory knowledge (Adickes, 1924–1925). However contestable that conclusion, its importance to Kant remains strangely unexamined in latter-day philosophy—Kant's forty years of lectures on physical geography at Königsberg have never been published in English and are rarely acknowledged in the original—and this translates into a public sphere literature with little interest in or seeming rationale for investigating the spatiality of the public sphere.

In other words, the lost geography of the public sphere comes with a concurrent loss of politics, however partial. Abstracting from the location of real events and social relations removes an entire dimension of political relationality. It is an underlying conviction of this volume that the respatialization of our sense of the public brings the opportunity of a more complete repoliticization of the public than would otherwise be available. Investigating the means of making and remaking public space provides a unique window on the politics of the public sphere, suggesting an even more powerful imperative to the focus on public space.

Before laying out the specific contributions to this volume, it is important to raise one other analytical issue. The following essays span a range of spatial scales from the highly localized scale of the play space to the neighborhood and the urban to the national and indeed global. Two decades of research rooted initially in the geographical literature has emphasized that spatial scales are neither simply a conceptual convenience nor simply given, but rather are socially generated in response to and often as solutions to specific social problems and contradictions. This notion is perhaps best explained by reference to the national scale. Although a few national states preexisted the seventeenth century, it was only after this period that national states began to fulfill their role as the pivotal players in the global political and cultural economy. City states, provinces, kingdoms and a host of other subnational units had previously fulfilled this role, but the expansion of capital accumulation associated with the advent of capitalism rendered these earlier scales of territorial organization incapable of managing the contradictory relations of cooperation and competition that undergirded the emerging socioeconomic order. The national state replaced an older order of provincialisms at lower scales, and the scale of the national was thereby produced in its modern form. A parallel if not identical argument might be made about the scale of the urban and the shift from the relatively small, walled cities of an earlier era to that of the modern metropolis, but the larger point is that the scale of public space and of the public sphere is socially produced, is a matter of intense political struggle, and an object of historical change (Smith, 1993; Marston, 2000).

This recent work—theoretical and empirical—on the production and politics of scale has not yet had a significant and direct effect in the literature on the public sphere, but insofar as global processes now threaten to circumscribe the power of the national and the urban scale enjoys a limited but undeniable reempowerment, the question of scale runs through many of the following essays even if it is not explicitly addressed. It would be facile to assume the withering away of the national state, and presumably with it the predominantly national definition of the public sphere. Yet in some arenas, the national definition of identities and power, sociality, and economy, has been widely challenged (if always unevenly and in different ways). Much as the preoccupation of public sphere writing needs to expand its scalar parameters beyond the national while resolutely not relinquishing that scale as obsolete, the public space literature needs to nest its traditional concern with the urban scale in a wider field of transformations spanning from the body to the global and even now supraplanetary. Even at the microscale of the urban plaza in Latin America, or the city square in North America, these political struggles can be traced historically as the venue for local, colonial, and global competition on behalf of capital with consequences for democratic practice and symbolic representation (Low, 2000).

David Harvey picks up the theme of the relationship between public space and the public sphere, touching on contemporary events such as the rebuilding of New York's Times Square and the design trend known as "the new urbanism," but he focuses especially on Second Empire Paris. The dramatic remaking of Paris in the 1850s and 1860s, at the behest of Napoleon III and at the hand of city builder Baron Haussmann, combined a spatial restructuring of the physical city with a revamping of the public sphere. Haussmann's new wide boulevards not only provided for military control over strategic streets but opened up areas of new commercial activity symbolized by the invention of department stores aimed explicitly at women. This was linked to a wider social restructuring, the emergence of a voluble middle class, the increasing segregation of the city by class, and a symbolic shift in the representation of urban space as spectacle. The Paris Commune of 1871 represented in part a popular resistance to this imbricated remaking of public space and the public sphere.

The chapter by Dolores Hayden implicitly combines the question of the production and politics of scale with that of public space. Suburbanization is traditionally treated as the means by which cities decentralized, but if we shift the scale of our gaze at suburbanization, in other words zoom out from the central core and see the metropolis at a wider metropolitan or regional scale, then suburbanization seems instead to be a powerful means by which in the twentieth century the scale of the urban has expanded dramatically compared with preexisting forms of urbanization. While the suburbs are still widely seen as a haven of private space in contradistinction to the chaotic publicness of the old city center, Hayden documents the ways in which, between the 1920s and 1950s, a plethora of public institutions vigorously subsidized the privatization of the new suburban spaces in the United States. If suburbanization represented a consumerist solution to the fear of economic depression, no inexorable logic was working here. Rather, the form taken by suburban privatization resulted from a series of political choices and struggles that cut through each other in discernable class, race/ethnic, and gender contours.

Perhaps inevitably, the new highly privatized metropolis has provoked a nostalgic reaction, an antisuburban suburbanism, if it can be put this way, represented by everything from gated communities to the so-called "new urbanism" as a design fashion. Elizabeth Blackmar examines one aspect of this reaction, the appropriation of the discourse of the commons, which found visceral expression in urban centers but especially at the metropolitan edge throughout the 1990s. Noting the classical correspondence between property rights and spatial relations, Blackmar provides a history of changing property rights as the basis for interrogating the new ideologies of the commons. If the reassertion of a concern with this category of property rights can be traced to Garrett Hardin's 1968 pastoral lament about "the tragedy of the commons," its conservative origins have blossomed not in opposition to but in consort with private property rights. Again, the public political sector—the state at all scales—colludes in this result, subsidizing ostentatious developments from Arizona and Texas to Maryland and New England. Such developments, advertised as a new "commons" and as a third-way alternative to the sterile opposition of private versus public space, are anything but "common" in the sense of allowing public access. Rather they reaffirm the rights of private property. Blackmar is explicit about the reification of politics that takes place when such property rights discourse is extracted from its spatial expression; respatialization, as Blackmar vividly demonstrates in her analysis of the meaning of the new "commons," raises the opportunity for repoliticization.

Setha Low picks up some of these same urban themes, directly tackling the question of the privatization of public space in the contemporary metropolis. Gated communities are her target. While there are certainly precursors, gated communities burgeoned in the U.S. urban landscape of the 1980s, especially in the south and west of the country where they now account for perhaps a third of new housing. Other regions are now following suit. Expressions of a broad malaise in the social order reflecting the insecurity brought on by the decay of the postwar economy, gated communities represent new privatized "enclosures" of public space aimed at enhanced, community homeowner control. Via ethnographic research in three urban areas, Low concludes that such developments sharpen the sociospatial segregation of the city, and shows how struggles emerge between communities and municipalities over tax payments for public services that have been privatized behind the gates and walls of such communities. Such struggles are played out at multiple scales up to that of national state policy. Indeed, gated communities are now a thoroughly internationalized phenomenon. Insofar as the failure and decay of liberal urban policy in much of the West has left the finances of municipalities tightly circumscribed, local administrations are not necessarily adverse to such privatized developments, especially if they can minimize the tax breaks provided to such developments while enhancing the local tax base and minimizing services provided to communities. There are signs, however, that many who have bought into gated communities are not especially content, feeling no significant increase in security and resenting the strict regulations that generally pertain. Privatization may not be the best alternative to the failure of public liberalism.

The question of security is central to the politics of public space and its privatization. Cindi Katz places this issue in a broad global context, arguing that the emergence of what she calls "terror talk" concerning children is intimately connected to shifts in the global positioning of the United States and consequent challenges to personal identities forged through identification with the national state. Further, as the focus on children suggests, the crisis of public space impinges on established norms of social reproduction. Since the late 1970s, she argues, in the wake of failure in Vietnam, the hostage takeover of the U.S. embassy in Tehran, and the so-called energy crisis in which President Carter compared the fight for cheap energy as "the moral equivalent of war," children and youth have been cast as especially vulnerable to forms of social terror—kidnapping, sexual assault, physical abuse, and so on—while also being cast as the source of certain kinds of terror, such as "wilding." Terror talk provides the broad ideological rationale for dramatically enhanced control over children's access to public space and their activities in privatized space. Children's public sphere is appreciably curtailed. At an intermediate scale, that of the urban park, Katz also documents ways in which the privatization of previously public functions further jettisons support for social reproduction, if in a highly uneven way. An essentially privatized Central Park in Manhattan thrives on the largesse of the elite (and subsidies from federal workfare funds), while adjacent Harlem and smaller neighborhood parks throughout the city are starved. The privatization of public space can only be understood as occurring at the nexus of global, national, urban, and neighborhood scales.

Ashley Dawson also approaches many of these and parallel issues through a global lens, emphasizing the increasing scalar dominance of urban governments in the global South. He focuses in particular on crime and security fears in postapartheid South Africa. Crime was of course a central mobilizing issue in Giuliani's remake of New York as revanchist city where reactionary revenge against those who had "stolen the city" was a central motif, and the general politics of revanchism in South Africa are parallel insofar as the state has asserted its right over that of the public in a thoroughly asymmetrical way. Much as in Harlem, racial containment and exclusion framed the urban experience of apartheid Johannesburg, and it continues today, albeit in altered form, in less direct but equally trenchant ways through the expression of class divisions in the postapartheid city. The spatial legacy of apartheid still dominates South African urbanism to a considerable extent, and this both exposes and exacerbates the high levels of violence in South African cities today (measured for instance by rates of murder and rape). Always historically high as an interstitial product of state-governed apartheid violence but rarely seen through the protective armor of apartheid policing and information control, interpersonal violence is now far more publicly visible while the stalled transition out of apartheid has severely exacerbated problems of employment, housing, education, and health services. Increased violence is one of the results, and the state struggles both to police and ameliorate its effects.

It is an obvious question to ask, then, and a central one in the public space discourse: what happens to those people excluded from the public spaces of the new private suburbs or the increasingly gentrified urban centers where the remaking of the public sphere displaces many from the resulting landscapes? This is the focus of the paper by Don Mitchell and Lynn Staeheli, who consider the geography of homelessness and the politics of homeless exclusionary practices in San Diego. Seen from this vantage point, that is the daily experience of homeless people in urban space, the privatization of the public sphere can telescope into the threat of the "end of public space," and for Mitchell and Staeheli this raises the question, first framed by French social theorist Henri Lefebvre: "Who has the right to the city?" The question of homelessness is inherently and simultaneously the question of property, and they explore these interconnections in ways that develop ideas from earlier chapters in the context of contemporary gentrification, homelessness, and the revanchist city. It is a cruel paradox that while redevelopment and gentrification cause homelessness, apologists for retaking the urban core often cite the need to rid the city of homelessness as a rationale for that same gentrification. Based on a series of interviews, Mitchell and Staeheli argue that the redefinition of property rights, combined with a changing regime of the public, has become highly visible in the exclusionary landscapes of the recolonized city. The rights of some are pitted against the rights of others, and as Marx once put it, against equal rights force decides. In this case again it is the force of the state—real and threatened—that secures the rights of private property against use, and again Mitchell and Staeheli demonstrate the way in which a spatialization of these issues highlights the political conflicts involved and provides political openings.

Public space and the public sphere represent conjoined arenas of social and political contest and struggle. As several of the chapters here suggest, the privatization of public space and the curtailment of the public sphere are certainly not a *fait accompli*. Indeed the dilemma of public space is surely trivialized by collapsing our contemporary diagnosis into a lament about private versus public. Insofar as the so-called public sector, represented by the state, often acts as the cutting edge of efforts to deny public access to places, media (themselves a part of the state according to classical definition), and other institutions, the contest to render spaces truly public is not always simply a contest against private interests. Union Square Park in New York City, following September 11, 2001, provides an exemplary case: There a spontaneous demonstration of public activism, commemoration, grief, and organization erupted, but was eventually circumscribed by the reasserted police power of the local state.

Less than three miles from where the World Trade Center had stood, Union Square is a highly symbolic space. As its name connotes, it had been a parade ground for the Union Army during the Civil War and still hosts statues celebrating that war. In subsequent years, presumably because of that history, it became a site of intense antiwar organization, and state efforts to suture the "official" symbolism of the space to its public popularity were periodically ruptured at the hands of a public with different ideas. The square was renovated in the 1980s in consort with the northward anchoring of gentrification in the Lower East Side, and as such became a low-intensity battleground over the rights of homeless people to occupy public space. In September 2001, it became the scene of a unique outpouring of public sentiment, a genuine and spontaneous, if rare, expression of the public sphere that for a while operated outside official control. Antiwar demonstrators mixed with religious proselytizers, peaceful candle vigilants with tripped-out babblers, angry anti-Muslim ranters and racists with socialists recounting the largely unpublicized history of U.S. imperial ambition in the Middle East that helped explain—though hardly justify—the 9/11 attacks. In those days and weeks, Union Square witnessed an especially poignant expression of public sentiment, given New York's aggressive policing of parks, its zero tolerance campaign aimed at strict official control of public space (a campaign that began with the

1990s repression of publicly visible homeless people), and its broad, energetic support for gentrification.

In Union Square after 9/11, by contrast, anything went. People stayed day and night, unconcerned by newly rediscovered curfew laws and unharassed by the revanchist mayor's police force, which only days earlier would have arrested many for the kinds of social events, gatherings, activities, proclamations, and public expressions that now transpired in the park. It took 9/11, in other words (and the response to it in Union Square Park), manufactured as a *national* rather than a local or global scale threat, and therefore one that could be parsed into a patriotic mold, to slice open the skin of repressive control and reveal so starkly the completeness of authoritarian command over public space that New Yorkers had come to experience as normal.

But the new spontaneous social and political energy of the Park and its revelatory apotheosis of a truly public sphere were too honest, too raw, and too threatening to be allowed to stand. After barely two weeks, the New York Police Department began to reimpose state authority by invoking specific regulations, beginning at the margins—geographically, legally, and politically—and working their way to the center until this unprecedented expression of the public sphere, occupying and remaking public space, was eventually closed down.

The same closure of public space has been orchestrated at various scales. The national boundaries are refixed against supposedly dangerous invasions of people, capital, goods, and ideas, much as the cities of "Fortress America" are increasingly gated within (Low, 2003). Even more sinister, the 2001 Patriot Act thoroughly spatialized its circumscription of the public sphere with the invention of "homeland security" as a cabinet level preoccupation. Consequently, the domestic public sphere suffered a clampdown, with library accounts, university computers, bank accounts, and even the normal modes of daily communication and movement placed under unprecedented surveillance. Whole new categories have been constructed beyond the traditional public sphere. The bureaucratic neologism designating prisoners of war as "enemy combatants" and their spatial incarceration in the legal limbo of Abu Ghraib and Guantánamo (not coincidentally a relict colonial outpost in Cuba), where they have absolutely no access to the supposed entitlements of the public sphere (legal representation, constitutional protection), is only the foremost means by which this circumscription of the (national) public sphere is globalized. The forced flight of prisoners to third countries where torture can be outsourced represents another. Here too it is not so much a matter of the privatization of the public sphere as of its global curtailment by the most supposedly public of all institutions, the national state.

The struggle for public space today has everything to do with contemporary debates pitting the public against the private, and vice versa, but it also has to do with the ways in which contemporary society is living a reprise of its liberal—as in conservative eighteenth century—origins. More than anything else, the Patriot Act and related legislation revisit the hypocrisy of that founding moment. In the eighteenth century, the founding rights lying at the base of the public sphere were supposed to be universal, but were of course highly restricted by class, race/ethnicity, and gender, not to mention national citizenship; assertions of universal rights coexisted quite sanctimoniously with class exploitation, slavery, and the oppression of women. Today the basic rights that undergird any coherent sense of the public sphere are also increasingly circumscribed, especially since 9/11, in terms of race and class especially, but also the geography of origin, real, suspected, or inherited, and in terms of other dimensions of social difference. The politics of public space today therefore express a deeper epochal shift.

That shift was long evident before 2001. Even as crime rates plummeted across the country in the 1980s and 1990s, the sense of insecurity was heightened, sentencing laws were escalated, and states were building more and more prisons. The underlying reasons for heightened angst in these decades probably had less to do with real threats to bodily or property security than with economic and deep-seated ontological security concerning identity. However that may be, the Bush administration has adeptly appropriated 9/11 to provide an ever-ready pushbutton source of widespread insecurity. This applies not just at the global scale but all the way down. Thus, in suburban Simi Valley, California, many new gated communities are actually faux fortresses. They exhibit all of the signs of a gated community—walls, gates, fences, guard houses—but without the guards, and they work insofar as the residents feel a sense of psychological security and a reaffirmation of class status (Low, 2003).

Early on, Habermas glimpsed that the blurring of boundaries between society and the state, which began to become apparent in the nineteenth century and was consummated in the twentieth, led to the end of a certain kind of liberal public sphere, first announced in the eighteenth century. He noted the progressive exclusion of the public from the resulting competition between and among private and governmental interests in a putatively postliberal public sphere. Today, however, a further element enters the equation. Since the 1970s, the social restructuring of economies in Europe, Asia, and the Americas has brought about a capitalization of social life that would have been inconceivable several decades earlier, from the biotechnological privatization of nature spanning from the entire Amazon to the human body, to the corporatization of the media and the financialization of everyday life (Frank, 2000; Martin, 2002), we now live in an era appropriately described, in starkly political economic terms, as neoliberal. Suddenly nothing is immune from appropriation as an accumulation strategy. This shift breaks the connection to twentieth-century American liberalism, which was in any case an extraordinary national anomaly in a wider global perspective, and reaches back to resuscitate the eighteenth-century liberalism, which, from the vantage point of the twentieth or twenty-first century, now looks jarringly conservative (Smith, 2005). Not only does society merge with the state, as Habermas intimated, but it increasingly and forcefully merges with the sphere of private capitalist economic calculation in a way that the theories of Adam Smith, a genuine progressive in his time, could hardly anticipate. The difference between now and the eighteenth century is that the infusion of society with the state and the economy is more complete than could have been dreamt of in that period, and the results are far from progressive.

What does this mean for the politics of public space? The outlook is not immediately optimistic. There is less and less room for the kind of ideal public sphere that Habermas envisages. The advent of neoliberalism clearly threatens a return to the exclusionary liberalism of its eighteenth-century template, but with the technology of the twenty-first century. It masquerades under the same pretension of universal democratic rights fused with the particular interests of an assertive and nationally rooted yet fundamentally transnational capitalist class. The heightened policing of public space at all scales is an integral result of the new political deep freeze. Today's neoliberalism may not divide the populace as bluntly as in the days of high liberal principle when slavery was legal, African Americans were counted as three-fifths of a person, and neither women nor the propertyless possessed a vote, but it makes its own discriminations.

As the papers in this volume suggest in various ways, the neoliberal regime that has taken hold of political and cultural power around the world involves the sharpening of social divisions, based especially on class, race/ethnic, national, and gender differences, but stretching much further into the fabric of social difference. The control of public space is a central strategy of that neoliberalism. For almost a million people deported from the United States in 2003, "America" is no longer part of their public space. Internally, antiglobalization and anticapitalist protestors, and social justice or antiwar activists, have borne the brunt of heightened assault on political dissent (invariably justified under the ludicrous rubric of antiterrorism). In September 2004 while the Republican National Convention (known locally as the Republican National Convulsion) was in town, midtown Manhattan was transformed into a police state (much as Boston had been weeks earlier for the Democratic convention), and the illegal sweep and detention of nearly 2,000 activists from New York City streets made clear the stakes over public space. Political movements are always about place and asserting the right, against the state, to mass in public space: Who can imagine the 1870 commune without Paris? The Russian revolution without the Winter Palace? The civil rights movement without the marches on Washington, Montgomery, and Selma? The British feminist antimilitary movement without Greenham Common? Gay, lesbian, and queer politics without Stonewall?

The neoliberalism of public space is neither indomitable nor inevitable, and however much public space is now under a clampdown, it is not closed. New events, new technologies, new ways of responding to the neoliberalization of public space, new forms of social organization—transnational labor organizing, indigenous rights and environmental justice movements, in addition to those cited above—are always creating alternative new spaces of and for public political expression. In addition to diagnosing the multi-faceted assaults on the public sphere, the central message of the essays in this volume is that whatever the deadening weight of heightened repression and control over public space, spontaneous and organized political response always carries within it the capability of remaking and retaking public space and the public sphere.

References

Adickes, Erich. 1924–1925. *Kant als Naturforscher.* 2 vols. Berlin: W. de Gruyter.

Cheah, Pheng and Bruce Robbins. 1998. *Cosmopolitics.* Minneapolis: University of Minnesota Press.

Foucault, Michel. 1980. *Knowledge/Power.* New York: Pantheon Books, 1980.

Frank, Thomas. 2000. *One Market Under God: Extreme Capitalism, Market Populism, and the End of Economic Democracy.* New York: Random House.

Fraser, Nancy. 1990. "Rethinking the Public Sphere: A Contribution to Actually Existing Democracy." *Social Text* 25/26, 56–79.

Giuliani, R.W. and W.J. Bratton. 1994. *Police Strategy No. 5: Reclaiming the Public Spaces of New York.* New York: Office of the Mayor.

Habermas, Jürgen, 2001. *The Structural Transformation of the Public Sphere: An Inquiry into a Category of Bourgeois Society.* Cambridge, MA: MIT Press.

Low, Setha. 2000. *On the Plaza: The Politics of Public Space and Culture.* Austin, TX: University of Texas Press.

Low, Setha. 2003. *Behind the Gates: Life, Security and the Pursuit of Hapiness in Fortress America.* New York: Routledge.

Marston, Sallie. 2000. "The Social Construction of Scale." *Progress in Human Geography* 24, 219–242.

Martin, Randy. 2002. *The Financialization of Daily Life.* Philadelphia: Temple University Press.

Mitchell, Don. 2003. *The Right to the City.* New York: Guilford.

Smith, Neil. 1993. "Contours of a Spatialized Politics: Homeless Vehicles and the Production of Geographical Scale." *Social Text* 33, 54–81.

Smith, Neil. 2001. "Global Social Cleansing: Postliberal Revanchism and the Export of Zero Tolerance." *Social Justice* 28, no. 3, 68–74 .

Smith, Neil. 2003. *American Empire: Roosevelt's Geographer and the Prelude to Globalization.* Berkeley, CA: University of California Press.

Smith, Neil. 2005. *The Endgame of Globalization.* New York: Routledge.

CHAPTER 2

The Political Economy of Public Space

DAVID HARVEY

The idea of the "public sphere" as an arena of political deliberation and participation, and therefore as fundamental to democratic governance, has a long and distinguished history. The imagery of the Athenian *agora* as the physical space wherein that democratic ideal might be attained has also had a powerful hold on the political imagination. As a result, some kind of association or even identity has been forged between the proper shaping of urban public space and the proper functioning of democratic governance. But the status of this association is often left vague. For some it seems to offer merely a convenient metaphor, and with the arrival of the Internet and the construction of "virtual communities" the physical materiality of spatial organization seems irrelevant. Others will ask more pointedly how it might be possible to encourage political participation in an urban world constructed out of segregated suburbs, gated communities, privatized spaces, and shopping malls under surveillance and downtown streets monitored (thanks, these days, to some shadowy form of governance in U.S. cities called a "business partnership") with a video camera at every corner.

While it may well prove impossible to sort out the relationship between the physicality of urban public space and the politics of the public sphere with any exactitude, there are, I think, some potent points of linkage between them. We do not, after all, experience the city blankly, and much of what we do absorb from daily life in the city (be it the long drag of the commute, the jostle of subway crowds, the blandness of the shopping mall, the elegance or grandeur of certain forms of urban architecture, the panhandlers on the sidewalk, or the peace and beauty of an urban park) surely has some kind of influence on how we are situated in the world and how we think and act politically within it. Conversely, firmly held conceptions filter our openness to and guide our interpretations of what the urban experience might be about. If, for example, suburbanites are consumed by mortal fear of someplace called "the inner city," and therefore avoid it like the plague, then not only do they cultivate material ignorance of that space while preserving stereotypical images of what it contains, but in so doing diminish the prospects for any kind of political alliance between city and suburban interests. If inner city residents view suburban life as flat, dull, homogenizing, and boring, then they too will be less likely to warm to the political agendas of their suburban counterparts. There is, therefore, an intriguing mix of sociogeographical perceptions, expectations, and material conditions at work that need to be unpacked if we are to think more cogently about how urban design in general, and the shaping of urban public space in particular, might influence politics in the public sphere.

A case study or two on this topic might in this regard be helpful. So, here I take up a particular example of how the radical reorganization of public space in Second Empire Paris might have had, directly or indirectly, political implications. I choose this case in part because I am reasonably familiar with it, and have often reflected, inspired by a wide range of penetrating commentators such as Walter Benjamin, Richard Sennett, Marshall Berman and T.J. Clark, on the political effects and meanings of Haussmann's works. But the case also has the advantage of being in some ways emblematic. Robert Moses, after all, studied Haussmann's works very closely and modeled his activities in the reshaping of New York on what he saw as Haussmann's virtues (he also copied some of his tactics and, at least in some people's eyes, repeated some of his more egregious errors).[1]

I begin with a consideration of a prose poem by Baudelaire entitled "The Eyes of the Poor," because it encapsulates a whole series of themes and controversies that accompanied Haussmann's interventions. Baudelaire opens the poem by asking his lover if she understands why it is that he suddenly hates her. Throughout the whole day, he says, they had shared their thoughts and feelings in the utmost intimacy, almost as if they were one. And then,

> That evening, feeling a little tired, you wanted to sit down in front
> of a new café forming the corner of a new boulevard still littered
> with rubbish but that already displayed proudly its unfinished

splendors. The café was dazzling. Even the gas burned with all the ardor of a debut, and lighted with all its might the blinding whiteness of the walls, the expanse of mirrors, the gold cornices and moldings.....nymphs and goddesses bearing on their heads piles of fruits, pates and game.....all history and all mythology pandering to gluttony.

On the street directly in front of us, a worthy man of about forty, with tired face and greying beard, was standing holding a small boy by the hand and carrying on his arm another little thing, still too weak to walk. He was playing nurse-maid, taking the children for an evening stroll. They were in rags. The three faces were extraordinarily serious, and those six eyes stared fixedly at the new café with admiration, equal in degree but differing in kind according to their ages.

The eyes of the father said: "How beautiful it is! How beautiful it is! All the gold of the poor world must have found its way onto those walls." The eyes of the little boy: "How beautiful it is! How beautiful it is! But it is a house where only people who are not like us can go." As for the baby, he was much too fascinated to express anything but joy—utterly stupid and profound.

Song writers say that pleasure ennobles the soul and softens the heart. The song was right that evening as far as I was concerned. Not only was I touched by this family of eyes, but I was even a little ashamed of our glasses and decanters, too big for our thirst. I turned my eyes to look into yours, dear love, to read my thoughts in them; and as I plunged my eyes into your eyes, so beautiful and so curiously soft, into those green eyes, home of Caprice and governed by the Moon, you said: "Those people are insufferable with their great saucer eyes. Can't you tell the proprietor to send them away?"

So you see how difficult it is to understand one another, my dear angel, how incommunicable thought is, even between two people in love.[2]

What is so remarkable about this prose poem is not only the way in which it depicts the contested character of public space and the inherent porosity of the boundary between the public and the private (the latter even including a lover's thoughts provoking a lovers' quarrel), but how it generates a sense of space where ambiguities of proprietorship, of aesthetics, of social relations (class and gender in particular), and the political economy of everyday life collide. It is also, incidentally, remarkable to think how easy it might be to transpose the incident and the diverse emotions expressed from 1860s Paris to, say, any upscale street café in 1990s New York ("history and all mythology pandering to gluttony" often seems a very apt expression for the decor), although it would then have been the mayor, Giuliani, who would be appealed to as "proprietor" to send the poor family away (as indeed he did with many of the homeless).

Plainly, the reshaping of Paris that Haussmann was undertaking was very much on people's minds (this is by no means the only time that the new boulevards loomed large in Baudelaire's work). And, if we are to judge from the sentiments expressed, the political reaction to them was rich with ambivalence. A new boulevard, ostensibly a public space, provides the setting for the poem. But the right to occupy it is contested by the author's lover who wants someone to assert proprietorship over it and control its uses. The café is not exactly a private space either; it is a space within which a selective public is allowed for commercial and consumption purposes. The poor family sees it as an exclusionary space, internalizing the gold that has been appropriated from them. The café projects an illuminated image outward onto the public space just as it spills outward onto the sidewalk. The poor can neither evade nor ignore it. They are forced to confront it in exactly the same way that the occupants of the café cannot avoid seeing them. The porosity of the boundary forms a zone of surprising and potentially conflictual contact.

So what, then, was this public space, the boulevard, and how did it come about? Everyone in Paris in Baudelaire's time was all too aware, of course, that the preexisting boulevards had run with workers' blood in the massacres of June 1848. The rights of those who sought a social and nurturing republic (as opposed to the rights of those looking for a purely political republic) had been violently denied upon the boulevards, and their access to the public sphere of politics thereafter strictly circumscribed. There were many then (just as now) who saw the new boulevards as spaces of militarization, surveillance, and control. The building of new boulevards in the Second Empire was considered strategic, designed to permit free lines of fire and to bypass the hard to assail barricades erected in narrow, tortuous streets that had made the military suppression of 1848 so difficult. The military coup that established the Second Empire in 1851 had first taken control of the boulevards. The new boulevards were construed as public spaces to facilitate the state's protection of bourgeois private property. They should not be open, therefore, to those who might challenge (or even appear to challenge by virtue of their rags) the bourgeois social order.

Military domination was, however, but a minor aspect of what the new boulevards were about. To begin with, they were public investments designed to prime the pump of private profit in the wake of the serious economic recession of 1847–1849. Deficit financed, they were a manifestation of what we later came to know as some mix of civilian and military Keynesianism. As such, they did much to revive the economy and enhance the values of private property both directly and indirectly. Land and property owners, some of whom early on resisted expropriation, came more and more to favor it as the Second Empire progressed (in part because they managed to inflate land and property prices to their own advantage). Clearly, the meaning of the new public spaces depended in large measure upon the private interests (such as landowners, developers, construction interests and workers, commerce of all kinds) they supported.[3]

But there were a whole series of secondary effects that had powerful reverberations for politics in the public sphere, and it is these cascading secondary effects upon which I wish to focus more closely here. Increasingly, Richard Sennett notes, the "right to the city" became more and more of a bourgeois prerogative. Social control and surveillance of who "the public" is (or is not) proceeded accordingly. The validation of the new public spaces (the splendor the boulevards displayed) was heavily dependent on the control of private functions and activities that abutted upon it. Haussmann set about a process of "embourgeoisement" of the city center that continued long thereafter. He sought to expel industrial activities (particularly noxious ones like tanning) and its associated working classes (often at the center of political revolt) from the center of the city. He strictly mandated design criteria and aesthetic forms for both the public and the private construction on and around the boulevards (with a lasting effect on Parisian architecture and aesthetics). Private activity was forced to support the political goal, which was to shape a certain kind of public space reflective of imperial splendor, military security, and bourgeois affluence. Haussmann sought to orchestrate the private and public spaces of Paris in mutually supportive ways. But he did so in class terms (as has happened recently in the reorganization of New York's Times Square). This is transparently so in the case that Baudelaire describes: Although unfinished, the boulevard is full of splendor, reflecting back the brilliance of the café's illumination. The café (an exclusive commercial space) and the boulevard (the public space) form a symbiotic whole in which each validates the other. But this presumes that the public space can be properly controlled. The poor, no matter how "worthy," must be excluded from it just as they are from the café.

But what might this mean politically and socially for those who either felt welcomed or (like the poor family in Baudelaire's account) excluded from such public spaces? In what ways did the experience of these highly stylized and controlled public spaces inflect consciousness, ways of thought, and even the possibilities for politics in the public sphere? And why do the two lovers react so differently to the scene before them?

Sennett, in *The Fall of Public Man* puts a very special gloss on these questions:

> [I]n the remaking of the city by Haussmann in the 1850s and 1860s the intermixing of classes within districts was reduced by design. Whatever heterogeneity occurred spontaneously in the division of private houses into apartments in the first half of the century was now opposed by an effort to make neighborhoods homogeneous economic units: investors in new construction and renovation found this homogeneity rational in that they knew exactly what kind of area they were putting their capital into. An ecology of quartiers as an ecology of classes: this was the new wall Haussmann erected between the citizens of the city as well as around the city itself.... [This] changed the very terms of localism and cosmopolitanism...[4]

Baudelaire's lover expresses sentiments consistent with these changed terms. She expects class homogeneity within the public space. This is what the new boulevard represents. Her deceived expectations lie behind the violence of her response. Baudelaire, on the other hand, is still in the old Paris, so brilliantly described by Balzac, and most famously represented by the iconography of the apartment building layered from a ground floor of tradespeople and artisans, through a first floor of affluent bourgeois or even aristocracy, a third floor of respectable clerks and government bureaucrats, a fourth floor of working class families, and finally to upper floors of starving artists, students, and the impoverished. Not only are cross-class encounters expected—they are also valued as part of the urban experience. The segregation that set in during the Second Empire was felt by many to have a deleterious political effect because the bourgeoisie no longer had contact with, and therefore lost its sense of obligation to and moral influence over the lower classes (Baudelaire's decanter and glasses "too big for our thirst" register the sense of obligation and mirror how the poor see all their gold upon the walls of the café). In contemporary terms, his lover wants the security of the gated community, while he values the mixing and diversity of a multicultural and class-variegated urban experience. Hers is exactly the sort of encounter that a bourgeois woman would fear (and the gender distinction is telling). Affluent New Yorkers, women in particular, are similarly grateful to Mayor Giuliani for removing the homeless and panhandlers from their paths en route to the boutiques of mid-town Manhattan.

T.J. Clark, in *The Painting of Modern Life*, provides another perspective on the depoliticization that flowed from "Haussmannization." This process may have brought modernity to Paris, he argues, but it also provided "a framework in which another order of urban life—an order without imagery—would be allowed its mere existence." Capital, Clark asserts,

> did not need to have a representation of itself laid out upon the ground in bricks and mortar, or inscribed as a map in the minds of its city dwellers.... [I]t preferred the city not to be an image—not to have form, not to be accessible to the imagination, to readings and misreadings, to a conflict of claims on its space—in order that it might mass-produce an image of its own to put in the place of those it destroyed.[5]

The new image was that of "the spectacle." Haussmann's rebuilding of Paris, writes Clark, "was spectacular in the most oppressive sense of the word." The mobilization of the spectacle (and splendor) of the boulevard and its luminous café was meant to mask and disguise the fundamentals of class relations, which is why the presence of the poor family on the boulevard comes as such a shock. The spectacle "was not a neutral form in which capitalism incidentally happened; it was a form of capital itself, and one of the most effective." Haussmannization was an attempt to put an image "in place of a city which had lost its old means of representation." What had been lost was the idea of the city as a form of sociality, as a potential site for the construction of utopian dreams of a nurturing social order. "The modes of political, economic and ideological representation in which the city had once been constructed, as a contingent unit in and through other social practices" had been dissolved in part by the repressions of 1848, but then further eviscerated under the transfixing power of spectacle. Once the city is imaged by capital solely as spectacle, it can then only be consumed passively, rather than actively created by the populace at large through political participation. In the previous social order, the city had been "a horizon of possible collective action and understanding." But, concludes Clark, "all such horizons must be made invisible in societies organized under the aegis of the commodity."[6]

It would be wrong, I think, to argue for a complete and radical break in political imagery after 1848.[7] With the "bourgeois" revolution of 1830, the social emphasis shifted from Court to boulevard, but it was solely the Boulevard des Capucines (North Side) outside of the celebrated café Tortoni's that became the place for everyone who was someone to be seen between four and seven of an evening (and then within Tortoni's after midnight). So the boulevard was not a Second Empire invention. But the habits of social display and bourgeois (as opposed to aristocratic) power spread rapidly outwards along the new boulevards with their new cafés to create a more dispersed pattern of social and political proprietorship. The revolutionaries (nurtured on the various utopian currents that circulated so strongly in France during the 1830s and 1840s) had, for their part, broadly construed the city and the republic as a potentially nurturing body politic. This motif was widespread in the thinking of the time: it exerts a powerful presence in the early works of Balzac, for example. Daumier's *Republic*, painted in response to the revolutionary government's call for suitable public art, illustrates the thought: A large bare-breasted woman, seated magisterially on a throne-like chair while gazing far into the distance, grasps the tricolor flag with one hand and suckles a sturdy child (by no means portrayed as young) at each breast while another sits reading at her feet. The city and the republic (often seen as an identity) should, the revolutionaries argued, provide sustenance in the face of hunger and distress, while the national workshops should provide work in the face of unemployment. All such hopes were crushed in the June days as the national workshops were closed, and the boulevards became sites for military massacres. Shortly thereafter, Napoleon III's election as president followed by the coup d'état put paid to all such hopes. It was then that public space began to be fashioned and orchestrated in fundamentally different ways. The spectacle took over. The sense of the city as a social body politic was laid low, or at least went underground only to be rediscovered and resurrected later in the tumultuous days of the Paris Commune.

But what kind of spectacle was constructed and what role did the shaping of public space have to play in its elaboration? And precisely how was the spectacle mobilized and controlled? For is it not also true that revolutionary action generates its own powerful sense of spectacle, that revolutions are, as Lenin put it, truly festivals of the people?

The spectacle of the Second Empire had, of course, a purely political aspect (which Clark largely ignores). This strongly focused on the populism of the Napoleonic legend and the idea of imperial power. The conscious plan for Paris to assume the mantle of imperial Rome and become the head and heart of civilization in Europe and beyond was central to Haussmann's efforts. The notion of a body politic was preserved but it was now construed as imperial rather than as social. The mobilization of spectacle, as in imperial Rome, became a crucial weapon in the struggle to maintain imperial power (recalling the famous slogan of "bread and circuses"). Court ceremonies, imperial marriages, burials, and royal visits, military parades (particularly to celebrate grand victories abroad with the emperor riding in the vanguard), and even boulevard openings, were turned into spectacular celebrations in which an adoring public was expected to bow down before imperial grace, munificence, and power.[8] Popular support for the emperor was often manifest through organized fêtes, galas, and balls (even the women of Les Halles, known for their republicanism, organized a grand public ball to celebrate the advent of empire). The more permanent monumentality that accompanied the reconstruction, even the monumentality of the new boulevards themselves, helped support the legitimacy and overwhelming mastery of imperial power. The flamboyance of the architecture—Garnier's elaborate Opera House comes very much to mind—mirrored the flamboyance of imperial spectacle more generally. Universal expositions, such as that of 1855 and 1867, added their weight to the glories of that power while simultaneously celebrating the city as a center of commodity circulation, technological innovation, and social progress. These universal exhibitions were, as Benjamin rightly remarks, "pilgrimages to the commodity fetish," but they also testified to the modernity of empire.[9]

Haussmannization also entailed, however, the reorganization of public space for the far more mundane purpose of facilitating the freer circulation of money, commodities, and people (and hence of capital) throughout the spaces of the city. Here, too, the sheer spectacle of that movement, the hustle and bustle of carts and public conveyances over newly macadamized surfaces, was not devoid of political meanings. Everything seemed to speed up; the stimuli of urban living became, according to many accounts, more and more overwhelming. What Simmel calls the "blasé attitude" took ever deeper hold on urban life (at least if we believe the innumerable tales of the flaneur and the dandy on the boulevards).[10] The arrival of the new department stores and the proliferation of cafés (of the sort that Baudelaire describes), cabarets, and theaters meant, furthermore, that the sociality of the boulevards was now as much controlled indirectly by the commercial activity around it as by police power.

The increasing power of the commodity itself as spectacle was nowhere better expressed than in the new department stores. The Bon Marché, opened in 1852, was the pioneer (although prototypes existed in the 1840s). Such high turnover stores needed a large clientele drawn from all over the city, and the new boulevards facilitated such movement. The department stores opened themselves to the boulevards and streets, encouraging entry of the public without obligation to buy. The shop window was organized as an enticement to stop and gaze upon and then enter and buy. The commodities visibly piled high inside the department stores became a spectacle in their own right. The boundary between public and private space was rendered porous; the passage between them became easy, although an army of ushers and salespeople (particularly salesgirls) patrolled behavior in that interior space (much as they continue to do to this day, although now armed with surveillance cameras and more prominent security guards). The effect, however, was to transform the citizen into a mere spectator and consumer. From this standpoint, the passivity of politics was tentatively and at least momentarily secured.

Women in this had a much more prominent role, both as sellers and buyers. The department stores, Zola noted in retrospect, particularly targeted women as consumers. In his novel *Au Bonheur des Dames*, Mouret, the proprietor of a pioneering department store (modeled on the Bon Marché), explains his "techniques of modern big business" to a baron (modeled, rather obviously, on Haussmann). Of "supreme importance," says Mouret:

> was the exploitation of Woman. Everything else led up to it, the ceaseless renewal of capital, the system of piling up goods, the low prices that attracted people, the marked prices that reassured them. It was Woman the shops were competing for so fiercely, it was Woman they were continually snaring with their bargains, after dazzling her with their displays. They had awoken new desire in her weak flesh, they were an immense temptation to which she inevitably yielded, succumbing in the first place to purchases for the house, then seduced by coquetry and, finally consumed by desire. By increasing sales tenfold, by making luxury democratic, shops were becoming a terrible agency for spending, ravaging households, working hand in hand with the latest extravagances in fashion, growing ever more expensive. And if, in the shops, Woman was queen, adulated and humoured in her weaknesses, surrounded with attentions, she reigned there as an amorous queen, whose subjects trade on her, and who pays for every whim with a drop of her own blood.... [Mouret] was building a temple to Woman, making a legion of shop assistants burn incense before her, creating the rites of a new cult; he thought only of her, ceaselessly trying to imagine ever greater enticements; and behind her back, when he had emptied her purse and wrecked her nerves, he was full of the secret scorn of a man to whom a mistress has been stupid enough to yield. "Get the women," he said to the Baron, laughing impudently as he did so, "and you'll sell the world."[11]

The art of enticement began with window display. Mouret, says Zola, "was the best window dresser in Paris, a revolutionary window-dresser in fact, who had founded the school of the brutal and gigantic in the art of display." But the boulevards also became public spaces for displays of bourgeois affluence, conspicuous consumption, and feminine fashion. The theatricality of the boulevards fused with the performative world inside the many theaters that sprung up along them. The boulevards became public spaces where the fetish of the commodity reigned supreme in every sense.

But note something very important here: It was the symbiotic relation between the public and commercial spaces that became crucial. The spectacle of the commodity came to dominate across the private/public divide giving a unity to the two. And while the role of bourgeois women was, in certain respects, much enhanced by this shift in emphasis from the arcades and many small shops as centers of commodity exchange to the department stores and larger-scale specialized commercial establishments, it was still their lot to be exploited, although this time as consumers rather than as managers of households. It became both necessary and fashionable for bourgeois women to stroll the boulevards, window shop, and buy and display their acquisitions in public space. They, too, became part of the spectacle (now heavily infused with overtones of sexual desire) that fed upon itself to create an entirely new sense of public space, but one that was defined in commercial and commodity terms overlaid with the intangibles of sexual desire. The direct encounter with femininity and fashion on the boulevard brought bourgeois men into these public spaces in droves.

Political pacification through consumption and arousal of erotic desire has long been a ruse to ensure capitalism's own survival (we live with it every day in our TV commercials). The successive targeting of vulnerable groups, such as bourgeois women in the Second Empire (now, of course, the slogan is "get the children [at the earliest possible age] and you'll sell the world") has long been a critical tactic of commerce. But behind all this, there always lies the symbiotic organization of public/private spaces under the aegis of commodification and spectacle. The hoped for effect is depoliticization. Sennett concludes:

> The capitalist order had the power to throw the materials of appearance into a permanently problematical, permanently "mystifying" state.... In "public," one observed, one expressed oneself, in terms of what one wanted to buy, to think, to approve of, not as a result of continuous interaction, but after a period of passive, silent, focused attention. By contrast, "private" meant a world where one could express oneself directly as one was touched by another person; private meant a world where interaction reigned, but it must be in secret.... In the spectacle few men play an active role.[12]

Yet in important ways the private world mirrored the public even as it inverted it. Baudelaire for one was explicit in acknowledging the power of the spectacle in relation to interior states of mind. "In certain almost supernatural inner states," he wrote, "the depth of life is almost entirely revealed in the spectacle, however ordinary, that we have before our eyes, and which becomes the symbol of it."[13] The poor family with their staring eyes are part of the spectacle for him (as the sight of the homeless may be for us); but how he or his lover sees them reflects and expresses their separate inner states. But what happens to those inner states when the proprietor sends the poor away, leaving only the boulevard and the dazzling café as spectacle?

The spectacle, Clark insists, "is never an image mounted securely in place; it is always an account of the world competing with others, and meeting the resistance of different, sometimes tenacious, forms of social practice." In Second Empire Paris, for example, it failed "to put together its account of anomie with that of social division, it [failed] to map one form of control upon another."[14] This failure, it seems to me, lies at the root of the lover's quarrel in Baudelaire's poem. The social control orchestrated through commodification and spectacle ("all history and all mythology pandering to gluttony" and the general glitter and splendor of café and boulevard) runs up against the clear signs of exclusion and exploitation of the poor to spark either anger ("send them away") or guilt ("I felt a little ashamed at our decanters and glasses...").

Governance by spectacle, it turns out, is a very chancy business, as it can all too easily spin out of control to produce unintended and sometimes quite surprising consequences. When the craft worker organizations were invited to attend the spectacle of the Paris Universal Exposition of 1867 and to deliberate collectively on their responses, the expectation seems to have been that they, like the bourgeoisie, would be so star-struck by the glamour and splendor of new technologies that they would overwhelmingly throw their support behind the imperial attempt to rival Britain in pursuing the fruits of technological progress. But the proceedings of the Worker Commissions tell a different story.[15] The workers for the most part resented the incorporation of a bowdlerized and crude version of their own craft intelligence into the machines and the standardized and, by their lights, inferior product that resulted. Commodities produced in such a way may have been suited to the emergent market represented by the department stores but they were not at all consistent with the sense of self-worth and the dignity of craft labor. The response, interestingly, was not to oppose the application of machine technology (no hint of Luddite sentiments can be found), but to look for new forms of labor organization that could ensure lower costs, an improvement in product, and enhancement of the dignity of labor. The most favored answer was to explore the idea of worker associations. This then became a hot topic of debate in the public meetings that were organized after 1868 and a nodal point of oppositional politics to the procapitalist politics of empire. The quest for worker association subsequently played an important role in the complex politics of the Paris Commune.

The mixing that went on in the exterior spaces—the boulevards and the public gardens (such as the Tuilleries)—was also not easy to control, despite the attempts to homogenize neighborhoods and to forge clearly demarcated public spaces. Fournel's 1858 account of what one was likely to encounter on the streets of Paris indicates an incredible mixing of types and genres that must have been a nightmare for the authorities.[16] Policing the public spaces became a problem. The boundary between respectable women and women of easy virtue called for stricter surveillance and the politics of street life—the activities of itinerant musicians and pamphleteers—were a focus of considerable police activity. From this there always arose a sense of insecurity and vulnerability, of bourgeois anxiety behind the turbulent mask of spectacle and commodification. To be effective in the public space, therefore, the network of informers and secret police agents had to penetrate deep into private spaces—concierges were activated as spies, informers were everywhere, and "even the walls," advised Proudhon, "have ears." The spectacle might conceal class relations (indeed, that was its primary purpose), but what else might hide within its complex folds? The informal regulation of the boulevards by the flows of commodities, traffic, and pedestrian activity made the task of surveillance and policing much more difficult. It was all too easy to disappear into the crowd. The remarkable reception given to the translation of Poe's story "The Man in the Crowd" is suggestive, as is Fournel's clear distinction between the "baudet" (the loiterer and spectator) and the "flaneur" (whose actions are mysterious but somehow purposive and perhaps, therefore, threatening and subversive). The concealing of class relations does not erase them. There is a story, possibly apocryphal, that the revolutionary Jacobin idol, August Blanqui (who spent more than forty years of his life behind bars), stood on the Champs Elysée while several hundreds of his followers paraded past him concealed within the milling crowd without the police ever noticing.[17]

In Baudelaire's prose poem, bourgeois anxiety (coupled with guilt) is palpable. It is almost as if the rising power of commodity spectacle to command the public and commercial spaces of the city produces deeper and deeper levels of anxiety and insecurity in the bourgeois personality. Reassurance then depends on "sending them away." Any continued sign of "their" presence produces a fear of that other who is otherwise concealed. The "other" is concealed behind the fetish of the commodity, as well as within the folds of the urban crowd.

But here we encounter the greatest difficulty of all for total bourgeois control over public spaces and the public sphere. The drive, spearheaded by Haussmann, to make the right to the city an exclusively bourgeois prerogative could not help but create its "other," primarily in the form of an increasingly homogeneous working class city where a quite different symbiotic relationship was set up between private, public, and commercial spaces. The division of Paris into a respectable west and a less fortunate and largely neglected east was broadly consolidated by Haussmann's policies (particularly in the field of social provision that Haussmann reorganized on neo-Malthusian lines, thus ending the right to sustenance and welfare as the poor had previously known it).

To be sure, the boulevards were everywhere used to penetrate and then colonize unfriendly territory in a generalized attempt to create spaces subservient to empire in both military and political economic terms. And if the boulevards could not penetrate unfriendly zones, then at least they could surround them. But the mass of workers, condemned for the most part to live on miserable wages and faced with notoriously insecure and often seasonally episodic employment, had to live somewhere. A predominantly male and heavily immigrant population crammed into overcrowded rooming houses in insalubrious conditions. With limited cooking facilities, they were forced to depend either on meals provided collectively in-house or go on the streets into the innumerable small eating and drinking establishments that became, as a result, centers of sociality and politics. To take their pleasures, this population relied heavily on dance halls, cabarets, and drinking establishments that proved adept at relieving the working classes of any surplus moneys they had when times were good. More fortunate workers, usually those with craft skills or occupying that peculiar mixed status of independent artisan or employee, could, of course, construct for themselves a different kind of life. Concentrated largely in the central districts, they nevertheless relied heavily on small-scale commercial establishments as centers of sociality and pleasure (often to excess, if many commentators at the time are to be believed). The dingy private and commercial spaces in these areas cast a shadow rather than a luster on the public spaces of the street, while the roiling turbulence and animation of street life in working class Paris, where the eyes of the poor were everywhere, could do little to reassure anyone with bourgeois pretensions that this was a secure world. Such spaces were to be feared, and most bourgeois steadfastly avoided them apart, that is, from the shopkeepers and small employers who dwelt within their midst.

In a way, this is an all too familiar and dismal story of the ghettoization and segregation of a city, in this instance almost entirely according to class interests and sentiments.[18] But in this case, the rambunctiousness of working class Paris provided a seedbed for the growth and expression of a wide range of oppositional political sentiments that later underpinned the complex politics of the Paris Commune of 1871. It was a radically different kind of spectacle that held sway here: a complex mix of what Marx termed "animal spirits" and street theater where intensity of local contacts and confusions masked all manner of plots, including those with political and revolutionary aims. As the dance halls and cabarets became the loci of public meetings on political topics after the liberalization of empire in 1868, and as political meetings proliferated throughout working class Paris, so bourgeois hegemony over the right to the rest of the city was challenged. Seeping outward from their own symbiotic fashioning of public, commercial, and private spaces, popular forces more and more asserted a public and collective presence on the boulevards of bourgeois Paris. The image of hordes of workers descending from the working class district of Belleville and pouring out onto the public spaces of the city, even, on one occasion in 1869 getting as far as the new Opera House, struck political fear into the bourgeoisie. The boulevards became spaces of political expression, albeit ephemerally, for those whom they were supposed to exclude or control. To this climate of insecurity was added the spectacle of public funerals of noted oppositional figures or even, for that matter, anyone who had participated in the events of 1848. The authorities had a difficult time repressing them or preventing graveside elegies veering off into political statements. The cemeteries, particularly Père Lachaise, opened up as public spaces where political memory of a different sort could be exhumed along with future hopes for the city as a body politic. Here was a crucial mobilizing occasion (much as we have seen more recently in Northern Ireland and among Palestinians) that allowed private grief to be parlayed into a public statement. The public spaces of Paris were transformed toward the end of empire into sites of geopolitical struggles between warring factions in ways that were intensely symbolic of clashing ideologies in the public sphere of politics. The eyes of the poor would not be averted. Nor could they be sent away. The anxiety of the bourgeoisie was justified. The spectacle of the commodity may mask, but it can never erase, the raw facts of class relations.

So what conclusions can be drawn from this particular case? Most important, I think, is this: The character of public space counts for little or nothing politically unless it connects symbiotically with the organization of institutional (in this case, commercial, although in other cases it may be religious or educational institutions) and private spaces. It is the relational connectivity among public, quasipublic, and private spaces that counts when it comes to politics in the public sphere. It was Haussmann's genius to orchestrate this symbiosis on the ground, while fortuitously facilitating the stronger presence of the commodity as spectacle in the new Paris that his works helped create. The bourgeoisie could thereby assert their hegemony in politics as well as in economy at the same time as they claimed privileged access to and control over the public spaces of their city. To back this claim they needed legitimate force, and this is what empire provided in Paris (in much the same way as Giuliani provided it in New York). But this privileged claim encountered two particular difficulties. First, since (as Balzac earlier asserted again and again) the bourgeoisie worshiped only money and commodities, they were less and less patient with the expense and spectacle of empire and pursued forms of market freedoms (including that of limited freedom of expression) that were hard to absorb within the repressive and authoritarian imperial frame of governance. The bourgeoisie undermined the legitimacy of the very force they needed to back their claims to hegemony over public space. The boulevards eventually became spaces hostile to imperial spectacle. But then the power to send the poor away and keep them under strict police surveillance also diminished, thus opening up the boulevards to a different kind of politics.

But the success of Haussmann's orchestrations also stopped short of that "other" Paris where workers, immigrants, and small entrepreneurs struggled to make some sort of living and were forced to generate a different connectivity between their private state of deprivation and their uses of both institutional (commercial) and public spaces. Here, too, the rule applies: that politics does indeed relate to the symbiotic connectivity across the public, institutional (commercial) and private realms. The rising tide of republican and working class protest, culminating in the endless political meetings after 1868 and the eventual proclamation of the Commune, cannot be understood without glancing back at the symbiotic connections between these different realms in that area of Paris that lay outside of bourgeois control and which relied entirely upon the Emperor's spies and police to maintain order. On both sides, therefore, politics was inflected by the experience of a symbiotic connectivity between private, public, and institutional spaces. The fierce clash of ideologies and ideals in the Commune of 1871 was at least partially explicable in these oppositional terms.

Contestation over the construction, meaning, and organization of public space only takes effect, therefore, when it succeeds in exercising a transformative influence over private and commercial spaces. Action on only one of these dimensions will have little meaning in and of itself. Attempts to change one dimension may prove worthless or even counterproductive in the absence of connectivity to the others. It is, in the end, the symbiosis among the three that matters.

To take a contemporary example, no amount of "new urbanism" understood as urban design, can promote a greater sense of civic responsibility and participation if the intensity of private property arrangements and the organization of commodity as spectacle (of which Disneyfication is the prime example) remains untouched. Empty gestures of this sort with respect to the organization of public space abound. But what the Second Empire case illustrates is that when connections are made, then the political consequences can be both intense and far-reaching. (I believe a parallel argument could be constructed with respect to the civil rights movement in the United States in the 1960s.) Both sides of the class divide in Second Empire Paris achieved some level of that symbiosis, but they did so in such a segregated way as to create a dual city with only a demimonde and a complex zone of mixing to separate them. The intensity of politics that flowed from this had immense consequences for the transformation of Paris as a city. But it also brought the potentiality of the city as a body politic (no matter whether of a social or imperial sort) into a violent confrontation with that conception of the city as a tabula rasa for the accumulation of capital and the bourgeois pursuit of wealth and power. I sometimes wonder if we have ever succeeded in moving beyond that polarity within the whole historical geography of urbanization under capitalism. But that is a thesis to be further investigated and not offered up as a firm conclusion.

Notes

1. R. Moses, "What Happened to Haussmann," *Architectural Forum* 77 (July 1942): 1–10. See also M. Berman, All That Is Solid Melts into Air. (New York: Simon and Schuster, 1982).
2. C. Baudelaire, *Paris Spleen*, edited and translated by L. Varese (1869; New York: New Directions, 1947).
3. D. Harvey, *Paris, Capital of Modernity* (New York: Routledge, 2003).
4. R. Sennett, *The Fall of Public Man: The Social Psychology of Capitalism* (New York: Vintage, 1978), 145–148.
5. T.J. Clark, *The Painting of Modern Life: Paris in the Art of Manet and His Followers* (London: Thames and Hudson, 1984), 36.
6. *Ibid.*, chapter 1.
7. In *Paris*, Harvey examines this process in depth.
8. M. Truesdell, *Spectacular Politics: Louis-Napoleon Bonaparte and the Fete Imperiale, 1849–70* (Oxford, UK: Oxford University Press, 1997).
9. W. Benjamin, *Illuminations*, trans. H. Zohn (New York: Schocken, 1968), 165–167.
10. G. Simmel, "The Metropolis and Mental Life," in G. Simmel, *On Individuality and Social Forms*, edited by D. Levine (Chicago: Chicago University Press, 1971).
11. E. Zola, *The Ladies' Paradise (Au bonheur des dames)*, trans. Brian Nelson (1883; Oxford, UK: Oxford University Press, 1995), 76–77; M. Miller, *The Bon Marché: Bourgeois Culture and the Department Store, 1869–1920* (Princeton, NJ: Princeton University Press, 1981).
12. Sennett, *Fall of Public Man*.
13. Baudelaire, cited in G. Bachelard, *The Poetics of Space*, trans. M. Jolas (Boston: Beacon Press, 1969), 192.
14. Clark, *Painting of Modern Life*, 49.

15. J. Ranciere and P. Vauday, "Going to the Expo: The Worker, His Wife and Machines," in *Voices of the People: The Politics and Life of 'La Sociale' at the End of the Second Empire*, edited by A. Rifkin and R. Thomas, (London: Routledge and Kegan Paul, 1988).
16. V. Fournel, *Ce qu'on voit dans les rues de Paris* (Paris: A. Delahays, 1858).
17. M. Dommanget, *Blanqui et l'opposition revolutionnaire et la fin du Second Empire* (Paris: Armand Colin, 1969).
18. J. Gaillard, *Paris, la ville: 1852–1870* (Paris, Honoré Campion, 1976); L. Lazare, *Les quartiers pauvres de Paris* (Paris: Bureau de la Bibliothèque Municipale, 1869); W. Haine, *The World of the Paris Café* (Baltimore: Johns Hopkins University Press, 1999).

CHAPTER 3

Building the American Way: Public Subsidy, Private Space

DOLORES HAYDEN

From the early seventeenth century through the 1920s, Americans created regional traditions of town design centered on public space. Residents of New England's villages grouped their houses around substantial town greens; builders of Southwestern towns and cities organized plazas with pedestrian arcades; designers of Midwestern county seats sited their public courthouses inside tree-shaded courthouse squares. Traces of these physical patterns linger in major urban centers such as Los Angeles and Boston as well as in smaller towns and villages, but in the twentieth century, town design in the United States largely shifted from public to private control.[1] Since 1945, complex public subsidies have buttressed many types of private real estate development. Americans have often made the mistake of condemning the low-grade products—badly-sited tracts, enormous parking lots, or gigantic malls—rather than attacking the process that has diverted public dollars to private rather than public space.

Between the mid-1920s and the mid-1950s, the National Association of Real Estate Boards (NAREB), an influential lobby, encouraged the federal government to enact five kinds of legislation: Federal Housing Administration (FHA) and Veterans Administration (VA) programs for mortgage loan insurance, homeowner mortgage interest deductions from income tax, interstate highway subsidies funded by gasoline taxes, and tax deductions for accelerated depreciation on commercial real estate. The first three subsidies led to the tract house suburbs of the 1940s and 1950s. The other two generated interstate highways in the 1960s and edge nodes consisting of malls, offices, and other commercial real estate projects at highway interchanges in the 1960s, 1970s, and 1980s. By providing subsidies indirectly, through loan guarantee programs or manipulation of the tax codes, the federal government avoided extensive scrutiny of the politics behind public funding for privately owned space. Few requirements for infrastructure (sewer systems, schools, transit), public amenities (open space), or public access accompanied indirect subsidy programs. While all of these programs have been critiqued, their cumulative impact on private and public space has not yet been fully assessed.[2] A brief history of three postwar developments—Levittown, Lakewood, and Park Forest—outlines the devastating economic and physical consequences of private, urban-scale construction.

Making the Rules: The Department of Commerce and the Real Estate Lobby

The federal government was first drawn toward urban planning and housing through Herbert Hoover's efforts to work with the real estate lobby to promote construction as secretary of commerce from 1921 to 1928 and then as president from 1929 to 1933. Hoover was an engineer, and his Commerce Department began by establishing a Division of Building and Housing that supported banking, building, and real estate activities. It developed a model zoning ordinance, a uniform national building code, and legislation to establish the Federal Housing Administration. Hoover also nurtured a private nonprofit group called Better Homes in America, Inc.[3] By 1930, Better Homes had organized over 7,000 local chapters composed of bankers, subdividers, construction firms, realtors, utilities, small businesses, and manufacturers advocating government support for the private development of small houses as a way to boost mass consumption. This coalition formed a "Growth Machine," a political machine promoting large-scale land development in many localities.[4] In 1931, Hoover ran the National Conference on Homebuilding and Home Ownership, which explored federal financing and construction of houses, subdivision layout, and the location of industry and commerce.

When Hoover became commerce secretary in 1921, the NAREB became "an important and highly favored trade organization, working with Commerce and other agencies."[5] Large developer/builders formed NAREB in

1908, and they assisted the federal government with housing issues during World War I. By 1931, NAREB was "a key national lobbying force." Its leaders included major developers such as Harry Culver of Culver City near Los Angeles, and J.C. Nichols of the Country Club District in Kansas City.[6] In 1927, NAREB worked jointly with the American City Planning Institute (ACPI) on the document that became the Commerce Department's *Standard City Planning Enabling Act.* Interestingly, planners wanted to require subdividers to dedicate some portion of all new tracts to parks and open space for public use. The realtors thought the planners too idealistic—they wanted to get paid for every bit of land.[7]

President Franklin D. Roosevelt followed Hoover and launched a number of New Deal programs in planning and housing during the Depression years.[8] The National Housing Act created the FHA in 1934. Realtors had worked on drafting the rules for the FHA and were active in administering the agency once it was established. Other New Deal efforts stressed public construction and public space, and realtors fought against them. The Resettlement Administration, created by executive order in 1935, sponsored the Greenbelt Towns, planned towns that were soon attacked by the real estate lobby as "too expensive." The U.S. Housing Act (Wagner Act) created the U.S. Housing Authority to sponsor public housing in 1937, soon attacked by the real estate lobby as "un-American." Activists such as Catherine Bauer (RPAA member) and other members of a group called the Labor Housing Conference had long campaigned for the design of multifamily housing with child-care centers and recreational amenities including swimming pools and meeting rooms. Projects such as the Hosiery Workers Housing in Philadelphia and the Harlem River Houses for African Americans in New York, designed by teams of noted architects in the 1930s, pointed to what could be achieved. Nevertheless, NAREB lobbyists held to the Hoover programs and fought hard against any alternatives to the single-family tract house purchased on a long mortgage. Conservative Republicans defeated the Wagner Act in 1935 and 1936, burdening its passage in 1937 with severe cost restrictions, means testing for tenants, and slum clearance to protect private landlords.[9] These provisions meant that public housing design would be minimal and residents would be poor. FHA would be the dominant program. Kenneth T. Jackson has shown that FHA's concern for appraised value was expressed as a prohibition on people of color in white neighborhoods.[10] As a result, postwar housing was dominated by private developers who created vast new tracts segregated by government policy.

None of this was inevitable—there was a moment after World War II when housing activists again challenged federal policy, and real estate interests fought hard to control the issue. Historians Rosalyn Baxandall and Elizabeth Ewen document the lobbying by bankers and builders behind the hearings on housing dominated by Senator Joseph McCarthy in 1947 and 1948.[11] McCarthy developed his "sledgehammer style" hassling proponents of public housing and planned towns as socialists and communists. McCarthy also attacked building workers in traditional craft unions in the AFL as incompetents who produced low-quality work and who would impede the postwar housing process. McCarthy found developer William Levitt an ally who would testify that only federal aid to large private builders could solve the postwar housing shortage. McCarthy and his allies also attacked the expansion of benefits for the poor in the 1949 Housing Act. FHA remained dominant in the housing area, and Title I of the 1949 housing legislation opened the way to land clearance in big cities for the benefit of private developers, later called "urban renewal."

Following the Rules: Postwar Suburbs

In the vast new tracts produced in the late 1940s and 1950s, public and private were redefined. With populations between 50,000 and 80,000, the largest of the post-World War II subdivisions were the size of cities, but they looked like overgrown subdivisions. Ten million new homes built between 1946 and 1953 were the products of a newly restructured private housing industry working closely with the federal government. Before the war, the average builder made a few houses a year. By 1949, the majority of new dwelling units in the United States were produced by very large builders.[12] Levitt and Sons of New York, Weingart, Taper, and Boyar of Lakewood, California, and Manilow and Klutznick's American Community Builders (ACB) of Park Forest, Illinois were typical. At 70,000 to 80,000 residents apiece, Lakewood and Levittown, New York, were the two largest suburbs of this era. In these suburbs, the federal government provided massive aid directed at developers (whose 90 percent production advances were insured by the FHA). They also subsidized veterans (who could get VA guarantees for mortgages at 4 percent with little or nothing down), and white male homeowners (who could deduct their mortgage interest payments from their taxable income for the next thirty years).

Levittown, Nassau County, New York

William Levitt and his brother Alfred were college dropouts. Their lawyer father, Abraham Levitt, encouraged them to stay busy by forming a building company during the Depression, and after the war they emerged as major developers. Levitt and Sons promoted a brand-name product to promote the community of over 17,000 houses that they built on Long Island for about 77,000 people.[13] A reporter described William Levitt as a hoarse-voiced chain smoker of three packs a day, with "a liking for hyperbole that causes him to describe his height (5 ft. 8 in.) as 'nearly six feet,' and his company as the 'General Motors of the housing industry.'"[14] Alfred, the firm's designer, said, "As in your car, the parts in a Levitt house are standardized; each part will fit any house of the same model." He added that "the Levitt factory … is the land on which we assemble our houses."[15] William Levitt developed a public relations campaign promoting every last step in the house building process, as well as every supplier. Bendix washers, General Electric stoves, and Admiral televisions were installed in the houses. Levitt houses endorsed the advertised products, and the products were often selling points for Levitt houses.

Although they are often credited with this, Levitt and Sons did not originate the methods of organizing the rapid production of houses in a continuous production process. Fritz Burns in California seems to have been first, but Levitt and Sons was pushing in the same direction in a 1942 project for 750 FHA Title VI houses in Norfolk, Virginia, where they systematized over two dozen basic tasks of house building.[16] Alfred Levitt styled their first Cape Cod to recall Sears, Roebuck mail order houses like "The Nantucket." Levitt and Sons stood behind the product with an unwritten one-year warranty, and began to sell 800-square-foot houses for $6,990 in the late 1940s. The Levitt "ranch" that followed included a carport. Levitt and Sons also relied on some sweat equity, giving veterans and their wives the chance to personalize their houses. They could convert the attics of their houses into additional bedrooms, build garages or porches, and landscape the yards. "No man who has a house and lot can be a Communist," claimed William Levitt. "He has too much to do."[17] Stories of customers standing in line for days appeared in the press. Happy purchasers posed in front of houses. By October 1952, *Fortune* magazine gushed over "The Most House for the Money," and praised "Levitt's Progress," publishing William Levitt's complaints about government interference, that is, strict FHA and VA inspections and standards. Said Levitt, with a straight face, despite hundreds of millions of dollars of FHA financing: "Utopia in this business would be to get rid of the government, except in its proper function of an insurance agency."[18]

Levitt and Sons never talked about urban planning. They were far more conservative than someone like NAREB's J.C. Nichols, who took pride in designing his developments well. Levittown was a large, unincorporated community of 80,000 people, straddling several towns including Hempstead and Oyster Bay. It had no master plan and no government of its own. Land purchases were not always contiguous—arterials with commercial strip development owned by others often intersected residential areas. Between 1947 and 1951, Levitt and Sons constructed seven small shopping areas, a few stores each.[19] They also built nine swimming pools and seven small parks with children's playgrounds and some baseball fields. What the Levitts did not build was infrastructure, according to a study made by New York University students and faculty in 1951.[20] Levitt failed to integrate their road systems with county and state highways. Levitt and Sons did not plan for urban-scale sewage disposal. They did not even use septic tanks—historian Barbara Kelly has noted they used individual cesspools attached to each house, rather than sewers.[21] Engineers in the Nassau County Department of Public Health protested the problems of ground saturation without success.[22] No sewers were built until the 1960s, when the federal government provided aid to suburbs around the country to eliminate health hazards and install sewers retroactively.[23] Similarly, the Levitt firm left trash removal up to private contractors, whose private waste removal services would be paid for by the residents.[24] Levitt and Sons boasted that they "set aside" land for schools to both towns, but they paid for nothing and built nothing.[25] Towns had to assess the taxpayers in special districts to pay for the land, school buildings, and operations. The state government provided financial aid to avoid a crisis. By 1951, Alfred Levitt learned from his mistakes, and proposed a new planned community called Landia. Bill Levitt then claimed he and his brother could no longer make decisions together. He split from Alfred and built two more Levittowns emphasizing houses plus more shopping.[26]

Lakewood, California

Lakewood developed a little bit more slowly than Levittown, but eventually it was slightly larger, about 80,000 people.[27] The three developers, Ben Weingart, Mark Taper, and Louis Boyar bought ten square miles of flat land near Long Beach.[28] The entire area was gridded with streets meeting at right angles, lined by lots of 50 by 100 feet, the smallest size permitted in Los Angeles County. It held 17,500 frame and stucco houses of 1,100 square feet. There were sewers, required by the county, and a Waste King electric garbage disposal in every kitchen. O'Keefe and Merritt gas stoves, Norge refrigerators, and Bendix "Economat" washers could be added to the purchase price at a hefty extra charge of $9 per appliance each month.[29] Each house was provided with one small tree in the planting strip between front sidewalk and street.[30] The developers were stingy with recreational facilities, but a county supervisor did browbeat the developers into building one swimming pool in a local park. The developers hired William Garnett, the noted aerial photographer, to fly over the land recording their progress. His chilling images of rows of houses sprouting from fields became famous, but not for the reasons he had been hired.

In contrast to Levittown, Lakewood also included, from the start, a highly profitable regional shopping mall surrounded by 10,580 parking spaces, as well as sixteen small commercial centers within walking distance—one-half mile—of the houses.[31] The shopping mall was anchored by a branch of the May Company, designed by architect Albert C. Martin with four giant neon "M's" sixteen feet high, facing north, south, east, and west. Opening in February 1952, the shopping center offered the goods new residents might need and also drew in outside customers.

With the mall, a private store became a public landmark, pointing to the directions that real estate would soon take across the country. The housing around it fueled controversy.

In *Holy Land*, D.J. Waldie relates that in 1954 Ben Weingart and Louis Boyar were subpoenaed to testify before Homer Capeheart's Senate subcommittee on "irregularities in their federally backed mortgages and construction loans."[32] The developers had not gotten FHA Title VI funding for a 90 percent guarantee. Instead, they had proceeded under the National Housing Act, Section 213, asking for 100 percent financing by pretending to be the organizers of "mutual homes." They got their employees to front dummy corporations, using a New Deal program planned for rural cooperatives with a maximum of 501 houses apiece. Using this deception over and over, they built the largest suburban community in America. It didn't cost them any jail time.

Park Forest, The GI Town

Some developers tried to do better. American Community Builders (ACB), a private development firm headed by Philip Klutznick, a former federal government official who had served in the Roosevelt and Truman administrations, created Park Forest, Illinois. He said, "We aren't interested in houses alone. We are trying to create a better life for people. In our view, we will have failed if all we do is to produce houses."[33] Approached about fronting a "GI town" by Nathan Manilow, a major Chicago real estate developer, Klutznick said he would only be interested if it were a real town, not an overgrown suburban development. According to landscape architect Gregory Randall, ACB selected a site of over 3,100 acres about thirty miles south of Chicago on a railroad line. The firm added experienced public housing architects Jerrold Loebl and Norman Schlossman. Elbert Peets, the noted Washington, D.C., landscape architect, co-author of *The American Vitruvius*, and co-designer of Greendale, Wisconsin, did the basic town plan for a "garden city" with a nearby railroad station, sites for industry, a shopping center, and several smaller commercial areas, parks, schools, and many types of single-family and multi-family housing.

ACB decided to begin with the construction of rental housing. Using Clarence Stein's Baldwin Hills Village as a model, a variety of two-story townhouses and flats were grouped in courtyards and superblocks. This phase included 3,010 units. By 1948, tenants were moving in, the Klutznick family first among them. At the first barbecue, the developers pressed residents to vote for incorporation as a village. Many volunteers stepped forward and began to run the town and its committees. Meanwhile, the company began to develop a town center with government offices, a department store, and forty-four smaller stores. By trying to build a town center (although it was similar to a mall) and set a higher standard for postwar development, ACB attracted other developers to the fringes of their area, smaller firms that would build only houses and sell them more cheaply. Those who thought sound neighborhoods turned few profits challenged Peets' residential neighborhood concept.[34] Under pressure to avoid slow home sales, ACB discarded Peets's elegant scheme of small residential neighborhoods with a hierarchy of streets, parks, and pedestrian circulation, in favor of Levitt-like streets with no connecting greenbelt and fewer landscape buffers. Costs were slashed at every turn—houses were moved closer to the streets to save on piping, planting strips were removed, sidewalks were combined with curbs to save on concrete work. Over time, the houses were all sold, and the town filled out to a population of 30,000. By the late 1950s and early 1960s, ACB began to dissolve, selling various parts of the village that had not been on the market before, including the rental housing. The partners became wealthy men. In time, Klutznick became the developer of Chicago's Water Tower Place, and then secretary of commerce in the Carter administration.

Keeping the Postwar Boom Going

In the mid-1950s, American politicians and business people worried about how to keep mass consumption going in a "consumer's republic" where white male citizens were encouraged to see purchasing things as a patriotic duty.[35] Could families who owned houses, cars, and consumer goods be persuaded to keep on buying? In the 1950s, Americans owned three-quarters of the appliances and gadgets produced in the world. As the 1950s wore on, the attention given to houses, appliances, and consumer products turned explicitly political in the televised 1959 Nixon/Khrushchev "Kitchen Debate" in Moscow.[36] At this exhibition, Nixon boasted to Khrushchev that a model house, "Splitnik," an all-electric kitchen, and dozens of small appliances provided material evidence of the superiority of the way of life of an ordinary American worker.

But could one more appliance keep consumers happy? Back in the 1930s, GE and other manufacturers had lobbied the FHA to get appliance costs included in mortgages.[37] Energy consumption soared as part of this strategy. The problem two decades later was to find novel ways to keep appliance consumption rising, and the strategy backfired. The introduction of air conditioning in the early 1950s (first room air conditioners and then central cooling) was followed by campaigns for electric heat (to balance the cooling load in summer with a comparable demand for power in the winter). The "all-electric home" was promoted by utilities and manufacturers looking for more business. They offered so many sweetheart deals for tract builders, as well as coercive measures, that their promotional practices generated congressional hearings.[38]

One alternative route to high consumption of appliances and energy was building bigger houses. Would families trade up their houses the way they did with automobiles? Those families who owned houses were encouraged to spend more with the "mansion subsidy," because tax deductions for mortgage interest rose with the cost and size of the house. The average size of a new house in 1950 was 800 square feet; in 1970, 1,200 square feet; and in 1990, 2,100 square feet. Estimated at $81 billion in 1994, the mansion subsidy remains larger than the annual budget of the department of Housing and Urban Development.[39] As house sizes rose, household size was decreasing and more and more mothers were engaging in paid work. By 2000, close to 60 percent of mothers of children under one year old were in the paid labor force.[40] While white male–headed households were often homeowners, households headed by persons of color and women lagged in their rates of home ownership—and still do. Rather than extend housing to those not housed, the next two federal subsidies went to support more development on urban peripheries.

Highways and Edge Nodes

Historians have often suggested that from the late 1920s on, cars enabled people to move to suburbs. Another way to understand the car–house relationship is that the FHA model of hidden subsidies for private housing was, in the mid-1950s, applied to asphalt, trucks, and automobiles, when the Interstate Highway Act provided for the construction of 42,500 miles of roads with 90 percent federal financing. Legislation specifically excluded public transportation from sharing in the subsidy.

From the mid-1950s on, developers responded to the infrastructure of interstate highways, and the lack of planned centers in existing suburbs, by large-scale construction of commercial real estate at highway off-ramps. These anchored dozens of non-places that Joel Garreau called "edge cities" in 1991, and Robert E. Lang recently expanded to "edgeless cities."[41] Terms such as "outtowns" and "outer cities" did not explain them. Perhaps "taxopolis" would have been better. As Tom Hanchett has shown, federal tax policies between 1954 and 1986 offered accelerated depreciation for new commercial real estate in greenfield locations. Developers received huge tax write-offs for "every type of income-producing structure," including motels, fast food restaurants, offices, rental apartments, and of course, shopping centers. As Hanchett notes, "Throughout the mid-1950s, developers had sought locations *within* growing suburban areas. Now shopping centers began appearing in the cornfields *beyond* the edge of existing development." This tax write-off cost the federal government about $750 million to $850 million per year in the late 1960s.[42] Accelerated depreciation also encouraged cheap construction and discouraged adequate maintenance. Obsolescence was rapid.

Over time edge nodes expanded, adding new building types such as "category killers" (big box discount stores) and "power centers" (groups of big boxes), plus disguised boxes and outlet malls trying to look like villages. Less and less was local. Businesses were increasingly tied to national or international chains, part of an expanding global economy, often requiring airport access as well as access by truck. Warehouse-like buildings were dictated by management protocols about "facilities" having nothing to do with the towns where they operated.[43] Millions who worked in edge nodes refused to live in places like Tyson's Corner, Virginia, or Schaumburg, Illinois. Instead, many Americans chose to drive to residences located on the rural fringe.[44] The 2000 Census showed rural fringes as the fastest growing areas in the country. (Myron Orfield's *American Metropolitics* critiques the way that residents of older, inner-ring suburbs are often subject to state and local taxes that subsidize the extension of infrastructure to the affluent outer fringes, but these state and local subsidies are beyond the scope of this paper.[45])

The American Way: Growth Machines

The Hoover era established a national pattern of urbanization based on federal subsidies to stimulate the consumption of houses, cars, and consumer goods by white, male-headed households. The visions of the "growth machines" never included public space. Without a federal commitment to economic equity, and without urban and regional planning and design controls, growth machines surrounded older city centers with low-density, low-quality greenfield construction, undermining their economic vitality. Oblique methods of delivering federal financial support to private developers made frontal attack difficult, so many reformers targeted narrower single issues. Since the 1950s, conservationists have campaigned for more open space in suburbs. Environmentalists have critiqued the wasteful use of land and energy in suburban development and struggled to get federal regulations to protect soil, water, and wildlife. Political activists have decried racism and campaigned for fair housing legislation. Architects have proposed pedestrian-friendly mixed-use neighborhoods. There have been relatively few critiques of broad spatial impact of the real estate lobby, its close ties to the federal government, and its definitions of building the American way.

In *Modern Housing in America: Policy Struggles in the New Deal Era*, historian Gail Radford defines the 1930s as the time when Americans developed a "two-tier" policy to subsidize housing. Cramped multifamily housing for the poor, the elderly, female-headed families, and people of color would be constructed by public authorities, and more generous single-family housing for white, male-headed families would be constructed by private developers with government support.[46] The split had profound implications for urban design—inadequate financial resources behind one effort and wasted material resources behind the other. And worst of all, it mystified many working-class and middle-class Americans, who saw minimal subsidies for the poor but never understood their own tract housing, highways, and malls were far more heavily subsidized.

As Barry Checkoway has noted, back in the 1950s *Fortune* was fond of portraying suburbs as "exploding" over the landscape, as the happy result of consumer preferences that created a boom. But, he says, "ordinary consumers had little real choice."[47] There were no well-designed multifamily housing projects in urban settings. There were no well-designed single family houses in integrated new towns with substantial public space.[48] Instead urban-scale places like Levittown, Lakewood, and Park Forest were constructed without much input from architects or urban designers, as if they were subdivisions of houses rather than cities. Design and construction were even worse a decade or two later, in edge nodes identified as hot spots for commercial real estate. Small town Main Streets withered, and urban commercial neighborhoods declined, as businesses moved to subsidized edge nodes. Although private investors made money, even the largest of these edge nodes, such as Tyson's Corner and Schaumberg, were monotonous landscapes of windowless malls, windowless big box stores, cheap office buildings, and logo buildings housing food franchises, all designed for constant automobile and truck traffic.

Coupled with earlier subsidies for massive, new urban-scale housing tracts in suburban locations, more recent subsidies for edge nodes and rural fringes surrounding them have devastated the centers of older cities and towns. A few decades of subsidies for greenfield growth reversed centuries of concentrated, locally regulated urban development. By 2000, metropolitan regions had expanded into urbanized areas 200 miles in diameter. Beyond the village greens of New England, the plazas of the Southwest, and the courthouse squares of the Midwest, beyond the centers of new towns established before 1920, public places built to attract citizens are scarce.

Legal scholar Carol Rose has written about "property as storytelling."[49] "Property is process," argues natural resources specialist Louise Fortmann.[50] Sketched here is the story of federal policies to stimulate the real estate and construction sectors of the economy, policies that granted large private developers a lavish sequence of subsidies without incentives to create well-designed residential neighborhoods, transit, and public space. To understand why public space is missing, Americans must remember that after 1945, most of the built environment was never planned or designed—it was shaped by old Commerce Department programs devised with the aid of the real estate industry just before the Depression. It would be funny if it were not so unfair.

Notes

This paper is drawn from my book, *Building Suburbia: Green Fields and Urban Growth, 1820–2000* (New York: Pantheon Books, 2003).

1. Public space is defined as publicly owned space accessible to all citizens—for example, parks, public sidewalks, and city hall. A shopping mall is private commercial property open to customers at the discretion of the owners. A highway is public property, but it is accessible chiefly to private cars and trucks. For an extended but somewhat abstruse theoretical discussion, see Andrew Light and Jonathan M. Smith, eds., *Philosophy and Geography II: The Production of Public Space* (Lanham, MD: Rowman and Littlefield Publishers, Inc., 1998).

2. Tom Lewis, *Divided Highways: Building the Interstate Highways, Transforming American Life* (New York: Penguin, 1997); Hayden, *Building Suburbia;* Hayden, *A Field Guide to Sprawl* (New York: Norton, 2004).

3. Gwendolyn Wright, *Building the Dream* (New York: Pantheon, 1981), 197–198; Gail Radford, *Modern Housing in America: Policy Struggles in the New Deal Era* (Chicago: University of Chicago Press, 1996), 51–53. Radford emphasizes Hoover's interest in standardization.

4. On "growth machines," also sometimes called "sprawl machines," see John R. Logan and Harvey L. Molotch, *Urban Fortunes: The Political Economy of Place* (Berkeley, CA: University of California Press, 1987), 52–98.

5. Marc A. Weiss, *The Rise of the Community Builders: The American Real Estate Industry and Urban Land Use Planning* (New York: Columbia University Press, 1987), 28–29.

6. NAREB became the National Association of Realtors (NAR), and today has 800,000 members, the largest trade organization in the United States. In the early 1940s, NAREB spun off the Urban Land Institute (ULI) and the National Association of Home Builders (NAHB) as additional lobbying groups. Both are still active today.

7. Weiss, *Rise of the Community Builders*, 75–76.

8. John Hancock, "The New Deal and American Planning: The 1930s," in *Two Centuries of American Planning*, edited by Daniel Schaffer, (Baltimore: Johns Hopkins University Press, 1988), 197–230.

9. Radford, *Modern Housing*, 188.

10. Kenneth T. Jackson has traced the federal redlining policies and their influence on the FHA in *Crabgrass Frontier: The Suburbanization of America* (New York: Oxford University Press, 1985), 190–218.

11. Rosalyn Baxandall and Elizabeth Ewen, *Picture Windows: How the Suburbs Happened* (New York: Basic Books, 2000), 87–116.

12. Weiss, *Community Builders*, 161.

13. Baxandall and Ewen, *Picture Windows*, 125, quoting his testimony at the McCarthy hearings.

14. "Housing: Up from the Potato Fields," *Time*, July 3, 1950, 67, 72.

15. Alfred Levitt, "A Community Builder looks at Community Planning," *Journal of the American Institute of Planners* 17 (spring 1951), 81.

16. Peter S. Reed, "Enlisting Modernism," in *World War II and the American Dream: How Wartime Building Changed a Nation*, edited by Donald Albrecht (Washington, DC: National Building Museum; Cambridge, MA: MIT Press, 1995), 30.

17. Eric Larrabee, "The Six Thousand Houses That Levitt Built," *Harper's*, September 1948, p. 84. For an account of the transformations of the houses, see Barbara M. Kelly, *Expanding the American Dream: Building and Rebuilding Levittown* (Albany, NY: State University of New York Press, 1993).

18. "Levitt's Progress," *Fortune*, 46, October 1952, p. 158. Also see "The Most House for the Money," in the same issue, 151–154.

19. When other developers began to build larger shopping facilities on the Sunrise Highway, the small Levitt commercial strips were in trouble, and vacant stores have remained a problem, according to Alexander Garvin, *The American City: What Works and What Doesn't* (New York: McGraw Hill, 1996), 337.

20. Charles E. Redfield, et al., "The Impact of Levittown on Local Government," *Journal of the American Institute of Planners* 17 (summer 1951), 130–141.

21. Kelly, "Expanding the American Dream," 218, n. 91: "Kitchen and bath waste were exhausted to a cesspool just outside the kitchen wall."

22. Redfield, "Impact," 137.

23. Adam Rome, *The Bulldozer in the Countryside: Suburban Sprawl and the Rise of American Environmentalism* (Cambridge, UK and New York: Cambridge University Press, 2001), 87–118.

24. By 1951 all of the local haulers were told that facilities in Oyster Bay were overtaxed. A quarry in Hempstead was used as a temporary dumping area, while Hempstead struggled to build a disposal plant.

25. Redfield, "Impact," 134.

26. Herbert Gans, *The Levittowners: Ways of Life and Politics in a New Suburban Community* (1967; New York: Columbia University Press, 1982), 3–5.

27. D.J. Waldie, *Holy Land: A Suburban Memoir* (New York: St. Martin's Press, 1996), 91.

28. Ibid., 89.

29. Ibid., 35–36.

30. Ibid., 37.

31. Ibid., 101.

32. Ibid., 164–170.

33. *Collier's Magazine*, February 14, 1948, quoted in Gregory Randall, *America's Original GI Town: Park Forest, Illinois* (Baltimore: Johns Hopkins University Press, 2000), 157.

34. Randall, *America's Original GI Town*, 164–166.

35. Lizabeth Cohen, *A Consumer's Republic: The Politics of Mass Consumption in Postwar America* (New York: Knopf, 2003).

36. Karal Ann Marling, *As Seen on TV: The Visual Culture of Everyday Life in the 1950s* (Cambridge, MA: Harvard University Press, 1994), 242–283.

37. Rome, *Bulldozer*, 38.

38. Hearings held in 1968. Rome, *Bulldozer*, 45–86.

39. Vicky Kemper, "Home Inequity," *Common Cause Magazine*, 20, summer 1994, pp. 14–26.

40. Tamar Lewin, "Now a Majority: Families with 2 Parents Who Work," *New York Times*, October 24, 2000, p. A20.

41. Robert E. Lang, *Edgeless Cities* (Washington, D.C.: Brookings Institution Press, 2003). See also Bruce Katz and Robert E. Lang, eds., *Redefining Urban and Suburban America: Evidence from Census 2000* (Washington, DC: Brookings Institution Press, 2003).

42. Thomas Hanchett, "U.S. Tax Policy and the Shopping-Center Boom of the 1950s and 1960s," *American Historical Review* 101 (October 1996), 1082–1110.

43. Keller Easterling, *Organization Space* (Cambridge, MA: MIT Press, 1999.)

44. Tom Daniels, *When City and Country Collide: Managing Growth in the Metropolitan Fringe* (Washington, DC: Island Press, 1999).

45. Myron Orfield, *American Metropolitics: The New Suburban Reality* (Washington, DC: Brookings Institution Press, 2003). It is also routine for a state like Connecticut to offer $60 million as in "economic development" subsidy to a mall developer. It is more controversial for the city of New York to offer a $1 billion subsidy for a privately owned team.

46. Radford, *Modern Housing*, 180–198.

47. Barry Checkoway, "Large Builders, Federal Housing Programs, and Postwar Suburbanization," in *Critical Perspectives on Housing*, edited by Rachel G. Bratt, Chester Hartman, and Ann Meyerson (Philadelphia: Temple University Press, 1986), 119–138.

48. Title VII towns including Columbia, Irvine, and the Woodlands, were intended to correct some of these faults. Government funds were used to provide infrastructure. Private developers built the towns in the late 1960s and early 1970s with mixed results. Ann Forsyth, *Reforming Suburbia: The Planned Communities of Irvine, Columbia, and The Woodlands* (Berkeley, CA: University of California Press, 2005).

49. Carol M. Rose, "Property as Storytelling: Perspectives from Game Theory, Narrative Theory, Feminist Theory," *Yale Journal of Law and the Humanities* 2 (1990), 37–57.

50. Louise Fortmann, "Bonanza! The Unasked Questions: Domestic Land Tenure through International Lenses," in *Who Owns America? Social Conflict over Property Rights*, edited by Harvey M. Jacobs (Madison, WI: University of Wisconsin Press, 1998), 5–7.

CHAPTER 4

Appropriating "the Commons":
The Tragedy of Property Rights Discourse

ELIZABETH BLACKMAR

In the last decade of the twentieth century, a new feature sprang up on the American landscape, a space designated "the commons." In Fort Worth, Texas, the Spring Garden Commons, a subdivision of new houses ranging in size from 1,700 to 3,000 square feet, stands at the intersection of Bankhead Highway and Highway 180. The Kierland Commons in Phoenix, Arizona, is described by its developer as an "urban village with space for retail, restaurants, offices, and possibly at a later time, multi-family." In Los Angeles, the city council authorized a $43.9 million subsidy for a $219 million Southland revitalization project called NoHo Commons. In the Atlanta metropolitan area, the eighteen-acre East Lake Commons won a prize for "mixed income" development ($90,000 to $300,000) and environmental protections, including nine acres set aside for a pond, garden, and woodlands. In Westchester County, New York, the abandoned Baldwin Place Mall has been resurrected as the Somers Commons.[1]

Like "country estates," "galleria," "festival marketplace," or "rancho verdes," the term "commons" identifies precisely what the space is not. The label's proliferation suggests the popularity of an imagined "third way" for ordering the landscape: a commons is said to be neither public nor private space. It implies open access and shared participation without

49

the shadow of the state (with its heavy-handed powers to tax or regulate); and it implies a space for community assembly apart from the hard sell of the market. New mall-like student centers feature a commons to invoke a tradition of medieval collegiality; within urban design circles, the notion of commons offers an antidote to the anomie of suburban subdivisions. But in contrast to England's Greenham Common, a space claimed for the purpose of mounting sustained political resistance to nuclear weapons in the 1980s, the third way of the contemporary commons disavows politics altogether. True, there is an implicit gesture toward New England town meetings, but there is no more expectation of political deliberation on the new commons, enclosed by stores, condominiums, doctors' offices, or computer labs, than there is of grazing cows.

The commons is perhaps unusual within the lexicon of American place names because it refers to a kind of property rights as well as a site. Nonetheless, common properties in the United States have been enclosed—that is, appropriated—since the nineteenth century; their vestiges—whether communal water or land rights in New Mexico or properties of certain Indian reservations—are seen as just that, the residue of archaic social relations. "Commons" as a place name is meant only to conjure up pleasant feelings of connection, not to describe or empower claims on shared resources.

"Commons" has become a sign of the times in scholarly discourse as well as in the vernacular landscape. Political science, anthropology, environmental studies, law, and economics abound with discussions of both theoretical and actual regimes of common property that govern territory or natural resources. Scholarly discourse, too, poses commons as an alternative to central state power, on the one hand, and the market (or, more often, market failure) on the other. But whereas the vernacular usage is mostly sentimental in projecting a shared, conflict-free community space, the academic concepts, working within neoliberal economic paradigms, have been more ideological, displaying antipathy for historical analysis of the contests over power and property rights within actual markets or government regimes.

What brings vernacular and scholarly use of "commons" together is the way in which the concept has been deployed to discount older institutions of public property—and hence public space—in order to affirm the essential benevolence of private property and, by extension, of capital. Indeed, the revival of the language of commons in the 1990s followed on a quarter century's campaign to suppress claims of common property in the environment, as well as to discredit claims that state-owned property can be organized to provide public benefits, including democratic public space. In this essay I want to look at how the discourse of property rights has evolved in order to account for the neoliberal appropriations of the concept of common property, appropriations that I believe have left their mark on the politics of public space today.

There are of course many ways to define public space, and few of them rest on the status of ownership and control established through property rights. Still, placing the politics of public space in the discursive frame of political economy highlights questions about the organization and reach of proprietary power, questions that often recede from discussions that equate public with amorphous community, on the one hand, or the realm of commercial spectacle, on the other. Politics within this frame entails contests over the power to collect and distribute resources to build and maintain public spaces—not just space in a territorial sense but space as a feature of all public institutions. Political negotiations also determine who has access to public spaces and how they can be used. But perhaps most important, the politics of public space center on how publicly controlled resources and institutions work together to create an arena of deliberation and accountability. Exploring the politics of any particular public space sheds light on broader historical conditions of access, participation, and accountability. But by looking at the way the language of property rights has shaped the kinds of claims that are made on and about public property in its broadest sense, I hope to call attention to one way the possibilities of democratic public space have been opened up and shut down.

The Ascendancy of Private and Public Property

At the outset, I want to offer some classic definitions of property rights taken from political theorist C.B. Macpherson.[2] Property can be thought of as enforceable claims to the benefits of resources. These claims carry with them duties and liabilities. The Anglo-American legal tradition has recognized essentially three kinds of property rights. Private property is the right of individuals to exclude others from the uses or benefits of resources. (Legal individuals can be human or "artificial persons," as in the case of corporations.) Public property, owned by governments, gives state officials the right to determine who has access to resources held on behalf of a wider constituency. Common property is an individual's right not to be excluded from the uses or benefits of resources. Historically, common property rights were recognized and enforced for members of a bounded community. Thus, common property is usually distinguished from "open access" or unappropriated resources that are beyond a prescribed political jurisdiction (as might be the case with fish outside territorial waters).[3] However sharp the distinctions among these different rights in theory, enforceable claims to property—whether rights to land or to revenues or goods—have been the subject and the product of ongoing contest. Indeed, the fact of such contests has given rise to theories that aim to justify particular property rights by showing how they derive from nature or from reason and sound social policy. A quick historical sketch illustrates the uneven ways that history and ideology have intersected to shape understandings of property rights and with those understandings, the spaces that they govern.

Common property was a feature of the agrarian landscape in seventeenth- and eighteenth-century England. When landlords acted under new laws to enclose common fields, wood lots, marshes, and pastures, they dispossessed rural families of their claims not to be excluded from these resources. As gentry proprietors asserted their individual political rights against the Crown as well as their economic power against longstanding tenants, political theorists such as John Locke explained the intersection of proprietorship and sovereignty by locating them in a natural order. Men's claim to property derived from the exertion of their own (and their dependents') labor in improving land or other resources; they formed governments to protect these rights. In the late eighteenth century, William Blackstone most boldly articulated the possessive individualism that underlay Lockean ideology: "There is nothing which so generally strikes the imagination, and engages the affections of mankind, as the right of property; or that sole and despotic dominion which one man claims and exercises over the external things of the world, in total exclusion of the right of any other individual in the universe."[4] Early American republican discourse echoed this rendering of proprietorship as the essential expression of individual independence, and also as evidence of men's capacity for citizenship.

Yet, by the early nineteenth century, English utilitarian thinkers who wanted to link private property rights to expanding markets chafed at the claims of parasitic landed elites to rights of absolute dominion. Jeremy Bentham offered a definition freed from the land and from nature. "Property is nothing but the basis of expectation," according to Bentham, "consist[ing] in an established expectation, in the persuasion of being able to draw such and such advantage from the thing possessed."[5] And positive law or policy determined what those advantages could be. Although Bentham himself believed that limited government interference with private property fostered the greatest economic growth, other nineteenth-century liberals advocated using state power and state property (the building of roads, canals, ports, and the acquisition of new territory) to promote economic development.

There is no simple story of progress in the evolution of property rights, whether public or private, to maximize social wealth. Claims to the benefits of land, water, or public improvements were as contested during the era of industrial expansion as they had been at the peak of English enclosures. Nor did American judges follow a linear progression from natural rights to utilitarian logic when enforcing particular claims. In the antebellum period, judges who favored a utilitarian conception of property—and the expectations of entrepreneurs—expanded the rights of manufacturers and railroads by limiting their common law liabilities for nuisances or trespass at the expense of neighbors, whose lands had been damaged by floods or fire. In Europe, such privileges were linked to the power of the state, for railroads were both public property and created quintessential public spaces. In their first generation, state-chartered, privately owned American railroads, far from representing purely private property and enterprise, were subsidized by local, state, and federal governments and hence taxpayers. Intense debate over access and accountability arose again and again with respect to location, rates, labor, monopoly, and rules of use. Courts and legislatures at all levels of government variously invoked private rights of dominion and contract or a countervailing public good and utilitarian policy, depending as much on the balance of political power as any stable doctrine of public and private property rights.[6]

Thinking of railroads as an example of public space—what historian Wolfgang Schivelbusch calls "mechanized territory"—highlights political dimensions of production, governance, and use that are sometimes lost in discussions of public space more conventionally defined as government–owned land.[7] While the uses of such transportation facilities were instrumental rather than deliberative or social, and thus loses the ready association of public space with collective assembly or self-conscious display, the politics never strayed far from property rights, encompassing debates over the distribution of public lands and monies, police protection (whether against Indians, bandits, or striking workers), the conditions and value of labor, farmers' and merchants' access to markets, and the civil rights of passengers. Two broad impulses established the comparable political terrain of public space as territory in the nineteenth-century United States. On the one hand, the federal government expropriated land into a public domain and redistributed it to private proprietors; on the other, local and state governments appropriated private lands through eminent domain to create streets, waterways, parks, schools, and welfare institutions. As was true of railroads, in both instances the politics of property were linked to issues of labor, maintenance, and governance as well as redistribution.

The politics of space and resources played out unevenly in many venues in the nineteenth-century United States. Still, as an overall trend, the rights of private property and public property expanded together, in both a dialectical and a complementary relation. Property-owning Americans, who as taxpayers dominated the political process, wanted autonomy in their exclusive control of resources, and also wanted governments, which they believed they controlled, to promote private economic activity and to establish public institutions—again, public space in its broadest sense.

Indeed, the American concept of public space as public institutions owned, managed, and maintained by government bodies on behalf of a larger citizenry came out of a distinctly bourgeois confidence in the value of state-sponsored improvements for property owners' own well-being. In some instances, the self-interest was specifically material, as when proprietors saw the value of their own land increase due to streets, parks, public water works, or schools. Sometimes the self-interest was cultural, as public venues provided a site for personal improvement, display, or recreation. Yet, nineteenth-century entrepreneurs' endorsement of an expanded public sector also registered the value they attached to the assimilative power of public institutions, which had a scope and reach that could not be matched by private proprietors. Radical social movements might call for the socialization of property in order to redistribute the means of production. But to many entrepreneurs and wealthy taxpayers, the creation of public parks, schools, waterways, or forests, as well as the traditional public properties of streets and wharves, represented a different logic of redistribution, an investment in the infrastructure of social peace and democratic capacity as well as in the infrastructure of production or markets.

Or this at least is what the political rhetoric that accompanied the rise of public property said. The public domain was not just the land acquired through conquest that awaited distribution to private proprietors. When wealthy merchants, bankers, or industrialists consented to taxes to create urban parks, or when—as was true of the New York Chamber of Commerce, perhaps the most powerful businessmen's association in the country—they endorsed national and state parks and public ownership and preservation of forests in the late nineteenth century, they saw this public property as enhancing American capitalism. This is not to say that there were not intense disputes over the costs of managing and maintaining public property throughout the nineteenth century, or that precisely because property was public, it was not also claimed by working-class Americans to their own ends and sometimes democratized in its access and uses. But it is to say that the economic practice of classical liberalism allowed space for a public realm that was valued for more ends than simply maximizing individual wealth.

It is perhaps difficult in our own time to grasp how and why bourgeois Americans invested themselves in expansive ideas about democratic public space—in both a literal and figurative sense—which could only provide seeds of future dispute. Yet, in the absence of a well-established ruling elite, public space and public institutions sustained both the opportunity and opportunism of many propertied Americans in the volatile age of capital. Moreover, with the state at all levels of government making relatively few demands on its citizenry, universal white manhood suffrage established strong expectations of access and accountability within the halls of public power, especially in the free-labor North. And even when some elites fought state regulations—for example, of railroad rates—precepts of free market liberalism aggressively asserted with respect to private property could coexist with the building of public institutions, which, proponents argued, would pay for themselves out of the future prosperity they helped foster.

Still, as public and private property rights expanded together in the nineteenth century, they left little room for the long-established common property rights of Indian societies, Mexican villages, or Southern farmers. The federal government expropriated Indian territories and granted or sold land from this new public domain in the name of yeoman democracy, on the one hand, and industrial empire, on the other. It also retained jurisdiction over vast amounts of western territory as public, not common, property. Settlers engaged in a range of enterprises—farming, mining, ranching, lumbering—may have worked out different ad hoc strategies or rules to secure private stakes in western water, fertile soil, grasslands, or timber, but the actions of public agencies (armies, land offices, courts, and later government forest, park, or reclamation services) underwrote and arbitrated those private claims. And these public agents also dismantled common property on behalf of private proprietors by overturning formal rights, as when American courts rejected the common property claims of villagers in territories acquired from Mexico, despite treaty provisions that called for recognizing the property rights of new subjects.[8] Suppressing common property entailed changing other customary usages. Thus, in the South following Reconstruction, state legislators who embraced a new industrial order passed fence laws to dismantle common rights to hunt and fish as well as to graze livestock on the open range.[9] The most dramatic American dispossession of common rights remained, of course, the wholesale displacement of American Indian societies from their historical territories.

None of these examples show that people ceased to assert claims to the benefits and resources that they believed should be common property, but fewer and fewer of these claims arose out of bounded communities or were enforceable by other means than temporary possession. Yet, even as public and private property rights expanded together and often at the expense of common property, the dominant discourse of property rights at the end of the nineteenth century came to rest on a simple opposition of public and private. As the example of the railroads had long suggested, that rhetorical binary was itself inherently unstable, especially as rights to property were spatialized or transformed into metaphor. The opposite of "public" could be a realm of domestic relations or it could be the market, unincorporated businesses, or the secrets of an individual body. The opposite of "private" could be the state, but it could also be "publicly held" corporations, publicity, the market, or any promiscuous, crowded social space. As high rhetoric, the discourse of property rights that vacillated between dominion and expectation was losing its descriptive as well as its prescriptive power.

In the early twentieth century, legal theorists adopted a new, much more prosaic trope of property rights as a bundle of sticks. The metaphor aimed to set aside Blackstonian notions of absolute dominion, whether private or public, and to capture instead the multiple claims that could adhere in the same piece of land, institution, or stream of revenue.[10] Property rights included an owner's right to sell and a tenant's right to occupy; a right to minerals below the surface could be bought and sold apart from the right to occupy the surface. A builder's right to develop a lot existed alongside city government's right to establish building codes. Most significantly in the minds of many progressives, the owners of corporate stock or bonds had different rights than the managers who controlled the company's operations. In other words, the proprietorship of capital was no longer modeled on proprietorship of land.

As a metaphor, the bundle of sticks was itself explicitly antispatial. And yet it gained currency precisely because contests over land use—whether nuisances, zoning, or public health regulations—exposed the contingencies of public and private claims. The metaphor allowed theorists to configure multiple claims to property and spaces, and in this sense to recover the complexity of property as an institution. Progressive theorists viewed property rights as the consequence of both social relations and social policy (a revived utilitarian conception), implicitly acknowledging their political as well as historical character. At the same time, the eclipse of the Lockean association of proprietorship with dominion and sovereignty was also part of a larger shift toward talking about property primarily according to market value, which according to theories of marginal utility, derived from relative demand for use or location, not from labor that created or maintained any particular use or value. The market was said to sort information and desires in such a way as to push private property to its highest and best—that is, its most profitable—use. Thus, the Progressives helped recast the public–private binary, which had been drawn sharply to authorize either political protest (the public good) or private appropriation (private right), into a functional distinction: Public power over property established rules; private power over property fueled the market. In this splitting of political economy, contests specifically over how public space was produced, managed, or maintained became less prominent; the public function of proprietorship was custodial or programmatic (with regulations fulfilling the program of conservation, or park workers fulfilling the function of recreation); and the private function was generative and wealth maximizing.

By the 1920s, leading land economists such as Richard Ely articulated the importance of a public domain over natural resources and of public spaces for recreation and championed government planning to preserve the efficiency of all land use.[11] But Ely's confidence in public oversight of the rational ordering of space in no way contradicted the work of other economists, who were busy constructing mathematical models for determining value and price and who treated property itself as essentially private. Still, alongside the narrow utility calculations of economists, as Progressive legal realists depoliticized the discourse of property rights in the 1920s and 1930s, the essential fitness of public space as property owned by government on behalf of the citizenry did not trouble most observers. Debates continued over specific dominion—for example, whether utilities or radio airwaves should be publicly or privately owned—and fights continued over the rules that governed the landed public domain, especially when aggrieved private proprietors found themselves on the losing end of public officials' policies governing use rights. But the New Deal's expansion of state power to preserve the capitalist economy brought with it a literal expansion of public space in the form of new parks, highways, schools, and a host of publicly funded, built, and operated facilities for recreation, sanitation, public health and incarceration. Through World War II, the existence and desirability of public space as public property were not widely questioned. Nor does one find much discussion of common property rights, though Ely acknowledged their "historical" existence in his textbooks on land economics.[12] In the aftermath of the war, however, property rights once again became the overt subject of political arguments and actions; and with these disputes came a new interest in the concept of common property and commons as a metaphorical space.

Public space was repoliticized in the postwar era through demands of access to the uses and benefits of resources that, whether publicly or privately owned, presented themselves as public spaces. Ending Jim Crow required making visible the relation between discriminatory public policies and private profit—whether government sanction of commercial proprietors' exclusionary practices or the direct subsidies of Federal Housing Administration redlining. The civil rights movement challenged the prerogatives of private proprietors on multiple fronts. Thus, for example, after hard battle, activists persuaded judges to limit the powers of transportation companies to humiliate customers on the basis of race; and Congress followed with the 1964 Civil Rights Act that banned all private proprietors of "public accommodations" from invidiously excluding customers. Older powers of property owners to refuse to sell houses to African Americans gave way to laws against discrimination. The civil rights movement moved from issues of access to public space and public markets to access to and accountability for public resources. In response to the welfare rights movement, for example, courts also expanded the property rights of recipients of social security benefits by guaranteeing them Fifth Amendment protections of due process before the state could discontinue their "public transfer payments."

Historians have long seen the Great Society as the climax of a New Deal order that expanded the public domain and individual rights of access to the benefits of the welfare state. But what has become more apparent in recent years is the steady and coincident organization of opposition in the 1950s and 1960s to just this expansion.[13] If the civil rights movement's greatest victories came with claiming public authority to pry open the private sector—the housing market, the job market—the political reaction against democratization focused in on the public sector, where access was less readily regulated by price and where all forms of public finance implied a transfer out of the pockets of the wealthiest taxpayers, whether corporate or individual. Although historians have contrasted the politics of the civil rights movement to an older (class) politics of property, it was against the backdrop of democratization and redistribution implied by equal protection of the law that the discourse of property rights was not only reanimated but expanded to reintroduce the concept of common property rights.

The revival of discussions of commons came from three disparate directions in the 1960s and 1970s. Environmental activists invoked common rights in a clean and healthy environment to counter what they saw as the depredations of private companies, on the one hand, and the indifference of government agencies on the other. Socialist historians, restoring a critique of political economy, recovered the early modern destruction of commons as a chapter in capitalist class formation that also gave rise to collective resistance, and thus revealed the historically grounded power relations underlying markets. And neoliberal or libertarian economists, themselves still aiming to naturalize markets, began to deploy the concept of commons to show how private property rights clarified and allocated claims to resources more efficiently than state actions. For all the talk of these different groups, however, common property rights were not themselves revived, only the idea that their possibility illuminated fundamental failures in private and public realms. The fact that the discourse of commons was never clearly centered meant both that its different speakers talked past each other and that it traveled quickly across disciplines. Ultimately, it was its very fuzziness that gave commons currency in fashioning opposition to both the concept and the institutions of public space.

The Revival of Common Property

Armed with an appreciation of the essentially political character of property rights, environmental activists in the 1960s revived a rhetoric of common property that had virtually no legal authority but which had great popular appeal. The notion that people had a right not to be excluded from the benefits of clean air or clean water was not the only way in which activists sought to contest the exploitation of the natural world. Aldo Leopold's land ethic, for example, did not presume that human beings had common rights that came at the expense of other species. But common property rights offered a way of arguing that those who were systematically polluting the air or water should be stopped from imposing harm on other members of their "community." Just how accessible the notion was, was made evident when Richard Nixon declared in his 1970 State of the Union address: "Clean air, clean water, open spaces—these should once again be the birthright of every American. If we act now—they can be."[14] If implicitly the state had a duty to protect the common birthright, nature itself seemed to place these rights above politics.

By appealing to the environmental movement's largely middle-class constituency, Richard Nixon himself sought an end run around the polarized antiwar, civil rights, and labor politics of the late 1960s. Even in the 1960s, the "environment" was not just the concern of suburbanites, as the tenant activist Jesse Gray aptly demonstrated when he dumped dead rats on the desks of public housing authority administrators in New York City. But Nixon's advisors did not see environmental regulations as a policy that would entail a redistribution of wealth or a major expansion of federal power. Moreover, as Luc Nadal has shown in his history of the discourse of public space, the notion of "open spaces" that circulated in liberal urban planning and design circles in the late 1960s implied enlightened alternatives to the aggressive state programs of urban renewal and highway construction.[15] The political key to Nixon's endorsement of a common birthright to a healthy environment, then, was that in a polarized era it did not imply any politics at all. But it did imply a recognition of the value of public space.

"Common" and "public" stood in ambiguous, almost interchangeable, relation to one another within popular environmental discourse. The use of "common" operated rhetorically at the level of "the people," that distinctly American expression of vaguely socialized collectivity that had taken shape in the nineteenth-century populist movement and reemerged in the 1960s in the language of the New Left. But unlike "the people" of the nineteenth-century movement, who as citizens denounced the political power of monopoly capital, for the most part the claims of the commonality in the late twentieth century came to be associated with a consuming public.

The ambiguities of the concepts of commons and public emerged more clearly as activists developed a political program to deal with environmental degradation. Some lawmakers and judges implicitly recognized common rights of individuals not to be excluded from clean and safe natural resources, by, for example, giving ordinary citizens standing to sue polluters. But environmental lawyers built their cases on a doctrine of "public trust," which, backed by nineteenth-century precedents concerning waterways, ultimately imposed a duty on government to guard certain resources for current and future generations.[16] By reaching back to a doctrine of "public *trust*," these advocates aimed to insulate public properties of natural resources or public space as much from government officials as from private exploiters. Fights with public agencies—the Army Corp of Engineers, the National Forest Service—that promoted development as the goal of conservation left many environmentalists with a deep skepticism concerning the protections secured to public space or natural resources by virtue of being public property. As the campaign for regulations and new environmental agencies to enforce them built on New Deal liberalism, the revival of the concept of common property rights as a metaphor for public accountability thus also stood in tension with the New Deal rhetoric of positive state action on behalf of a larger, undivided public good.

Meanwhile, in academic circles in the 1950s and 1960s, more overt political stakes in the discussion of property rights became apparent in the fundamentally opposed inquiries of socialist historians and libertarian economists as to what had happened to "the commons" as an institution of property rights and a feature of past landscapes.

For English historians working within and seeking to revise the Marxist tradition, what happened to "the commons" mattered as a way of understanding the class relations of industrial capitalism and, implicitly, the possibilities for a revival of class politics in their own time. England's permanent wage-earning class was formed by the expropriation of people from land and natural resources. Christopher Hill, E.P. Thompson, and Raymond Williams charted the commodification of land and the destruction of customary rights not as a socially neutral commercial revolution that promoted economic growth and opportunity, but as a violent dispossession. The historical tragedy of commons was the displacement of people from their livelihoods and the denial that they had had any claims worth valuing. ("The social violence of enclosure consisted precisely in the drastic, total imposition upon the village of capitalist property-definitions," wrote Thompson in *The Making of the English Working Class*.[17]) Nonetheless, enclosure and the contests over customary rights left a memory that could sustain oppositional consciousness. Indeed, in the historians' dialectic, the end of commons pointed less toward a public or a private property regime than toward the collectivity of class that challenged the reduction of all social life to property rights.

(It was in this tradition of collective action that the radical English historians and other scholars supported women peace activists who marched to Greenham Common in 1981 to protest the North Atlantic Treaty Organization's introduction of cruise missiles to an army base that had been placed on the town common during World War II. Women established camps on the common land outside the base that lasted for more than a decade, despite the town's own effort to claim ownership of the common and evict the protesters, an effort that was itself blocked by the House of Lords.[18])

Libertarian economists heard the arguments of socialist English historians and their American followers as an attack on the legitimacy of capitalism. "It is unfortunate that the study of the underpinnings of capitalism has been left by default to its critics on the left," economists Armen Alchian and Harold Demsetz wrote in an article offering a new "property right paradigm" in 1973.[19] The neoclassical economists had themselves taken up the quest for such a paradigm as part of a larger project of reestablishing the primacy of free markets as the motor of prosperity; and though they covered many fields, environmental issues offered one illustration of how public limits placed on private property rights should be reexamined.

Even before the environmental movement took off, economist J.R. Coase had posed new questions about the desirability of government regulating social costs of the unfortunate consequences ("externalities") of private enterprise—for example, pollution—that seemed to harm the general public. From a free market perspective, one person's harm was another person's profit. If all individual members of the public held clearly defined property rights to such resources as clean air, then they could enter into direct negotiations with polluters and bargain their way to a resolution of conflicting interests. The market would weigh the value of dirty emissions to the polluter—that is, what was gained by not having to introduce new cleansing technology—against the value of clean air to neighbors—what was gained by not having to move to a new location to escape the pollution. Rather than let the state place the cost of clean air on the polluter, which might come at the expense of an enterprise's contribution to aggregate social wealth, a bargained outcome would determine what pollution was worth to society as well to individuals. Still, individual economic actors could enter into contracts only if each held clearly defined private property rights that could be exchanged. If individual property rights could not be enforced (who owns the air?), or if there were too many parties to such exchanges, the costs of transactions could outweigh the benefits, so that "market failure" would give rise to new inefficiencies.[20]

Coase and libertarian economists associated with the University of Chicago rejected the idea that the state served as the representative and agent of a collective public interest, arguing instead that government was merely one economic actor or proprietor among many, but one unfairly insulated from the market's accounting of the true costs and benefits of its actions. Even New Deal liberals had come to question an "idealist"—or socialist—conception of the state as embodying a single public will and producing a uniform public good. But in the 1950s and 1960s, economists Milton Friedman and James Buchanan and political scientists Gordon Tullock and Mancur Olsen, Jr. advocated a radical individualism to counter the liberal paradigm of a broker state mediating among competing group interests. The ideology of "public choice" applied the logic of the market to governments, arguing that rational wealth-maximizing individual citizens expected and were entitled to a strict quid pro quo for their taxes.[21] Public choice theorists emphasized the added costs that arose from private interests seeking to "capture" regulatory agencies or special benefits from public policies. Public officials also operated out of bureaucratic self-interest rather than on behalf of any wider constituency. In order to prevent the inevitable corruptions of public power ("rent seeking"), wherever possible public policies had to be evaluated by the same standards as private enterprise. In most instances, such an evaluation would demonstrate that private proprietors working through the market could provide comparable goods and services more efficiently.

Broad conceptions of "public space" as government-owned and managed institutions or resources open to all, as a sum larger than its parts, or as the product of collective effort had no place in such analyses. Indeed, by the 1970s, public choice was preoccupied with determining what—if any—goods or services could be considered inherently public and therefore worth their weight in taxes. Not anticipating Dick Cheney's and

Donald Rumsfeld's Pentagon, even the neoliberals agreed that national defense was one state service that individuals could not efficiently secure outside the public realm, offering, in effect, a perpetual Cold War prospect of military bases as the last fortress of American public space. (Nor did they anticipate a world that would come to view "failed states" as a far greater danger to security than market failure.)

Neoliberals' arguments that the market offered the most efficient means of allocating costs and maximizing individual and hence social wealth did not initially foreground property rights. Still, Chicago School economists who had resurrected economic man as a matter of faith also aspired to describe the dawn of private property on which markets rest. Common property had no theoretical status, institutional form, or practical power that had to be confronted by these economists, but it did have rhetorical value as the emblem of a primitive order from which private property evolved, not as a consequence of Lockean man mixing his labor with nature, but as a result of strategic calculations and rational choices.

In his 1967 "theory of property rights," Harold Demsetz used a story of an Indian commons to illustrate how property rights were fashioned out of "legal and moral experiments."[22] According to anthropologist Eleanor Leacock, he reported, when Montagnais Indians entered the fur trade, they divided a previously shared hunting territory into private property in order to avoid one hunter's bounty or initiative exhausting the opportunities of others. (Noting that not all American Indians strategically embraced private property, he added that the absence of woods and a fur trade in the Southwest obviated the need for such a conversion.) The larger point of Demstez's heuristic invocation of commons as a new "state of nature," of course, was to reclaim the inherent rationality and efficiency of the institution of private property and thus to remove it—like the market—from history as well as from politics.

The neoliberal economists walked a narrow line as they challenged the New Deal order and worked to reestablish the market as the dominant institution of a well-ordered universe. On the one hand, they wanted to end the "inefficient" public property regime of regulation and redistribution; on the other, once state intervention was rolled back, they imagined ideal markets operating free of further historical—which is to say political—disruptions. The economists couched their own political project in the scientism of Pareto optimality, and their discussion of property rights became more and more abstract as they reverted to decision-making models emptied of recognizable human agency as well as of three-dimensional space and history.[23] And yet, the terms of those discussions also had very real consequences for the politics of public space in the last third of the twentieth century.

The Suppression of Public Space as Public Property

The scholars' contest over whether "the commons" would be understood as a historical set of social relations, as a metaphor for a primitive past that spawned an enlightened future, or simply as a scenario for decision making was overtaken in the late 1960s with the rise of a new trope, which continues to circulate to this day. In a 1968 article in *Science* magazine, the biologist and environmentalist Garrett Hardin illustrated his argument on behalf of regulating population growth by describing a "tragedy of the commons." Hardin said he wanted to "exorcize the spirit of Adam Smith," especially "the tendency to assume that decisions reached individually will, in fact, be the best decisions for the entire society." In fact, he resurrected Adam Smith's economic man as he directed his readers to "picture a pasture open to all." Individuals would rationally increase the number of cattle they grazed on the commons in order to maximize their personal benefit; the sum of such rational individual strategies was the exhaustion of the resource held in common. What made this scenario "tragic," Hardin wrote, quoting Alfred Whitehead, was "the remorseless working of things," the "futility of escape." "As a rational being, each herdsman seeks to maximize his gain.... [Thus] each man is locked into a system that compels him to increase his herd without limit—in a world that is limited." If one took the earth as the shared property of all, "freedom in a commons brings ruin to all."[24]

Hardin's article was the work of an appropriative mind; he drew as readily on the rising discourse of game theory as he did on Malthus and Hegel. It was also the argument of an illiberal mind. As with the arms race, Hardin argued, overpopulation had no "technical solution," and therefore required "mutual coercion, mutually agreed upon." Such a stance explicitly rejected the Universal Declaration of Human Rights, which held, for example, "that any choice and decision with regard to the size of the family must irrevocably rest with the family itself and cannot be made by anyone else." Under the welfare state, Hardin insisted, there was no way of dealing with "the family, the religion, the race, or the class (or indeed any distinguishable and cohesive group) that adopts overbreeding as a policy to secure its own aggrandizement."

A biologist venturing into social policy, Hardin was not in full control of either his logic or his metaphors; and his arguments stirred debates across the political spectrum.[25] But what interests me about Hardin is less his specific arguments than the way his trope of commons traveled in the 1970s and 1980s into the literature of a loosely but self-defined "property rights movement" and also ended up in the mouths of formerly New Deal liberals who left the state behind for nongovernment organizations (NGOs).

Although "mutual coercion, mutually agreed upon" implied a field of state action, the "tragedy of commons" was used both to attack the public sector and to celebrate the stewardship of private property, supporting the "nontechnical solution" of privatization.[26] Moreover, by associating "the commons" with the exploitation of natural resources, Hardin's metaphor implicitly disarmed other environmentalists' rhetorical claims on behalf of common rights in a healthy ecology. The environmental movement's vague association of commons rights with a generalized public good had in effect embraced all kinds of "public space," from the "open space" of parks and preserves to better managed (i.e., "freed") space of wild rivers. Now, by Hardin's reasoning, public space might be no better than a commons, destined to be overrun.

Among the first groups to respond to Hardin's metaphor in the early 1970s had been political scientists enamored of game theory as a way of representing how individuals weighed their options and made "public choices." Recognizing the "tragedy of commons" as a subset of the "prisoner's dilemma" (and doubtless tantalized by the prospect of "no technical solution"), experts in "conflict resolution" retold Hardin's cautionary fable of how rational decisions could transform a commons into a desert.[27] But as the trope traveled, the moral of the story also began to change.

Charting how language moves through a culture and gradually transforms common sense and suppresses dissent is difficult. As was true of "systems analysis" or "action programs" in the late 1950s and 1960s, or of "win–win" situations in the 1980s or "taking ownership" of a problem in the 1990s, millions of people find themselves talking in ways (often in a managerial vocabulary) that they hardly recognize. In the 1970s, the basic vocabulary of neoclassical economics—cost-benefit analysis, efficiency, and rational choice—moved into popular—as well as scholarly—American discussion of how the world worked in part because these were the terms that self-appointed experts used to explain how and why the world wasn't working. Against the backdrop of the fiscal crisis in cities, fierce fights over busing, and declining real wages, perhaps neoliberals did not have to work hard to argue that the Great Society had failed. But it was a much larger project to propose that government and the public sector were by nature inefficient or to persuade Americans that no rational person would choose to pay taxes to sustain public institutions open to all.

The ideological discrediting of common property, of rights not to be excluded from the use and benefits of resources, then, was aimed not at a latent tradition of communalism or collectivity in the United States, but rather at the regulatory welfare state and, by extension, public property rights. During the Cold War, business leaders had attacked the expansion of the public sector, for example, public housing, as creeping socialism. But so long as the federal government made it possible for millions of Americans to participate in the abundance of education and suburban home ownership, it was difficult to discredit the state head-on. At the local level as well, few questioned the benefit of governments overseeing the expanded public space initially funded by the New Deal. The lagging capitalism of the 1970s, however, made questioning the value of public institutions easier. Deindustrialization was sapping the labor movement; the federal government was reeling from Vietnam and Watergate; the oil crisis and stagflation were eating into profits; and local governments responded to fiscal crisis by cutting "inessential" services, including the maintenance of parks and other public spaces.

Against a backdrop of political disaffection and economic vulnerability, the CEOs of leading corporations launched a new campaign to lobby on behalf of deregulation and fiscal retrenchment. The environmental movement, with its foundation funding, broad constituency, and strong media ties, retained political access where other movements lost resources and steam. Had business leaders not faced a particular problem in contesting regulations that had been adopted in the name of all Americans' "birthright" to clean air or open space, it is unlikely that "property rights" would have become a prevalent political discourse in the late twentieth century.

David Vogel and others have shown that the organization and dissemination of knowledge was an essential part of the business campaign to change the hearts and minds of the voting public on environmental matters as well as other features of the welfare state. The American Enterprise Institute had paved the way for more than twenty years when, in 1973, the Heritage Foundation was established as a conservative think tank to counter the perceived influence of liberal and left-leaning public interest foundations, think tanks, law firms, and activists. By 1980, more than a dozen institutes and foundations—funded by contributions from leaders of the oil, energy, chemical, and timber industries—sponsored libertarian, neoliberal, and conservative policy studies, and provided both lobbyists and expert witnesses to lawmakers. William Simon, head of the Olin Foundation, led the way in providing financial backing for libertarian entrepreneurs who produced the texts and organized the conferences, institutes, journals, and small publishing houses that circulated neoliberal "paradigms" as definitive social knowledge. Business-backed legal foundations took test cases to court to challenge environmental regulations and zoning laws.[28]

Economists associated with the Chicago School provided the framework for all aspects of the campaign against the regulatory welfare state, of course, but their conceptualizations of social costs, rational choice, and property rights were especially important in the two initiatives that together remapped public space in the United States and influenced how public space is talked about internationally. A loosely defined "property rights movement" ran variations on the theme of the "tragedy of commons" as it fashioned solutions that ranged from "free market environmentalism" to World Bank–sponsored ecological management. At the same time, although efforts to privatize state services and property received their greatest boost from the hard facts of fiscal crisis, that movement also scored points off the trope of commons in ways that helped usher in the public–private partnership as a model for governance of public property and hence public space.

A number of ideological entrepreneurs launched their careers by weighing in on the "debate" over Hardin's "Tragedy of Commons." In 1977, John Baden, who three years later established the Foundation for Research on Economics and the Environment (FREE), based in Bozeman, Montana, joined Hardin in publishing a collection of articles titled *Managing the Commons*.[29] Hardin's occasional essays on many themes dominated the first edition, but its other essays sketched what would become the property rights movement's rhetorical trajectory from the fringe to the center of discussions of environmental protection and of property regimes as key to the governance of resources and space. When Baden coedited a second edition in 1998, Hardin receded as other authorities declared their higher levels of definitional precision and fuller command of institutional solutions to the tragedy he had unleashed.

In the first edition, economists Terry Anderson and P.J. Hill applied the narrative of "commons" to land, livestock, and water in the nineteenth-century American West in an essay reprinted from the *Journal of Law and Economics*, the product of Chicago School economists' collaboration with legal scholars.[30] In effect retelling Harold Demsetz's story two centuries later, the authors explained how the "extent of tragedy" of miners, cattlemen, or farmers overrunning common resources was modified by settlers devising different rules to establish private rights and enter into transactions that allowed them to lift the (public) domain to a higher and better use. Anderson wrote another book retelling American Indian history not as dispossession but as strategic negotiation over the allocation of resources, and he coedited numerous volumes on property rights under the sponsorship of the Political Economy Research Center (PERC). Founded in 1980 in Bozeman, Montana, PERC is still directed by Anderson, who also serves as a research scholar at the Hoover Institution. PERC describes itself as "the nation's oldest and largest institute dedicated to original research that brings market principles to resolving environmental problems ... the approach known as free-market environmentalism."[31]

In addition to providing numerous links to other think tanks, including the Cato Institute, Manhattan Institute, Fraser Institute, Competitive Enterprise Institute, the National Center for Policy Analysis, and FREE, the website lists PERC's tenets: "private property rights encourages stewardship of resources," "government subsidies often degrade the environment," "market incentives spur individuals to conserve resources and protect environmental quality," and "polluters should be held liable for the harm they cause others," this last a gesture to a pre-state common law tradition, although only other proprietors were in a position to assert this claim against polluters.

The discussion of Hardin's *Tragedy of Commons* in the 1970s, however, also gave rise to other modes of institutional (and interdisciplinary) analysis. Political scientists, sociologists, and anthropologists endorsed common property regimes as antidotes to conditions when resources, especially "common pool resources" that stood outside a clear political jurisdiction, could not be efficiently appropriated. That might be the case when the terrain was so extensive that no one could patrol and restrict its use to private proprietors. In the first edition of *Managing the Commons*, Elinor Ostrom initiated the search for examples of non-state means of "governing the commons," as she later titled her book, and suggested that Hardin may have been too "pessimistic."[32] Many fishing or herding communities maintained common property without exhausting their resources. Marshaling empirical evidence of practices that did not conform to dominant models of property relations, Ostrom also brought public choice into closer dialogue with the neoliberal Law and Economics school of jurisprudence. Given the nature of many resources, scholars in both fields found they could not afford a strict private–public binary when developing their paradigms for property rights. The examples of successfully administered common property regimes uncovered by Ostrom, her followers, and dozens of anthropologists investigating societies around the world demonstrated that "market failure"—that is, problems governing or allocating many resources that the market could not efficiently organize—could be solved through nonmarket mechanisms other than a central state.

A third wing of a property rights movement, not represented in the published forum on Hardin's essay or initially recognized within the academy, emerged more directly out of opposition to federal management of forests, grazing lands, and water in the West, the so-called "Sagebrush Rebellion." Long after Ronald Reagan's Secretary of the Interior James Watt had been removed, the legacy of this mobilization was felt in the formation of the self-proclaimed "Wise Use Movement." Also funded by business, its leaders Ron Arnold and Alan Gottlieb advertised their cause as part of a grassroots movement of small property owners intent on defending themselves against elitist environmentalists.[33] Wise Use advocates did not linger long over "the commons" as either a wedge against the bureaucratic excesses of the state or a hedge against market failure. But they did use the trope to give an environmental spin to the rhetorical tradition of possessive individualism: "While the 'commons' will always be at the mercy of politically powerful special interests who may hold no stake in the land, it should be recognized that exclusive ownership of property creates the only effective, long-term incentive to conserve resources and minimize pollution," Nancie Muzulla typically wrote.[34]

By the mid-1980s, property rights discourse linked American universities and the shadow academy of "free enterprise" institutes. Scholars taking a Law and Economics approach joined law faculties (where in the field of environmental law, they countered "public trust" doctrines) and, in several noteworthy Reagan appointments, moved on to the federal bench. One key moment in the advance of the libertarian discourse of property rights came with the publication of Richard Epstein's *Takings* in 1986, which took as its own target not simply the broad Progressive constructions of the doctrine of eminent domain, but all public regulations that diminished rights of dominion and reduced an owner's purported expectations for benefit from property.[35] When published, *Takings* was received as transparently ideological; a decade later, parts of its arguments had not only been endorsed by judges, they were churning the doctrinal waters of environmental law, leaving hundreds of law review articles in the wake. Indeed, "takings" became a kind of corollary to "the tragedy of commons": if unappropriated resources posed a special risk of depreciation or degradation, government rules only increased the burden of that risk to private proprietors. In the early 1990s, the Foundation for Research on the Environment and Economy started sponsoring summer seminars for federal judges and law professors at a ranch in Montana to introduce them to the precepts of property rights and environmental law from a Law and Economics perspective.[36]

During the Reagan and first Bush administration, the "wise use" advocates gained their own symbolic clout with executive orders and state laws mandating that a "takings impact statement," analogous to an environmental impact statement, be issued for any new government regulation to expose its "true" economic cost. The antiregulation regulations never went far beyond symbolism, but neither have their advocates disappeared. On the contrary, when George W. Bush appointed Gail Norton as interior secretary, it was widely seen as a green light to a "wise use" approach to overseeing—privatizing—the public domain as well as dismantling environmental regulations.

At the same time that the property rights movement systematically challenged state control of natural resources or public space, the failings of public property were also being worked out both narratively and institutionally in local and in global politics. In seeing how the discourse of property rights played out at these two scales, we also return to questions of the social relations that produce, maintain, and govern any public space. It was primarily at the local level that the question of the relationship between ownership and labor emerged from the haze of the neoliberal property rights paradigm.

It is noteworthy that Hardin's "tragedy of commons" was a pastoral tale. No labor was implied in the decision of how many cattle to graze on the commons. But the classic utilitarian association of property and labor discipline came to the forefront when economists elaborated on the commons' tragic features. Common property offered no incentive to labor, and without incentives to labor, society faced the problem of "free riders" and "shirkers," two groups who turned the *public* domain itself into a wasteful commons by taking something for nothing.

The free rider was someone who did not pay his or her way. The worry that taxpayers might be supporting "freeloaders" preoccupied public choice theorists, intent as they were on viewing government as nothing more than a direct quid-pro-quo service provider for wealth-maximizing individuals. The term "free rider" itself had first emerged in labor circles to describe workers who didn't join a union and pay dues but benefited from its presence. But by the early 1970s, the "free rider" had transmogrified into a vague cross between Dennis Hopper and a welfare queen, a figure who undermined the very definition of self-interested human nature, to say nothing of the actual maximization of social wealth, by sponging off and depleting a public domain paid for by other people's money. One of the few groups worse than free riders in the writing of neoliberal economists and political scientists were inefficient or opportunistic ("rent-seeking") public bureaucrats. Thus, a kind of Hobbesian self-defense prompted those public bureaucrats to eliminate free riders in the 1970s by charging user fees for access to all kinds of public space and public institutions—zoos, forests, museums—once supported by tax dollars and open to all visitors. At a minimum, public space would no longer connote rights of free access or assembly.

As management experts applied neoliberal economics to public administration, they were quick to note that "free riders" were not the only group getting something for nothing from the public domain and thus turning it into a commons. Equally troubling were the "shirkers"—for example, the recently unionized public workers—who cost too much and did too little. If government was regarded as a firm like any other firm, its officials had to make decisions about whether they could most efficiently produce services from within or by contracting out. The political fight over which services would be contracted out continues, department by department, to this day, but the calculus itself was said to be neutral, a matter of weighing competing bids and the efficiency of different "providers."

In retrospect, we can see that removing public labor from public property lifted a very big stick out of the bundle that historically had comprised American public space by integrating matters of governance, maintenance, use, and accountability. And in retrospect, we can also see that what was at stake in cracking the whip on shirkers and free riders was a determination that the politics of public space would no longer at its heart be a contest over the redistribution of wealth, even at the most basic level of paying public workers a fair wage.

In the aftermath of the fiscal crisis in New York, when public agencies competed for severely constricted funds, taxpayers' reluctance to pay for the labor necessary to maintain public space offered a starkly visual iteration of a tragedy of commons in park meadows turned to sand lots or recreational facilities abandoned to arsonists. But the deteriorating condition of Central Park, for example, was attributed as much to mismanagement that permitted "overuse" as an unregulated commons as to cutbacks in its maintenance force.[37] It was a small step to the conclusion that government officials could not be trusted with the public property of an exemplary public space, which in any case needed protecting from an indiscriminate public.

In 1980, in the name of restoring public space to its earlier glory, the Central Park Conservancy became a flagship for a new model of governance of the public space of parks, an experiment that was also being advocated for housing and schools (if not for hospitals and prisons, which were more aggressively privatized). The idea of creating new "public–private partnerships" for the provision and management of what had been public institutions came from many directions. Business school professor E.S. Savas is often credited with developing the idea for Central Park in the mid-1970s.[38] At the same time, when David Rockefeller's Partnership for New York City, modeling itself in part on the national Business Round-table, took over New York's old Chamber of Commerce, the CEOs of major companies proposed partnership programs as alternatives to public housing, summer job training for youth, and later schools.[39] In the 1990s, the Partnership for New York City, like the Central Park Conservancy, posed itself to other cities as a model for governance based on rational business principles and freed from politics. As partnerships and conservancies steadily increased their control over budgets, maintenance, and rules of parks and other public institutions, they eroded the historical def-inition of public space as public property.

One key to the rise of partnerships, of course, is that the private part-ners' contributions—their "taxes"—are voluntary and discretionary. As one advocate of public–private partnerships for land conservation put it, "Donors, whether foundations or corporations or individuals, are usually more comfortable making gifts to a non-profit organization, even if the donation eventually supports a government project."[40] The public–private partnership of land trusts also expanded dramatically in the 1980s as the best means of preserving open or natural space in rapidly developing sub-urbs. Their advocates followed conventional wisdom in concluding that government lacked "agility" or the ability to "create an 'atmosphere of possibility'" to undertake such projects. Moreover, the labor of "volunteer land stewards," who worked through partnerships, did not tax the public purse. Why have a partnership at all? In keeping with law and economics reasoning, the public sector could establish rules and hence predictability: "[A] certain amount of bureaucratic uniformity is a necessary protection from a program made impossible to administer by unlimited variations in legal documents, funding arrangements, or management practices."[41] In other words, government could reduce the transaction costs that might undermine a free market regime.

The neoliberal paradigm for administering local public spaces removes their governance from direct public accountability and their use from an open public political process. At the other end of the geographic scale, property rights discourse has aimed to remove the very prospect of public space—that is, lands brought under state administration on behalf of specific constituents. Indeed, new models of governing common property, public property, and unappropriated land or resources have gained their greatest momentum from international environmental activists' collabo-ration with the sponsors of global development. Thus, for example, in the early 1990s, the Beijer International Institute of Ecological Economics, supported by the World Bank and the MacArthur Foundation, engaged nearly fifty scholars to explore "the notion that a significant cause of much biodiversity loss lies in inadequate institutions, in particular, ill-defined property rights."[42] Crediting Hardin with having posed a significant ques-tion about sustainability, the scholars nonetheless concurred that histori-cally "the use of common property resources has rarely been a free for all."[43] The revelation did not modify the neoliberal economic premises from which they worked however. ("The correct economic valuation of environmental and sociocultural assets, and their internalization in the price system, is one means of ensuring that market forces lead to more sustainable resource use.") One team sympathetically evaluated the free

market environmentalists' proposal for handling environmental degradation through "individual transfer quotas" (ITQs), which could, in effect,
commodify the right to pollute alongside the right to fish.[44] Other scholars
stuck with the question of how the commons could be managed through
"local knowledge," customary institutions, and "nested decision-making
power" rather than a central state.[45] Still, with the World Bank aspiring to
track (and hence manage) the management of natural resources everywhere in the world, little in their approach moved away from Hardin's prediction of coercion as the only solution to his imagined tragedy of
commons.

Meanwhile in the United States, the property rights movement, which
might be regarded as parochial were its echoes not heard around the
world, today runs an endless loop of propaganda, continuing to invoke the
tragedy of commons to discredit any economic regime other than that of
the free market while paying lip service to voluntary community control
where the market doesn't quite work. A curious person who ventures into
the web-page world of libertarian institutes quickly feels lost in a hall of
mirrors; not only do the same authors and directors move from institute
to institute, they generate hundreds, if not thousands, of books, pam-
phlets, op-ed articles, speeches, letters to the editors, and talk-show transcripts arguing that private property offers the key to American freedom,
prosperity, and self-realization. When the most strident members of the
Competitive Enterprise Institute invoke the unnuanced tragedy of commons, they advocate "privatization" as the solution for everything from
endangered species to the condition of the central cities. Given that nearly
15 percent of Americans live in private communities, Robert Nelson
argues in *Privatizing the Inner City*, equal opportunity requires that residents be allowed to enclose the commons of city streets and create their
own private neighborhoods, with "physical barriers so that entry was controlled through a few access points."[46] The logic of much of this transparently ideological literature is incoherent, but coherence is not the point.
The Competitive Enterprise Institute will recommend an expert who will
confirm whatever a libertarian lawmaker needs to hear in order to promote markets or block public regulations.

It is against this drumbeat that liberal planners have regrouped to
propose the alternative of "smart growth." Distancing themselves from the
gloominess of a "limits" mentality, they work on how capitalist development can be rendered kinder and gentler to the land, to cities, and to the
dispossessed. Within these circles, "the commons" has become the
progressive urbanist label for pedestrian-friendly, mixed-use, mixed-
income, in-fill developments that project an idea of "Main Street" as the
center of community life. There are other efforts to revitalize a tradition of

commons as a creative expression of shared obligations that arise from shared labor. Thus, Brian Donahue suggests that small farms and community gardens can attach people to one another as well as to land.[47]

It might be easy to dismiss such efforts as exercises in nostalgia, but I hesitate to do so if for no other reason than out of respect for the practice of alternatives. One thinks of Raymond Williams' effort to imagine that "in some places still, an effective community, of a local kind, can survive in older terms, where small freeholders, tenants, craftsmen and laborers can succeed in being neighbors first and social classes only second. This must never be idealized, for at the point of decision, now as then, the class realities usually show through." Nonetheless, Williams warned, "when the pressure of a system is great and is increasing, it matters to find a breathing-space, a fortunate distance, from the immediate and visible controls. What was drastically reduced by enclosures was just such a breathing-space, a marginal day-to-day independence for many thousands of people."[48] It is just such intellectual breathing space that the property rights movement has reduced today through its appropriation of the concept of commons. And yet, there is one more aspect of this story.

Lifted out of history, severed from place, detached from the labor of real people, private property rights skip across our discursive landscape as the pacemaker of free enterprise. But then, so too do property rights themselves skip across the globe through all manner of market transactions. The proprietorship of land is now modeled after the proprietorship of capital; and the same quarter century that has relentlessly celebrated the creative power of individuals to rationally and freely buy and sell claims on the uses and benefits of resources has also seen the overwhelming institutional consolidation of proprietorship and the spectacular fragmentation of that which is owned. I dare say that any American scholars who look closely will find they own shares in a "commons" in Arizona or North Carolina, for proprietorship is managed by pension funds that, in turn, invest in real estate investment trusts, mortgage-backed securities, and environmental insurance—and perhaps even ITQs—and these are the financial building blocks and tokens of ownership for all the new "commons" on the American vernacular landscape.[49]

Thus, what is perhaps most remarkable about the discourse of property rights that has girded the transformation of American politics in the last quarter of the twentieth century is the tenacity with which its legitimating metaphors cling to conventions from a landed social order even as financial markets have left land far behind. The critics are perhaps no better than the advocates in this respect. To try to make sense of the new political economy that frames public space by relying on vocabulary derived from an earlier era is to risk irrelevance. But to disregard those past meanings—and the contests on which they rested—is to risk the cognitive blankness that comes from believing that a meaningful world can exist without history, labor, or connection to specific places.

What difference, then, does this revival of a language of commons, however inconsistent its meanings, make to concepts, institutions, or politics of public space? Governments at all levels will continue to own and manage land or resources, often in the name of a commonality, but this literal public space has itself become ever more narrowly bounded, with no presumption that land or resources or social institutions belong in a public domain. Rather, public jurisdiction designates administrative authority. Public property, thus, does not imply a collective will and sovereignty projecting itself over time through space on behalf of future generations. An older expansive discourse of public space as a site of political contests and sometimes democratic processes has run up against not only the material and rhetorical power of advocates of the free market, but also against empire as the dominant expression of state power. Locally, public spaces continue to offer arenas of assembly and can even prompt meaningful political fights on behalf of access, fairness, accountability, or redistribution. Beyond local settings, however, public space as public property has become as vulnerable as common property was in early modern England. And within a capitalist logic, if it cannot grow, it will die.

The language of commons has contributed to this circumscribing of public space, pushing it to the margins of its old binary opposition to private space. Whether commons represents an alternative to market failure or commons prescribes market salvation, what it does not represent in the discourse of contemporary social science or law or even popular common sense is a property regime that can evolve into public property and hence public space. There is no expectation of a continuum of space, whether institutional or temporal; that is to say, the creation of new parks or waterfront promenades does not carry with it a promise that schools, libraries, hospitals, or other institutions will follow and also be supported through public monies collected from individual citizens. Moreover, the existence of these institutions places no burden on citizens to fight for the public domain as a whole. Indeed, a fragmented, residual public domain leaves everyone to think of themselves as free riders, illicit beneficiaries of an unexpected abundance that they did nothing to produce. After management consultants have finished advising parties to "take ownership" of whatever matters to them, to exercise the strategies of voice and exit alongside those of bargaining, what is left most depleted is the language of a public realm itself.

We might ask, was it ever truly otherwise? When was the public domain and public space experienced as more than a slice of quotidian affairs, a slice that seldom elicited the kind of loyalty and labor associated with family, or work, or even community? When did people not resist paying into a common fund in order to sustain facilities that they only partially used themselves and that might be widely used by people they did not know? Taxpayer revolts ran as a strong current through the era of creating an expansive public sector in the United States. Those revolts reined in local governments, which was where most of the fight over public space took place prior to the income tax. Local governments were reined in, but also financed. Bourgeois Americans may have seen themselves as buying off a noisily disgruntled working class; they may have seen themselves as unifying people into a "civil society" that could enjoy public goods in order to assuage divisions and temper conflicts; they may simply have seen their own individual advantage in paying a little into a public purse that brought back an extraordinary return in schools, parks, libraries, and health, to say nothing of rising land values, reduced transportation costs, or easier communication. But the question remains: What happened to that class and what happened to the idea that socializing public goods yields both private and public benefits?

Some have suggested that the fantasy of limitless private wealth has distorted the vision and values of propertied Americans, turning self-interest into a crabbed and literal-minded miserliness. Cold War anticommunism, the economic trauma of deindustrialization, and the political disruptions and gains of social movements in the 1950s and 1960s left economic elites fearful rather than confident in the assimilative powers of public institutions. And, as was true among environmental activists, leftists as well as libertarians thought that public officials could not be counted on to protect or advance the common good. Some scholars suggest that with abundance, Americans outgrew their collective need—even their capacity—for a public realm. Others argue that the public itself was felt to have become too large, too inclusive, its rewards too widely disseminated in too many forms—too democratic. Whatever the cause, the demise of the idea of a democratic public domain in the United States is a loss that extends beyond its borders.

It is not possible, of course, to construct a global public; at a global scale, the ideas of democratic access and accountability associated with public space stretch beyond recognition, for people do not live their lives as members of abstract communities or spaces. Of necessity, common property regimes around the world are represented as sharply bounded, local, and delimited, usually with reference to particular kinds of resources, such as fish, land, and forest. The discourse of property rights has created ways of imagining that those independent systems of allocating property rights and sharing resources might continue at the sufferance of international proprietors—the NGOs who are taking figurative ownership of the globe's "future" and who in their capacity as guardians have set about evaluating the efficacy and efficiency of any given system to determine which should be left in place and which should be reformed. Local practices can create their own space for unexpected contingencies, new openings that can redirect strategic calculation on a larger scale, of course. But without larger institutions of government, there are not many ways most ordinary people with limited means can collectively deliberate over what they wish to control or leave for their descendants by way of shared resources, institutions, or public spaces.

Historically, public space was created as public property, and if that institution has run its course, if there is no language or theory that affirms that people can build and maintain governments that can build and maintain public space, we should all pay attention, for we have observed one more tragedy in our own time.

Acknowledgments

Jessie Alpaugh helped me look for commons; I finished this essay to honor her memory. I thank Jeffrey Sklansky, William Leach, and Roy Rosenzweig for their comments on a draft.

Notes

1. Aside from the Somers Commons, these samples come from Lexis-Nexis searches. Personal observation in cities across the country and the scanning of real estate sections of newspapers in any region yield numerous examples.
2. C.B. Macpherson, *Property: Mainstream and Critical Positions* (Toronto: University of Toronto Press, 1978), 1–13.
3. Elinor Ostrom, "Common Property and Private Property," in *Encyclopedia of Law and Economics*, edited by Boudewijn Bouckaert and Gerrit De Geest. Available at: *www.encyclo.findlaw.com*. Some scholars further distinguish between depletable and nondepletable common properties.
4. Robert W. Gordon, "Paradoxical Property," in *Early Modern Conceptions of Property*, edited by John Brewer and Susan Staves (New York: Routlege, 1996), 95–115, quote on 95. See also Patricia Rose, "Canons of Property Talk, or, Blackstone's Anxiety," 108 *Yale Law Journal* (December, 1998), 601; and C.B. Macpherson, *Possessive Individualism: Hobbes to Locke* (New York: Oxford University Press, 1962).
5. Joshua Getzler, "Theories of Property and Economic Development," *Journal of Interdisciplinary History* 26(4) (1996), 639–669; Jeremy Bentham, "Security and Equality of Property," an edited excerpt from *Principles of the Civil Code* (1830), in Macpherson, *Property: Mainstream and Critical Positions*, 41–58, quote on 51.
6. Morton Horwitz, *The Transformation of American Law* (Cambridge, MA: Harvard University Press, 1981); William J. Novack, *People's Welfare: Law and Regulation in Nineteenth-Century America* (Chapel Hill, NC: University of North Carolina Press, 1996); Arnold Paul, *Conservative Crisis and the Rule of Law, 1887–1895* (Ithaca, NY: Cornell University Press, 1960).
7. Wolfgang Schivelbusch, *The Railway Journey: The Industrialization of Time and Space in the Nineteenth Century* (Berkeley, CA.: University of California Press, 1977).
8. On fights over the Mexican grants of common property to villages, see Maria E. Montoya, *Translating Property: The Maxwell Land Grant and the Conflict over Land in the American West, 1840–1900* (Berkeley: University of California Press, 2002).

9. Steven Hahn, "Hunting, Fishing, and Foraging: Common Rights and Class Relations in the Postbellum South," *Radical History Review* 26 (1983), 13–34; for a Law and Economics riposte, see Shawn Everett Kantor, *Politics and Property Rights: The Closing of the Open Range in the Postbellum South* (Chicago: University of Chicago Press, 1998). Carol Rose proposes that residual common rights in roads represent, in effect, a public property in commerce as a means of realizing a public good; "The Comedy of the Commons: Custom, Commerce, and Inherently Public Property," in *Property and Persuasion: Essays on the History, Theory and Rhetoric of Ownership* (Boulder, CO: Westview Press, 1994), 105–162.

10. Barbara Fried, *The Progressive Assault on Laissez Faire: Robert Hale and the First Law and Economics Movement* (Cambridge, MA: Harvard University Press, 1998), offers an excellent analysis of Progressive legal theories of property.

11. Richard T. Ely and Edward W. Morehouse, *Elements of Land Economics* (New York: Macmillan, 1926).

12. Richard T. Ely and George S. Wehrwein, *Land Economics* (New York: Macmillan, 1940), 77–78.

13. Kimberly Phillips-Fein, "The Roots of Reaganism: Business Backlash in the Liberal Age, 1945–1964," Ph.D. diss., Columbia University, 2004.

14. David Vogel, *Fluctuating Fortunes: The Political Power of Business in America* (New York: Basic Books, 1981), 71.

15. Luc Nadal, "Discourse of Urban Public Space, USA 1960–1995: A Historical Critique," Ph.D. diss., Columbia University, 2000.

16. For public trust doctrine, see Joseph L. Sax, *Defending the Environment: A Strategy for Citizen Action* (New York: Knopf, 1971), and "The Public Trust Doctrine in Natural Resource Law," *Michigan Law Review* 68 (1970), 471. On the environmental movement more generally, Samuel Hays, *Beauty, Health and Permanence: Environmental Politics in the United States, 1955–1985* (New York: Cambridge University Press, 1987); and Adam Rome, *The Bulldozer in the Countryside: Suburban Sprawl and the Rise of American Environmentalism* (New York: Cambridge University Press, 2001).

17. E.P. Thompson, *The Making of the English Working Class* (1963), 238, cited in Getzler, "Theories of Property and Economic Development," 668. See also E. P. Thompson, *Customs in Commons* (New York: New Press, 1991); Raymond Williams, *The Country and The City* (New York: Oxford, 1973); Christopher Hill, *Reformation to Industrial Revolution, 1530–1780* (New York: Viking/Penguin, 1967, 1969), 61–71, 146–156, 268–274.

18. See the notes for The Greenham Common Collection, 1982–1983, in AIM 25 Archives in London and the M25 Area. Available at:*www.aim25.ac.uk/cgi-bin/search2?coll_id=6849&int_id=65*.

19. Armen A. Alchian and Harold Demsetz, "The Property Right Paradigm," *Journal of Economic History* 33, no. 1 (1973), 16.

20. R.H. Coase, *The Firm, The Market, and The Law* (Chicago: University of Chicago Press, 1988) reprints Coase's major essays, including "The Problem of Social Cost" (1960). Steven G. Medema offers a very lucid summary of Coase's theories in *Ronald H. Coase* (New York: St. Martin's Press, 1994).

21. Hugh Stretton and Lionel Orchard, *Public Goods, Public Enterprise, Public Choice: Theoretical Foundations of the Contemporary Attack on Government* (New York: St. Martin's, 1994) offer an excellent assessment of public choice theory. Key texts include Mancur Olson, *The Logic of Collective Action: Public Goods and the Theory of Groups* (Cambridge, MA: Harvard University Press, 1965); James Buchanan and Gordon Tullock, *The Calculus of Consent: Logical Foundations of Constitutional Democracy* (Ann Arbor: University of Michigan Press, 1962).

22. Harold Demsetz, "Toward a Theory of Property Rights," *American Economic Review* 57, no. 2 (1967), 347–359. The flavor of this economic analysis can best be conveyed through a direct quote: "A primary function of property rights is that of guiding incentives to achieve a greater internalization of externalities. Every cost and benefit associated with social interdependencies is a potential externality. One condition is necessary to make costs and benefits externalities. The cost of a transaction in the rights between the parties (internalization) must exceed the gains from internalization.... In a lawful society the prohibition of voluntary negotiations makes the cost of transacting infinite" (p. 348).

23. See, for example, Erik G. Furubotn, "Property Rights and Economic Theory: A Survey of Recent Literature," *Journal of Economic Literature* 10, no. 4 (1972), 1137–1162.

24. Garrett Hardin, "The Tragedy of the Commons," *Managing the Commons*, 2d ed., edited by John A. Baden and Douglas S. Noonan (Bloomington, IN: Indiana University Press, 1998), 6–7.

25. He placed himself beyond the liberal pale in a 1974 article that envisioned the United States as a lifeboat: Although developed nations, and especially the United States, had two-thirds of the world's wealth, he argued, scarcity meant that it could neither effectively share that wealth nor admit newcomers to its benefits. Garret Hardin, "Living on a Lifeboat," *Managing the Commons*, 210–226.

26. Hardin called for "world government" as the only effective solution to global environmental crisis, and he also suggested that "under a system of private property the man or group of men who own property recognize their responsibility to care for it, for if they don't they will eventually suffer." *Managing the Commons*, 213.

27. See, for example, Mark Sproule-Jones, "Strategic Tensions in the Scale of Political Analysis: An Essay for Philomophalasceptics," *British Journal of Political Science* 2, no. 2 (1972), 173–191; Thomas C. Schelling, "Hockey Helmets, Concealed Weapons, and Daylight Saving: A Study of Binary Choices with Externalities," *The Journal of Conflict Resolution* 17, no. 3 (1973), 381–428. For an excellent analysis of discourse formation in Britain, see David Toke, *Green Politics and Neo-Liberalism* (New York: St. Martin's Press, 2000), including discussion of public choice and market theory, 75–85.

28. David Vogel, *Fluctuating Fortunes: The Political Power of Business in America* (New York: Basic Books, 1989), 213–227; Hays, *Beauty, Health and Permanence*, 287–328; Sharon Beder, *Global Spin: The Corporate Assault on Environmentalism* (White River Junction, Vt.: Chelsea Green Publishing Co., 1997).

29. For the Foundation for Research on Economics and the Environment, see *http://www.free-eco.org/*.

30. Terry Anderson and P.J. Hill, "From Free Grass to Fences: Transforming the Commons of the American West," *Managing the Commons* (1977), 200–216.

31. See *www.perc.org/about.htm*. PERC's precepts are also summarized in Terry L. Anderson and Donald R. Leal, *Free Market Environmentalism* (San Francisco: Pacific Research Institute for Public Policy; Boulder, Colo.: Westview Press, 1991). See also the codification of the property rights approach to economics in Terry L. Anderson and Fred S. McChesney, *Property Rights: Cooperation, Conflict and Law* (Princeton, NJ: Princeton University Press, 2002).

32. Elinor Ostrom, "Collective Action and the Tragedy of Commons," 173–181; and Vincent Ostrom and Elinor Ostrom, "A Theory for Institutional Analysis of Common Pool Problems," 157–172, in *Managing the Commons* (1977). Elinor Ostrom, *Governing the Commons: The Evolution of Institutions for Collective Action* (New York: Cambridge University Press, 1990). For comprehensive bibliographies on commons from multiple disciplines, see the Digital Library of Commons, available at: *http://dlc.dlib.indiana.edu/*, produced under the auspices of the Workshop in Political Theory and Policy Analysis at Indiana University, which Ostrom co-directs. The anthropological approach is well illustrated in Bonnie J. McCay and James M. Acheson, eds., *The Question of Commons: The Culture and Ecology of Communal Resources* (Tucson: University of Arizona Press, 1987).

33. Alan M. Gottlieb, *The Wise Use Agenda* (Bellevue, WA: Free Enterprise Press, 1989); Harvey Jacobs, "The 'Wisdom' of the Wise Use Movement," in *Who Owns America?*, edited by Havey M. Jacobs (Madison, WI: University of Wisconsin Press, 1998), 29–44; Philip Brick and R. McGreggor Cawley, eds., *A Wolf in the Garden: The Land Rights Movement and the New Environmental Debate* (Lanham, MD: Rowman & Littlefield, 1996); John Echeverria and Raymond Booth, eds., *Let the People Judge: Wise Use and the Private Property Rights Movement* (Washington, DC: Island Press, 1995). Gottlieb and Arnold are affiliated with the Center for the Defense of Free Enterprise.

34. Nancie G. Marzulla, "Property Rights Movement: How It Began, Where It Is Headed," in *A Wolf in the Garden*, 55. Marzulla heads the Defenders of Property Rights, a legal foundation in Washington, DC. Gail Norton, Secretary of the Interior, had previously served as a board member. Available at: *www.defendersofpropertyrights.org/*.

35. Richard Epstein, *Takings: Private Property and the Power of Eminent Domain* (Cambridge, MA: Harvard University Press, 1986).

36. The program for the summer sessions can be found on FREE's website, such as *www.free-eco.org/agenda_seminar_law_july24_2001.htm*. Funders have included the Olin Foundation,

the Claude R. Lambe Foundation (which has contributed $7 million to the Cato Institute), and Liberty Fund, Inc. See also Douglas T. Kendall and Charles P. Lord, "The Takings Project: A Critical Analysis and Assessment of the Progress So Far," *Boston College Environmental Affairs Law Review* 25 (1998), 509.

37. Roy Rosenzweig and Elizabeth Blackmar, *The Park and the People* (Ithaca, NY: Cornell University Press, 1992), 501–502.

38. Emanuel S. Savas, *A Study of Central Park* (New York: Columbia University Center for Government Studies, 1976); *Privatization and Public–Private Partnerships* (New York: Chatham House, 2000).

39. Elizabeth Blackmar, "Exercising Power: The Business Elite and the Public Realm," in *Picturing Power: New York's Chamber of Commerce*, edited by Karl Kusserow (New York: Columbia University Press, forthcoming).

40. Eve Endicott, ed., *Land Conservation Through Public/Private Partnership* (Washington, DC: Island Press, 1993), 5.

41. Ibid., 9.

42. Susan Hanna and Mohan Munasinghe, eds., *Property Rights and the Environment: Social and Ecological Issues* (Washington, DC: World Bank, 1995), v. For a critical assessment of global managers' deployment of property rights rhetoric to manage ecology around the world, see Michael Goldman, ed., *Privatizing Nature: Political Struggles for the Global Commons* (New Brunswick, NJ: Rutgers University Press, 1998). Goldman and his co-authors themselves use the discourse of commons in describing local struggles to control natural resources.

43. Carl Folke and Fikret Berkes, "Mechanism that Link Property Rights to Ecological Systems," in *Property Rights and the Environment*, 123.

44. Michael D. Young and Bonnie J. McCay, "Building Equity, Stewardship, and Resilience into Market-Based Property Rights Systems," in *Property Rights and the Environment*, 87–102.

45. Elinor Ostrom, "Designing Complexity to Govern Complexity," in *Property Rights and the Environment*, 33–45. My point here is not to dispute the persistence or value of common property regimes around the world, but rather to illustrate how empirical findings lend themselves to theoretical conclusions that are uncritically governed by neoliberal premises.

46. Availble at: *www.cei.org/utils/printer.cfm?AID-1303*. For Robert J. Smith's "Resolving the Tragedy of Commons by Creating Private Property Rights in Wildlife," see *www.cei.org/utils/printer.cfm?AID-1457*.

47. Brian Donahue, *Reclaiming the Commons: Community Farms and Forests in a New England Town* (New Haven, CT: Yale University Press, 1999). David Bollier also deploys the tropes of commons and enclosure in *Silent Theft: The Private Plunder of Our Common Wealth* (New York: Routledge, 2004).

48. Williams, *Country and the City*, 106–107.

49. For pension funds and the relation of financial property to land development, see Elizabeth Blackmar, "Of REITs and Rights: Absentee Ownership at the Periphery," in Jeffrey M. Diefendorf and Kurk Dorsey, eds., *City, Country, Empire: Landscapes in Environmental History* (Pittsburgh: University of Pittsburgh Press, 2005).

CHAPTER 5

How Private Interests Take Over Public Space: Zoning, Taxes, and Incorporation of Gated Communities

SETHA LOW

This chapter began when my mother sent me a clipping from the *Los Angeles Times* about Broad Beach in Malibu, "where non-resident sunbathers, picnickers and others are booted off the dry sand, which the community considers private property" (Weiss, 2003: B1). California's public access law guarantees beach access only seaward of the mean high-tide line, the portion of the beach with damp sand. But many oceanfront communities—including Broad Beach—have granted public easements to an additional 25-foot strip of dry sand. Yet Broad Beach is littered with no-trespassing signs to keep the public away from the homes of celebrities such as Steven Spielberg, Danny Devito, Goldie Hawn, and Dustin Hoffman. These wealthy homeowners assess themselves $3,000 to $5,000 per year to maintain security guards who harass visitors even when they have the right to be there. Earlier this year there was another confrontation concerning access to the Malibu Beach when two homeowners obstructed the public easement that ran between their houses.

The Malibu article arrived shortly after residents of Georgia Estates, a private community best known for its Hollywood entourage, illegally dug a trench to drain East Hampton Town's Georgia Pond, because their basements were flooded from heavy rains. There is a long history of antipathy between townspeople and renters who use the public pond to supplement their diet with fish, crabs, and clams, and for weekend sailing and canoeing, and the elite homeowners who find the pond's high water table an annoyance. The pond is opened to the ocean every fall after the summer activities. But this year, Georgia Associates residents, who already restrict access to their private community by employing a guard to stop visitors from entering, wanted to reduce the water level to dry out their basements in the spring. The elected trustees in charge of natural resource decisions denied Georgia Associates' request, stating that the pond is for everyone's enjoyment. So the homeowners illegally cut a trench that emptied the pond for the entire summer. The police are still searching for the person who did the trenching, but no one has been charged in the case.

Beaches, ponds, and lakes are significant public places for residents of Los Angeles and the East End of Long Island, yet the wealthy homeowners who border them are successfully restricting their use. In both Los Angeles and New York, security guards and surveillance augment blatantly illegal actions—putting up no trespassing signs and fences and degrading the natural resource—used by private property owners to privatize public space.

This resurgence of urban privatization reverses a trend started in the mid-nineteenth century when water, sewer, street cleaning, policing, and fire protection were provided privately in cities. The first public police officers were hired in Boston in 1838, followed by New York in 1844, and Philadelphia in 1850. New York employed 5,000 street sweepers by 1900, and began designing a series of public parks (Cranz, 1982; Stark, 1998). The public realm continued to expand, encompassing most urban services and functions that we now take for granted. But recently the boundaries of what is private or public have become less clear, and increasingly incursions by privatization and other neoliberal practices have been transforming public space, placing it back in corporate or commercial hands.

During the past 20 years, privatization of urban public space has accelerated through the closing, redesign, and policing of public parks and plazas (Low, 2000), the development of business improvement districts (BIDs) that monitor and control local streets and parks (Zukin, 1995; Briffault, 1999), and the transfer of public air rights for the building of corporate plazas ostensibly open to the public (Kayden, 2000; Low et al., 2005). In the suburbs, privatization takes the form of conservation easements that restrict access to public lands, the creation of shopping malls and new town centers relocated within these private commercial developments, and the building of gated residential communities (Harvey, 1990; Low, 2003). Accompanying this expansion of private interests are changes in strategies of governance and regional differences in how local governments and residents encourage private encroachment on public space.

Private interests take over public space in countless ways. Don Mitchell, Neil Smith, and I have documented how sealing off a public space by brute force, redesigning it, and then opening it with intensive surveillance and policing is a common precursor to its private management. (Mitchell, 1995; Smith, 1999; Low, 2000). But these strategies are inadequate when dealing with large tracts of land or urban neighborhoods. When private interests orchestrate the takeover of the public space of entire communities, an expanded set of strategies are employed. For example, illegal actions combined with private security guards were used ex post facto to privatize Broad Beach and Georgia Pond. Restricting access through conservation easements or the buying up of private property encircling the public space or amenity works effectively to keep the public out, and privatizes its use. Of course, building walls and fences with gates and guards is a sensible way to exclude the public when there is a public amenity or resource inside. And policing and surveillance ensures that the mall, shopping center, or gated community will only allow a certain "public" to use its privatized public facilities.

These "physical" tactics, though, are bolstered by "legal and economic" strategies in which private interests coopt the public, placing public goods in the hands of a private corporation or agency. These schemes are harder to identify, as they utilize normative governmental procedures but are manipulated for private ends. For example, BIDs are private organizations allowed to tax local businesses and retail establishments to provide private services such as special policing, trash removal, or street renovation. The BID decides on the level of taxation and retains the right to use the money in ways that enhance their commercial interests. In this privatization scheme, public space is often lost, such as Herald Square in the Thirty-Fourth Street BID in Manhattan, which is now fenced, gated after 6 p.m., and guarded by private security guards to keep homeless people from sleeping there. Park conservancies also blur traditional public/private distinctions when the municipality—New York City in the example of Central Park or San Francisco for Golden Gate Park—gives over decision making to a group of private citizens who raise money and then use those funds to run what was formerly a public park.

Private gated communities employ still another set of practices connected with regional and municipal planning. Incorporation, incentive zoning, and succession and annexation recapture public goods and services, including taxpayers' money, and use these goods for the gated community and residents. These strategies are not illegal in the sense that they are not draining a pond or posting no-trespassing signs on land that is not theirs, and do not employ brute force, but they do mislead taxpayers and channel funds into amenities that the public cannot use, and instead contribute to the maintenance of private communities.

This chapter focuses on this last set of relatively unstudied privatization practices by focusing on how gated communities manipulate municipal and town planning laws and regulations to control public space and tax dollars. To accomplish this task, I discuss the emergence of gated communities as a new form of privatization of urban/suburban space and then tease out the legal and institutional underpinnings of this spatial governance. Case studies drawn from geographical research on gated communities in Greater Metropolitan Region of Los Angeles and an ethnographic study of residents living in urban and suburban gated communities in New York and Texas, illustrate how the strategies of private governance and exploitation of the public sector differ. I examine incorporation in Greater Metropolitan Region of Los Angeles, California, incentive zoning in Long Island, New York, and annexation in San Antonio, Texas. These manipulations of private land use controls in the United States are not necessarily new, but with gating there is an accelerating trend away from governmental and public control of land use toward an increased reliance on privately created controls. The consequences of this shift toward privatization of land use control are an impoverishment of the public realm and limited access to public resources.

The Case of Gated Communities

Defining the Gated Community

A "gated community" is a residential development surrounded by walls, fences, or earth banks covered with bushes and shrubs, with a secured entrance. In some cases, protection is provided by inaccessible land such as a nature reserve, and in a few cases, by a guarded bridge (Frantz, 2000–2001). The houses, streets, sidewalks, and other amenities are physically enclosed by these barriers, and entrance gates operated by a guard, key, or electronic identity card. Inside the development there is often a neighborhood watch organization or professional security personnel who patrol on foot or by automobile. Gated communities restrict access not just to residents' homes, but also to the use of public spaces and services—roads, parks, facilities, and open space—contained within the enclosure. Communities vary in size from a few homes in very wealthy areas to as many as 21,000 homes in Leisure World in Orange County, California—with the number of residents indexed to the level of amenities and services. Many include golf courses, tennis courts, fitness centers, swimming pools, lakes, or unspoiled landscape as part of their appeal, while commercial or public facilities are rare.

As commercial developments, gated communities are predominantly new settlements built as part of large-scale housing developments or "master-planned communities" (Frantz, 2000–2001). They are located mostly at the edge or just outside the city on rural or otherwise undeveloped land. Within any one master-planned community, there are various kinds of subdivisions built for different income-level buyers. Each has its own architecture, amenities, and facilities, but they are often connected by shared parks, golf courses, artificial lakes, or shopping centers.

Once the roads and lights are in, developers divide up an area into subdivisions, survey the individual house lots, and then sell the rights to builders who function as general managers. The developer also sets up the legal framework, the common interest development (CID) agreement, and the covenants, conditions, and restrictions (CC&Rs) for each private community. These rules and regulations stipulate how the houses and gardens will be maintained, and establish the homeowners association that will ultimately govern the community. A management company is usually hired to organize the necessary services until the lots are completely sold and the developer relinquishes financial and administrative control (Frantz, 2000–2001).

History of the Gated Community

Gated residential communities in the United States first originated for year-round living on family estates and in wealthy communities such as Llewellyn Park in Eagle Ridge, New Jersey built during the 1850s, and as resorts exemplified by New York's Tuxedo Park, which was developed as a hunting and fishing retreat with a barbed wire fence eight feet high and twenty-four miles long in 1886 (Hayden, 2003). Another early resort was Sea Gate in Brooklyn, established with its own private police force in 1899. The architect and real estate developer Julius Pitman designed the majority of St. Louis's private streets between 1867 and 1905, borrowing from the English private square to create exclusive residential enclaves for the business elite (Beito, 2002).

Planned retirement communities such as Leisure World in Southern California built in the 1960s and 1970s, however, were the first places where middle-class Americans walled themselves off. Gates then spread to resort and country club developments, and finally to suburban developments. In the 1980s, real estate speculation accelerated the building of gated communities around golf courses designed for exclusivity, prestige, and leisure.

Gated communities first appeared in California, Texas, and Arizona, drawing retirees attracted to the weather. One-third of all new communities in Southern California are gated, and the percentage is similar around Phoenix, Arizona, the suburbs of Washington, D.C., and parts of Florida. In areas such as Tampa, Florida, gated communities account for four out of five home sales of $300,000 or more. Since the late 1980s, gates have become ubiquitous, and by the 1990s they were common even in the northeastern United States (Dillon, 1994; Fischler, 1998).

The number of people estimated to be living in gated communities in the United States increased from 4 million in 1995, to 8 million in 1997, to 16 million in 1998. By 1997, there were in excess of 20,000 gated communities with over 3 million housing units. A census note by Tom Sanchez and Robert E. Lang provides more accurate demographic statistics based on two new questions on gating and controlled access that were added to the 2001 American Housing Survey (Sanchez and Lang, 2002). They found that 7,058,427 or 5.9 percent of households report that they live in communities surrounded by walls or fences, and 4,013,665 households, or 3.4 percent live in communities where the access is controlled by some means such as entry codes, keys cards, or security guard approvals. The West has by far the highest number of households living in walled or gated communities (11.1 percent), followed by the South (6.8 percent), Northeast (3.1 percent), and Midwest (2.1 percent). The metropolitan areas of Los Angeles, Houston, and Dallas have over 1 million walled residential units.

The Rise of Gated Communities: The Enclosure and Control of Open Space

The contemporary gated community as a sociospatial form is a response to transformations in the political economy of late twentieth-century urban America (Low, 1997; Harvey, 1990; Smith, 1984). The increasing mobility of capital, marginalization of the labor force, and dismantling of the welfare state began with the change in labor practices and deindustrialization of the 1970s, and accelerated with the "Reaganomics" of the 1980s. This economic restructuring and relocation of global capital weakened existing social relations and contributed to the breakdown of traditional ways of maintaining social order. Social control mechanisms and their associated institutions, such as police and schools, were no longer seen as effective (Foucault, 1975; Devine, 1996; Schlosser, 1998). This breakdown in local control threatened some neighborhood residents, and the gated residential community became a viable and socially acceptable option.

Racism is another major contributor to patterns of urban and suburban separation and exclusion in the United States. Cities continue to experience high levels of residential segregation based on discriminatory real estate practices and mortgage structures designed to insulate whites from blacks. Blacks are less likely to move to the suburbs in the first place, and then more likely to return to the city (Skogan, 1987, 1995: 66; Bullard and Lee, 1994; Denton, 1994; South and Crowder, 1997; Massey and Denton, 1998). Residential proximity to blacks intensifies whites' fear of crime, and whites who are racially prejudiced are even more fearful.

Residents of middle-class and upper-middle-class neighborhoods often cordon themselves off as a class by building fences, cutting off relationships with neighbors, and moving out in response to problems and conflicts. At the same time, governments have expanded their regulatory role through zoning laws, local police patrols, restrictive ordinances for dogs, quiet laws, and laws against domestic and interpersonal violence that narrow the range of accepted behavioral norms. Indirect economic strategies that limit the minimum lot or house size, policing policies that target nonconforming uses of the environment, and social ordinances that enforce middle-class rules of civility further segregate family and neighborhood life (Merry, 1993: 87, 2001). The gated community is an extension of these practices.

The creation of "common interest developments" provided a legal framework for the consolidation of suburban residential segregation. "Common interest development" describes "a community in which the residents own or control common areas or shared amenities," and that "carries with it reciprocal rights and obligations enforced by a private governing body" (Judd, 1995: 155). Specialized "covenants, contracts, and deed restrictions" (CC&Rs) that extend forms of collective private land tenure and the notion of private government were adapted by the lawyer and planner, Charles Stern Ascher, to create the modern institution of the homeowner association in 1928 (McKenzie, 1994).

The evolution of "pod," "enclave," and "cul-de-sac" suburban designs further refined the ability of land use planners and designers to develop suburban subdivisions where people of different income groups would have little to no contact with one another. Regulated resident behavior, house type, and "taste culture" are more subtle means of control. Even landscape aesthetics function as a suburban politics of exclusion, often referred to as making everything "nice" (Bourdieu, 1984; Duncan and Duncan, 2004). The number of legal proceedings in California courts has grown as some residents attempt to deregulate their rigidly controlled environments (McKenzie, 1994), but litigants have not been successful. Instead, common interest developments guarantee a "bundle of goods"

that includes security, exclusiveness, and an extraordinary level of amenities, and this promise is "nestled at the center of all advertisements for the
new walled cities" (Judd, 1995: 160).

Supply-side economic factors also figure prominently in understanding
the widespread expansion of these communities. Developers want to maximize their profits by building more houses on less land, and incentive
zoning packages for common interest development housing allow them to
cluster units and achieve this higher density within otherwise low-density
residential zoning areas. California and states that have experienced a
property tax revolt find CID housing particularly attractive because it
transfers the debt liability, building of infrastructure, and provision of services to private corporations, while at the same time the municipality col-
lects property taxes from residents (McKenzie, 1998; Webster, 2002).

Like gated communities, the number of homeowners associations has
also grown exponentially. In 1962, there were only 500 homeowners associations in the United States, but by 1970 there were 10,000; in 1980,
55,000; in 1990, 130,000; and by 1992, there were 150,000 housing over 32
million people. While only 1 percent of American housing units were
located in a homeowners association, condominium, or cooperative—the
three main instruments of collective private ownership of housing—in
1970, by 1998 this figure had risen to 15 percent. Today, in major metropolitan areas, 50 percent of all new housing units are being built and sold
as part of a collective housing regime (Kennedy, 1995).[1] This increase is a
social revolution in governance, with private organizations now responsible for collecting trash, providing security, and maintaining common
property. Private enforcement of covenants has replaced municipal oversight in regulating the environment by zoning, and new ground
rules—voting rights determined by property or home ownership and not
citizenship—are being put into place.

Cases

The case of incorporation of gated communities in the Greater Metropolitan Region of Los Angeles is based on the work of Renaud Le Goix, a
French geographer who has studied gated communities in Southern California for three years at the time of this writing, and Evan McKenzie, a
lawyer and political scientist, who has written extensively on homeowners
associations in California and Nevada (McKenzie, 1994, 1998, 2003; Stark,
1999; Le Goix, 2002, 2003). The cases of zoning variances in Long Island,
New York, and annexation in San Antonio, Texas are based on an ethnographic study that began with gaining entrance into upper-middle- and
middle-income gated subdivisions in 1994 and 1995: one in Nassau

County on Long Island, and three in the northern suburbs of San Antonio, Texas. Additional gated communities were added: an upper-middle- to middle-income community in Mexico City in 1998,[2] and a middle-income and middle- to lower-middle-income community in the New York City area in 2000.

Setting

Greater Metropolitan Region of Los Angeles, California

From 2000 through 2003, Le Goix studied the social and ethnic impact of gated communities within the metropolitan area of Los Angeles (Le Goix, 2002, 2003). He selected a sample of 219 gated communities and integrated geographic information systems (GIS) maps of these housing subdivisions with race/ethnicity, age, and socioeconomic status data from the 2000 census. With this database, he was able to describe the social and economic patterns of gating in the Greater Metropolitan Region of Los Angeles area locating 108 gated communities within the richest areas, thirty within dense, middle-income white suburbs, thirty-one on the edges of urbanization in desert areas with lower-income housing, and thirty-four within predominantly Hispanic or Asian neighborhoods (Le Goix, 2002). Through a cluster analysis of race/ethnicity, age, income, social status, and mobility, he demarcated the level of sociospatial discontinuity created by the walls and gates demonstrating the negative impact of gated communities on segregation patterns (Le Goix, 2003). As part of his inquiry, he critiqued "gated communities as predators of public resources" which I used as a starting point for this chapter (Le Goix, 2002: 8).

McKenzie (1998) has argued that California is the best place to study political incorporation as it is used in defense of CID interests. A statewide survey of California in 1987 located between 13,000 and 16,000 CIDs, and by 1993, 25,000. These figures suggest that approximately 13 percent of California's population and 16 percent of the state's housing units have homeowners associations, a large percentage that, according to McKenzie, influences electoral politics in favor of private interests.

These two studies illustrate how profoundly gating and private governance influence urban politics and spatial relations in the Greater Metropolitan Region of Los Angeles, providing a sociospatial model for how cities might be privatized and physically segregated in the future.

Nassau County, Long Island, New York

Nassau County, Long Island has experienced a resurgence of residential development, much of it gated, following the decline in the real estate market in the early 1990s. With a population of 1,298,842 in 1997, Nassau County abuts the eastern boundary of Queens. Although complete statistics for the number of gated communities in Nassau County have not been compiled, a 2001 survey of the Manor House neighborhood identified seven gated developments along the main road (Plöger, 2002a, 2002b), and in the Pine Hills area, at least three gated communities located in the immediate vicinity (Kirby, personal communication).

Manor House. Located in Nassau County, this mostly white and wealthy development of single, detached houses is situated on an old estate with the original manor house retained as a community center. There is a security guard at the entrance who controls the gate. The individual houses are large (3,250 to 4,500 square feet), generally two-story structures, built in a variety of traditional styles, and sell anywhere between $745,000 and $1,000,000.[3] Houses are organized along a winding thoroughfare with dead-end streets branching off, leading to groups of houses clustered quite close together on small lots, fifteen feet wide, on a quarter to a third of an acre. The built-out community will contain 141 houses, tennis courts, and an outdoor swimming pool, and the mansion has been renovated to accommodate an indoor pool, billiard saloon, library, conference rooms, sauna, and cigar-smoking rooms.

Pine Hills. Pine Hills is a gated townhouse development of eighty units completed in 1997. There is a gatehouse, and residents use electronic identity cards to raise the arm blocking the entrance. Located near the Long Island Expressway in Nassau County, Pine Hills is a middle-income, mostly white community made up of long rows of similar-looking attached houses in three basic styles. All the houses are two-story, white and beige clapboard, single-family townhouses with wood or stone trim and bay windows. There are few amenities except for the streets, sidewalks, and jogging paths. The location and quality of the townhouses have kept the prices in the $400,000 to $500,000 range, even though it is located in a prestigious, suburban neighborhood.

Waterview. Waterview is a gated condominium complex of 800 units located in the lower-middle to middle-class neighborhood of Bayside, Queens, near the Nassau County line. There is both a guarded entrance and a pedestrian entryway that can be opened with a key. Organized as a series of three-story buildings, each with three apartments arranged around a swimming pool with health club facilities and sauna, Waterview has been successful in maintaining its prices in the $350,000 to $450,000 range. Many of the apartments are rented by their owners, so that there is a broad spectrum of residents of various income levels and greater cultural diversity including African nationals, African Americans, Korean Americans, and white workers and professionals.

San Antonio, Texas

San Antonio is divided by Loop 410, a highway that circles the city and defines inner and outer loop differences in quality of life, schools, housing development, and municipal services. Inside the loop, 96 percent are non-Anglo and poor, and house prices average $20,000, while beyond Loop 410, residents are mostly Anglo and wealthy, and homes in newly constructed gated communities average $200,000. Inside Loop 410, 43.5 percent of people mention crime as a neighborhood problem, contrasted with 26 percent of residents outside the loop (MacCormack, 2000).

Sun Meadow. Sun Meadow is part of the master-planned suburban development centered on a private golf and tennis club with swimming pools, restaurant, and clubhouse. The subdivision includes 120 lots, a few fronting the golf course, surrounded by a six-foot masonry wall. The main entrance is controlled by a grid design gate that swings open electronically by a hand transmitter or by a guard who is contacted by an intercom and video camera connection. The single-family detached houses are large (3,000 to 6,000 square feet) two-story brick colonials or stucco Scottsdale designs, with a few one-story brick ranch-style houses, and sell between $275,000 and $650,000. These different models accommodate the mostly white and a few Hispanic upper-middle- and middle-income families.

The Links. The Links is a mostly white and upper-income, luxury gated community with a 24-hour guarded entrance. All of the twenty-two lots face the golf course. The single-family houses are large (4,000 to 6,000 square feet), and designed by individual architects to look like small mansions with French, Italian, or Southwestern architectural details. They sell for $500,000 to $750,000. These houses have large gardens as well as common landscape spaces that abut the clubhouse and tennis courts of the master-planned development.

The Lakes. The Lakes is a white and Hispanic, middle-income gated community in a northwestern central suburb of San Antonio. The fifty-nine lots are organized along a series of curving roads with three cul-de-sacs. The mixture of townhouse styles is unusual, and lower the overall house prices to the $250,000 to $300,000 level.

Methodology

For the ethnographic research in New York and Texas, family members, friends, and real estate agents were contacted to gain entry. Nonetheless, obtaining interviews was a slow and difficult process that stretched out over eight years. Open-ended, unstructured residential histories lasting over two hours each were conducted in the home, with the wife, husband, or husband and wife together for married couples, and with the three single female residents. The majority of the interviewees were European Americans and native born; however, of the fifty interviews completed in the United States, three interviews were in households in which one spouse was born in Latin America, one interviewee was born in the South Pacific, and one interviewee's spouse was born in the Middle East. Interviewees were aged twenty-three through seventy-five; all husbands were either professionals such as doctors or lawyers, businessmen, or retired from these same pursuits. In most cases, the wives remained at home while the husband commuted to his place of work. A few women worked part-time. There were three single women in the sample, one divorced, one never married, and one widow, and of these three, one was retired, while the other two worked in professional occupations.

Extensive participant observation in the surrounding neighborhood and shopping areas provided additional contextual data. Interviews with architects, builders, developers, and real estate agents, as well as town planners and government officials were completed in order to understand the underlying legal and economic structures of gated community development, supplemented by the collection of sales materials, advertising campaigns, and local planning documents.

Analysis

The ethnographic analysis of participant observation field notes focused on identifying empirical evidence of changes in the local environment. Further, it produced data on casual conversations and everyday observations that naturally occurred, and provided a test of ecological validity for data collected through the interviews. Field notes were coded by the themes that emerged during the research process.

A thematic content analysis of the interviews and documents collected from the media, marketing, and sales materials provided both a qualitative and quantitative understanding of the data. The interviews were coded based on themes identified in the interviews and the ethnographic fieldwork. Depending on the number and specificity of the themes, they were consolidated to allow for a quantitative (ranking, numbering, calculation of percentages) of the expression of those themes.

Incorporation: Greater Metropolitan Region of Los Angeles and Orange County, California

In the Greater Metropolitan Region of Los Angeles, the incorporation movement began between 1954 and 1970 sparked by the "Lakewood Plan," a state law that allowed small bedroom communities to incorporate and contract with counties for their urban services (McKenzie, 1998). It was a "quiet tax revolt" by homeowners who wanted to limit their property tax burden, expansion of government bureaucracies, and social welfare programs. Even though the creation of these "minimal cities" was an ineffectual land-use planning strategy, it benefited homeowners by ensuring that people who needed welfare benefits could not live within the local boundaries, protecting high property values without the assessments that would otherwise be taxed for extensive social services in the City of Los Angeles.

In 1961, one of the nation's oldest gated communities, Hidden Hills, incorporated as a city, but remained gated and left their private homeowners association in place (Stark, 1993). They divided up the provision of local services between the two government agencies, but placed most of their public functions, including the Fourth of July Parade and parks, roads, and horse trails, in the hands of the private government so that these activities and public spaces would not have to be open to all. More recently, the city hall has been relocated outside the gates, so that people could not demand to "go to city hall," and thus threaten Hidden Hills residents' security (Stark, 1993). Hidden Hills has been successful in privatizing everything but the seat of the public government.

Incorporation of Los Angeles–area gated communities continues to thrive as residents realize that they can transform their private governments into public entities that will fund and service their interests. It is a complicated strategy in which the voting power of gated community residents is drawn on to create a public entity that can tax all residents in its jurisdiction, and then use the funds exclusively for private community needs.

Gated community incorporations include a range of political involvement. Of the twelve major gated communities involved in incorporation in the Greater Metropolitan Region of Los Angeles area, Rolling Hills (1958), Hidden Hills (1961), Canyon Lake (1991), and Leisure World/ Laguna Woods (1999) created entire new cities, while in Indian Wells (1967), Rancho Mirage (1973), La Quinta (1982), Dana Point (1989), and Calabasas (1991), they included the majority of the housing stock. But in a few cases, such as Laguna Niguel (1989), Malibu (1991), and Rancho Santa Margarita (including Dove Canyon and Coto de Caza) (2000), the gated communities were the principal actors even though they represented less than 10% of the housing units (Le Goix, 2002).

In all three scenarios, however, there has been a shift in the use of city services, paid by taxpayers or by local grants, to the "exclusive use of gated enclaves" (Le Goix, 2002: 8). Gated communities have used incorporation to pay for their aging infrastructure, such as in the case of Rolling Hills where their leisure facilities are the property of the city, and the homeowners association rents exclusive rights to their use, while the city bears the cost of repairs and maintenance. In Calabasas, the gated community of Parkway Calabasas created a public "community facility district," and then took on a loan of $30 million to pay for parks, roads, and beautification of the gated community neighborhoods. It became so expensive for gated community taxpayers, however, that the loan was refinanced and paid for by the entire incorporated municipality, including the nongated community residents. The incorporation of Leisure World/Laguna Woods was motivated both by aging infrastructure and the rising costs of urban services, as well as their desire to fight the building of a public airport in nearby El Toro (Le Goix, 2002, 2003). And Coto de Caza would not allow a public school to be placed within its walls because the gates would have had to remain open for public access. The more recent example of Pelican Hills in the City of Newport illustrates just how complicated incorporation strategies can become. Newport Coast is proposing to annex the nearby developing gated communities to prevent them from opposing the airport, and enticing them by guaranteeing an $18-million gift to provide parks and a public library exclusively for their use.

Thus, the incorporation of gated communities reveals a new trend in the privatization of public space through the use of a land-use planning and municipal government strategy accompanied by active political involvement. While incorporation can be employed to reduce taxes and create a municipal government more responsive to local needs, in the Greater Metropolitan Region of Los Angeles gated community examples, it is a means of coopting public resources for private interests, to the detriment of surrounding neighborhoods and the city as a whole.

Incentive Zoning Variances: Nassau County, Long Island, New York

In Nassau County, where there is limited open land and strict zoning codes for new housing, developing a gated community can be a considerable undertaking. The architect John Gaines describes the history of the parcel of land and what he faced when developing Manor House in the early 1990s as a process of appeasing village officials.

The process of producing an acceptable plan, Gaines said, was relatively complex.[4] The village[5] had to approve the homeowners association, and there was a great deal of concern about the application of the "cluster zoning" open space ordinance. Cluster zoning allows increasing the density of buildings on one part of a site, while the remainder of the parcel is retained in its natural state, preserving forest and farmland, as well as historic structures and landscapes.[6]

Gaines said that he proposed small lot sizes, close together, but with detached houses. This kind of clustering had only been used with townhouses. He wanted to keep most of the land open with no fencing, owned communally through the homeowners association. It was an innovative plan that finally got approval in 1994.

He worked with the village to create a governance structure, a CID, that separated ownership of common areas from ownership of individual lots. Buyers purchase "fee-simple" lots, that is, they own their land and house. But they also purchase the right to be a member of the homeowners' association that collectively owns and oversees the mansion, tennis courts, pool, and common grounds.

But his description of the development process was incomplete. Gaines did not explain that in Nassau County gated developments are allowed only under incentive zoning regulations recently added to the village's original zoning and building codes. Interviews with the village planner and board officials uncovered how these zoning changes gave Gaines considerable economic concessions and freedom in the development of the site. For example, the incentive zoning allowed him to build more houses than allowed in exchange for the provision of amenities for the town or village. A payment of $510,000 in compliance with the new zoning code was made by Gaines to the village to be used to provide public amenities (Plöger, 2002b).

According to the local planner, developers usually approach the village board saying: "We need more flexibility in designing our subdivisions."[7] The village is willing to allow some relief, but wants to receive some benefit in exchange. Legally, the village cannot negotiate the fees paid in lieu of creating a public amenity, but asks the developer to create a park, library, or some kind of public facility. But in practice, negotiations with the village mayor occur throughout the review process, and in the end a compromise is reached that satisfies both parties. Thus, the fees paid to the village for zoning changes are completely negotiable, and there are no standards for the calculation of the fee. Every single item on the building application list, including the fencing, has to be approved or negotiated against a fee.

These quasilegal exchanges are considered acceptable because the village is trying to maintain very low taxes compared to other municipalities, and wants to keep the tax burden to a minimum. These low taxes are made possible by offering only a limited amount of public services, and the village uses the fees paid by developers to create whatever public amenities are needed. The reason that developers who apply for incentive zoning always paid a fee and never actually created any public amenity, is that this village has so little public land and the land that exists is almost entirely privately owned. In the few cases where an amenity was created—such as scenic open space, agricultural fields with a preserved farmhouse, jogging paths, or unspoiled forest—it was placed within the gated community, or located in such a way that a conservation easement of the surrounding area restricted public access.

The idea behind incentive zoning is that the public will be the beneficiary of additional open space or public amenities achieved through increased housing density or other zoning concessions by the municipality, town, or village. But like the New York City Plaza Bonus Zoning Ordinance that allows developers to build additional stories on their buildings, these "privately owned public spaces" are located and/or restricted in such a way to discourage public use (Kayden, 2000). Private interests are able to craft complicated deals that benefit the developer and the gated community residents without enhancing public space and at the expense of taxpayers who unwittingly are trading higher-density housing for privatized open spaces and reduced public amenities. Ironically, the taxpayers are subsidizing the creation of a secured residential enclave with private parks, tennis courts, club houses, and swimming pools.

Annexation and Adequate Services: San Antonio, Texas

Like Nassau County, many of the incorporated towns north of San Antonio's Loop 410 have amended their zoning ordinances to allow private subdivisions, but erecting gates around neighborhoods can be costly for residents, because they must pay for street maintenance and other expenses. Even though expensive, the demand for gating is increasing (Graham, 1999). New residential developments in the northern suburbs are almost all gated and built by a number of different architects and investment groups.

According to economists, the current growth in private communities—gated and nongated—is a response to municipal governments' failure to provide adequate neighborhood services because of "free riding," that is, services being used by those who do not pay for them, and the inability of local governments to supply services in rapidly growing areas. Instead, by "bundling up" a variety of public goods within a residential scheme and recovering costs through sale prices and fees, the house-building industry and market has become a "neighborhood"-building industry and market (Webster, 2001: 163).[8] For the people living inside gated communities it is an efficient solution, because of the legal requirement to pay fees, the homogeneity of the community needs and desires, and the fact that would-be residents can choose their package of communal goods according to their personal preferences (Webster, 2001: 164). Critics, on the other hand, are concerned that gated-community dwellers will vote to reduce municipal expenditures that they do not use. But from an economic point of view, the gated community is an opportunity to experiment with new solutions for the provision of goods and services that distribute them more efficiently, to those who can afford to join the "consumption club," than current governmental strategies.

The Mitchells who retired to Sun Meadow illustrate this point. They lived in an incorporated town within San Antonio where they liked the schools, had their own police department, and purchased services from the city. But they found the services supplied by San Antonio expensive yet merely adequate, and therefore decided to move to Sun Meadow where services were initially provided by the homeowners association.

Economic recession and the decline of real estate prices, however, have altered the level of services and tax structure, particularly in Texas, because Texas is extremely reliant on real estate taxes—rather than income taxes—like many other Sunbelt states. Because of this dependence on real estate taxes, Texas relies on privatization of municipal services in order to expand its public tax base. In an interview, urban planner Wayne Trestle, who lives in Sun Meadow, offered his perspective on how taxation, private governance, and land planning influence the fees and services in their gated development and other gated communities.

A lot of what's happening in these gated communities is that local government continues to annex.[9] As they annex, the level of service goes down, not only for the annexed areas, but also for the inner parts of the city. [The idea is that] we'll get more money and everybody will benefit. [But in fact] they get more taxes and dilute the level or quality of services.

So developers say, "Well, I have got to have my own amenity package, I have to have my own gated community." All that is, is a reflection of the inability of the government to deal properly with the problems at hand. They create another level of service: homeowners associations in these gated communities. So the type of [gated] development we get is because the city is ambitious in terms of annexation.

> I see problems with gated communities in the future.... The reality is that when gated communities are annexed, the city does not take responsibility for repairs of streets [and infrastructure]. Homeowners associations have to provide that.

Trestle believes that Sun Meadow will be annexed within two years. It means that residents will have to pay city and county taxes as well as their homeowners association maintenance fees. Tax assessments also will change with annexation, and resident taxes will increase. But the city will not take over responsibility if they have private streets, and even though the city offers police and fire protection, the gating prevents access.

While annexation bolsters municipal revenues and broadens the city's tax base, it has a downside for gated community residents in terms of double taxation—paying fees to the homeowners association and paying high real estate taxes. For example, Gilbert and Marie moved to Sun Meadow in an attempt to escape some of these taxes, and to purchase private services at a reasonable cost. Their motivation for moving to a gated community was that there is a private government, a homeowners association, providing services within the development. As Gilbert put it, "Anytime I can keep the government out of my business I do." His attitude reflects the Sunbelt conservatism and rightwing politics espoused by a number of San Antonio residents. He thought being in a gated community would keep the government out, but now Sun Meadow is to be annexed by the city. When he purchased his home, they were two and half miles outside the city limit. But now "we're going to be a gated neighborhood in the city."

Gilbert is disappointed that the city is going to annex Sun Meadow. He agrees with Trestle's prediction that Sun Meadow residents will be taxed for services they will not use. For Gilbert and Trestle, triple taxation (city taxes, county taxes, and homeowners association fees) is inequitable, especially when street maintenance and water are not provided. They expect that what city services they do get will be mediocre.

Some gated communities have applied to receive a rebate on their property taxes for services that they pay for privately. The executive director of Woodbridge Village in Irvine, California went to the state assembly in 1990 to make a case for deducting homeowners association dues from federal and state income tax, but was not successful. In New Jersey, though, a group of private homeowners associations succeeded in pushing the Municipal Services Act through the state legislature, which provides rebates on property taxes that residents pay for trash collection, snow removal, and street lighting. The New Jersey chapter of the Community Association Institute, the national association of homeowners associations, also continues to lobby for rebates on taxes paid to maintain public roads (Stark, 1998). If gated communities that are annexed are successful in reducing their taxes, it will also mean that they can use public highways, parks, and services without having to pay for them. Tax rebates will create the same kinds of public/private inequities and the loss of public space and resources as incorporation and incentive zoning

Conclusion

The sociospatial characteristics of gating in the Greater Metropolitan Region of Los Angeles are already anticipated in San Antonio, Texas as the rapid expansion of jobs and housing peaks, and annexation is no longer an adequate alternative for solving urban problems. New York and Los Angeles have already been through this phase of extreme urban growth, and as San Antonio's growth spurt slows, different planning strategies will emerge. Yet the Greater Metropolitan Region of Los Angeles still leads the way in its use of incorporation and municipal succession to solve an array of social, economic, and financial problems. Eventually San Antonio, and Nassau and Suffolk Counties in New York, will catch up with Los Angeles by having more than a third of their housing stock located in private gated communities. And when this happens, I expect there will be even greater similarity in the ways that private interests take over, manipulate, and/or overlay resources in the public domain.

Unfortunately, with this increase in private gated communities there will be increased social and economic segregation according to Le Goix's analysis, a public that votes for private interests from McKenzie's point of view, and an insecure and anxious gated world where residents are not safer, deplete their sense of community, and are disgruntled about the strict rules and regulations of private governance (Wilson-Doenges, 1995, 2000; Low, 2003). At many levels—political, legal, social, and psychological—residents are expressing disappointment with the outcome of these privatizing strategies for refashioning the urban and suburban fabric.

But from the perspective of cities, the building of private communities has the advantage of providing the "front-load" infrastructure construction costs. Municipalities and towns that cannot fund new development, but want to expand their tax base, rely on real estate developers to produce new housing through incentive zoning and annexation mechanisms. The benefits of these strategies became even more apparent after the passage of laws like Proposition 13 in California that restrict the power of local government to finance activities through property taxes (McKenzie, 1998). Thus, as states follow the lead of California's tax abatement, they will also increasingly privatize the provision of what are currently public services. Gated communities will gain even greater popularity as one of the only solutions for the failure of the public sector. And the public sector will become private by incorporation.

What happens to public space in this scenario? Based on the Greater Metropolitan Region of Los Angeles example, it becomes privatized, walled, and/or restricted for those who are "members" rather "citizens." But in this rather dark vision of the urban future, the latest trend in gated communities emerges, faux fortresses located in the Simi Valley called "neighborhood entry identities," which offer all the visible signs of gating, but without guards. Since functional gates come with problems such as the maintenance of private streets and the hiring of internal police, manager staff, and landscaping and trash services, these new residential developments are designed to look like a gated community, but in fact are not. For many residents, the walls, unlocked gates and guard house are enough to provide the sense of feeling special, exclusive, and secure. The unmanned guard house implies that it is a private community, but anyone is free to enter. These pseudo-gated communities provide the same housing and amenities without the additional costs. According to the *Los Angeles Times,* "Many who want to live in a modern-day fortress find the fake model just as good as the real thing" (Halper, 2002: B14). Do these fake fortresses mean that the costs of privatization and gating will ultimately outweigh their social and political appeal?

Acknowledgments

I would like to thank the Wenner-Gren Foundation for Anthropological Research and The City University of New York for funding this project. I am also indebted to Andrew Kirby, Elena Danaila, and Suzanne Scheld, graduate students in environmental psychology and anthropology at the City University of New York who collected many of the interviews cited in the New York section of this chapter. Many colleagues have read parts of this manuscript and offered their helpful comments, including Evan McKenzie, Dolores Hayden, and Richard Briffault. And finally, Renaud Le Goix and Jörg Plöger graciously allowed me to use data collected for their doctoral and master's theses, respectively. I am deeply appreciative of their support and assistance in completing this comparative project. I would like readers to know that I grew up in Los Angeles, although I currently live in New York City and the eastern end of Long Island.

Notes

1. Evan McKenzie puts this figure at one-eighth of all housing.
2. Not discussed in this chapter.
3. These prices are for 1995–1996. Jörg Plöger reported that in 2001 a house sold for as high as $1.8 million.

4. Like most towns on Long Island, there is a zoning review board that controls development in the village and the township.
5. I am not using the name of the village to protect the interviewees involved.
6. The developer calculates the maximum density allowed by local zoning standards, but distributes it differently. For example, two-acre residential zoning allows a developer to build ten houses on twenty acres, each house on a two-acre lot. With cluster zoning, a developer can build ten houses on quarter-acre lots, leaving the remaining seventeen and a half acres as open fields, woods, or setting for a historic structure.
7. From fieldnotes of Jörg Plöger.
8. According to Webster (2001, 2002), gated community debates frequently espouse overly simplistic notions of the private and public realms. Adding a third category, the "club" realm, modifies this dichotomy. From the point of view of public goods theory, access to and consumption of a good or service is what makes it public or private. "Public goods" have the quality of nonexcludability, so that once they have been provided, everyone benefits regardless of whether they pay or not. Cities or suburbs, in this scheme, are made up of small *publics*, each of which may be thought of as a collective consumption club.
   These "consumption clubs" assign legal property rights over neighborhood public goods by property market institutions (ownership, real estate assessments) and are not different from other governance institutions where included "members" (taxpayers) share goods and "nonmembers" (nontaxpayers) are excluded. A comparison can be made between municipal governments supplying collective services on the basis of taxes, and gated communities with their own management companies, local service budgets, and contractual regulations providing goods and services based on fees. Rather than focusing on the distinction between public or private, it is more fruitful to ask whether gated communities deliver more equitable services to "club" residents.
9. Annexation is a process by which a town, county, or other governmental unit becomes part of the city, in this case the metropolitan region of San Antonio.

References

Beito, David T. 2002. "The private places of St. Louis: urban infrastructure through private planning." In *The Voluntary City*, edited by D.T. Beito, P. Gordon, and A. Tabarrok, 47–75. Ann Arbor, MI: University of Michigan Press.

Bourdieu, Pierre. 1984. *Distinction.* London: Routledge and Kegan Paul.

Briffault, Richard. 1999. A government for our time. Business improvement districts and urban governance. *Columbia Law Review*, 99, 365–477.

Bullard, R. and C. Lee. 1994. "Racism and American Apartheid." In *Residential Apartheid*, edited by R.D. Bullard, J.E. Grigsby III, and C. Lee, 1–16. Los Angeles: Center of Afro-American Studies.

Cooper, Marc. 2000. "The Two Worlds of Los Angeles." *The Nation*, August 21/28, p. 15.

Davis, Mike. 1990. City *of Quartz: Excavating the Future in Los Angeles.* London: Verso.

Davis, Mike. 1992. "Fortress Los Angeles: The Militarization of Urban Space." In *Variations on a Theme Park*, edited by M. Sorkin, 154–180. New York: Noonday Press.

Denton, Nancy. 1994. "Are African-Americans Still Hypersegregated?" In *Residential Apartheid*, edited by R. B. Bullard, J.E. Grigsby III, and C. Lee, 49–81. Los Angeles: Center for Afro-American Studies.

Devine, John. 1996. *Maximum Security.* Chicago: University of Chicago Press.

Dillon, David. 1994. "Fortress America: More and More of Us Are Living Behind Locked Gates." *Planning* 60(6): 8–13.

Duncan, James S. and Nancy L. Duncan. 2004. *Landscapes of Privilege.* New York and London: Routledge.

Fischler, M. S. 1998. "Security the Draw at Gated Communities." *New York Times*, August 16, section 14LI, p. 6.

Foucault, Michel. 1975. *Discipline and Punish. The Birth of the Prison.* Trans. Alan Sheridan. New York: Random House.

Frantz, Klaus. 2000–2001. "Gated Communities in the USA—A New Trend in Urban Development." *Espace, Populations, Societes* 101–113.

Graham, Lee. 1999. "Straddling the Fence." *Dallas Morning News*, August 7, p. 1.

Halper, Evan. 2002. Communities Say Keep Out—By Bluffing. *Los Angeles Times*, May 28, p. B1.

Harvey, David. 1990. *The Condition of Postmodernity*. New York: Blackwell.

Hayden, Dolores. 2003. *Building Suburbia: Green Fields and Urban Growth*, 1820–2000. New York: Pantheon.

Judd, Dennis. 1995. "The Rise of New Walled Cities." In *Spatial Practices*, edited by H. Ligget and D.C. Perry, 144–156. Thousand Oaks, CA: Sage Publications.

Kayden, Jerold S. 2000. *Privately Owned Public Space*. New York: John Wiley & Sons.

Kennedy, David. 1995. "Residential Associations as State Actors: Regulating the Impact of Gated Communities on Non-Members." *Yale Law Journal* 105: 761–803.

Le Goix, Renaud. 2002. "Gated Communities in Southern California: Assessing the Geographical Aspects of Urban Secession." Paper presented at the International Conference on Private Urban Governance. Institute of Geography, Johannes Gutenberg Universität, Mainz, June 5–9.

Le Goix, Renaud. 2003. "Les 'gated communities' aux Etats-Unis, morceaux de villes ou territoires à part entiére" [Gated communities within the city in United States, urban neighborhoods or territories apart]. Ph.D. diss., Panthéon-Sorbonne, Paris.

Low, Setha M. 1997. "Urban Fear: Building Fortress America." *City and Society, Annual Review*, 52–72.

Low, Setha M. 2000. *On the Plaza: The Politics of Public Space and Culture*. Austin, TX: University of Texas Press.

Low, Setha M. 2001. "The Edge and the Center: Gated Communities and the Discourse of Fear." *American Anthropologist* 103, no. 1: 45–58.

Low, Setha M. 2003. *Behind the Gates: Life, Security and the Pursuit of Happiness in Fortress America*. New York: Routledge.

Low, Setha M., D. Taplin, and S. Scheld. 2005. *Rethinking Urban Parks: Public Space and Cultural Diversity*. Austin, TX: University of Texas Press.

MacCormack, John. 2000. District 6 faces its own great divide. *San Antonio Express-News*, May 22, 1–11.

Massey, D.S. and Nancy Denton. 1988. "Suburbanization and Segregation." *American Journal of Sociology* 94, no. 3: 592–626.

McKenzie, Evan. 1994. *Privatopia*. New Haven, CT: Yale University Press.

McKenzie, Evan. 1998. "Homeowner Associations and California Politics." *Urban Affairs Review* 34, no.1: 52–75.

McKenzie, Evan. 2003. "Private Gated Communities in the American Urban Fabric." Keynote presentation, Glasgow, Sept. 19.

Merry, Sally. 1993. "Mending Walls and Building Fences: Constructing the Private Neighborhood." *Journal of Legal Pluralism* 33: 71–90.

Merry, Sally. 2001. "Spatial Governmentality and the New Urban Social Order: Controlling Gender Violence Through Law." *American Anthropologist* 103, no. 1: 36–45.

Mitchell, Don. 1995. "The End of Public Space: People's Park, Definitions of the Public, and Democracy." *Annals of the Association of American Geographers* 85, no. 1: 108–133.

Nelson, Robert H. 1999a. "Privatizing the Neighborhood: A Proposal to Replace Zoning With Private Collective Property Rights to Existing Neighborhoods." *George Mason Law Review* 7, no. 4: 827–880.

Nelson, Robert H. 1999b. "Zoning by Private Contract." In *The Fall and Rise of Freedom of Contract*, edited by E.H. Buckley, 157–176. Durham, NC: Duke University Press.

Plöger, Jörg. 2002a. "Analysis of the Courses that Lead to a Concentration of Gated Communities in North Hills." Paper presented at Rights to the City Conference, Rome, May 29–June 1.

Plöger, Jörg. 2002b. "Gated Communities in North Hills." Diplomarbeit im Studiengang Diplom-Geographie. Hamburg: Universität Hamburg, Institut für Geographie.

Sanchez, T. and R. Lang. 2002. "Security versus Status. The Two Worlds of Gated Communities." Census Note 2:02. Alexandria, VA: Metropolitan Institute at Virginia Tech.

Schlosser, Eric. 1998. "The Prison-Industrial Complex." *Atlantic Monthly*, December, 51–77.

Skogan, Wesley G. 1987. "The Impact of Victimization of Fear." *Crime and Delinquency* 33: 135–154.

Skogan, Wesley G. 1995. "Crime and the Racial Fears of White Americans." *Annals of the American Academy of Political and Social Science* 539, no. 1: 59–72.

Smith, Neil. 1984. *Uneven Development*. Oxford: Basil Blackwell.

Smith, Neil. 1996. *The New Urban Frontier.* New York: Routledge.

South, S. and K.D. Crowder. 1997. "Residential Mobility Between Cities and Suburbs: Race, Sub-urbanization and Back-to-the-City Moves." *Demography* 34, no. 4: 525–538.

Stark, Andrew. 1998. "America, The Gated?" *Wilson Quarterly* 22, no. 1: 58–80.

Webster, Chris. 2001. "Gated Cities of Tomorrow." *Town Planning Review* 72, no. 2: 149–170.

Webster, Chris. 2002. "Property Rights, and the Public Realm: Gates, Green-Belts and Gemeinshaft." *Environment and Planning B: Planning and Design* 29: 397–412.

Weiss, Kenneth R. 2003. "A Malibu Civics Lesson: Beach Is Open." *Los Angeles Times*, Monday, August 25, p. B1–8.

Wilson-Doenges, Georgeanna. 1995. "The Fortressing of Residential Life: Effects of Guard-Gating on Sense of Community and Fear of Crime." Ph.D. diss., University of California, Irvine.

Wilson-Doenges, Georgeanna. 2000. "An Exploration of Sense of Community and Fear of Crime in Gated Communities." *Environment and Behavior* 32, no. 5: 597–611.

Zukin, Sharon. 1995. *The Cultures of Cities.* London: Blackwell.

CHAPTER 6

Power, Space, and Terror: Social Reproduction and the Public Environment

CINDI KATZ

The politics of public space, especially around its privatization, surveillance, and "security"' have concerned me for several years. Not only do these issues have profound implications for children's everyday lives—which is how I came to them—but in ricocheting around questions of social reproduction, they expose some of the most important contradictions of neoliberal globalism at a range of scales. This thorny nexus was brought powerfully home to me in a series of strange but somewhat startling little pieces in *The New York Times* in the fall of 1997 when I was in the thick of writing about the social, spatial, and cultural implications of the privatization of children's play. The first article to catch my eye, in October 1997, indicated that the Disney Corporation had hired Henry Kissinger to be its ambassador to China. They were anticipating a rough road ahead with the soon to be released Scorsese film on Tibet, *Kundun.* China—a vast and as yet unDisneyfied market, the possible location of a Disneyworld or two—was already grumbling about shutting Disney out if Scorsese's film hit the screen. Who better than Henry Kissinger to keep China safe for Disney? Not ten days later, I read that billionaire financier, George Soros, had pledged to donate $500 million over the next three years to Russia for health care, education, and retraining the military for civilian jobs. *The*

New York Times article pointed out that Soros's contribution would exceed that of the United States, which had spent a total of $95 million in foreign aid in Russia in 1996. All of this was happening less than a month after Ted Turner had promised $1 billion to the United Nations to fund various programs over the next ten years.

Each of these events made me think of Central Park. And not as a refuge.

Corporations developing what are essentially foreign policies with the likes of former secretary of state Henry Kissinger advising them, while the foreign aid of individuals outstrips that of nations the size and stature of the United States are of a piece with the private self-serving initiatives sponsored by organizations and "partnerships" such as the Central Park Conservancy. In each realm, we are witnessing nothing short of a wholesale reworking of the meaning of public life. As corporate income tax declines and the benefits of "tax reform" accrue largely to these outsized individuals and privatized outfits, we witness an increasingly strapped state at all scales. Public coffers are hurting relative to the level of circulating wealth, and government expenditures have been increasingly skewed toward "security." Policing, *carceral* (prisons, detention centers, etc.), and military expenditures continue to grow as other traditional areas of state expenditure are reeled in, while private initiatives to pay for what best serves the interests of the wealthy are on the increase almost everywhere. These initiatives—parks, playgrounds, museums, and the like—look good and seem swell, but I find myself skeptical to the point of feeling like a sore sport.

In this piece, I would like to unravel why. I want to argue that we are witnessing privatization on a world scale that speaks of an individualist neoliberal politics of choice rather than any notion of public or collective responsibility for social reproduction. The themes that I hope to touch on along the way include the nature of contemporary struggles over social reproduction, some of the stakes of a cultural politics of childhood, and the ways that these questions of power are inscribed on and furthered by particular landscapes.

I begin with a few telling tales from *The New York Times* that provoked me on this train of thought during the 1990s.

"Indoor playgrounds" or as they are known in the industry, "children's entertainment centers," had been introduced in the New York metropolitan area and elsewhere. *The New York Times* quotes industry officials and playground owners who reassure that indoor playgrounds offer "safe play" because all of the equipment is padded or cushioned. But their real attraction, as the 1994 article slyly suggests, is that they offer a "safe haven" for children whose parents are alarmed by news reports of children being abducted or harmed while playing outside. An echoing article noted how franchised indoor playgrounds, such as the now defunct Discovery Zone, were increasingly popular in the city. Again, the reason given was that they allay parental safety fears. Without so much as a whisper of concern for the broader implications of a city perceived as savagely unsafe, the article makes paying to play (at the time $6.00 an hour) sound thoroughly American, and takes pains to democratize fear—and its privatized mitigation—by highlighting the positive gush of a Latina mother in the Bronx shelling out the money.

In early summer of the same year, Sara Mosle, then a Washington Heights schoolteacher, wrote a column bemoaning the fact that children in that working class, largely Dominican, section of Manhattan do not have the opportunity for "normal childhood rambunctiousness," and in dangerous neighborhoods, sometimes live under what she called, "virtual house arrest." Too bad there's nothing virtual about it; not only are children without childcare routinely kept indoors, but in recent years a small but growing number of parents have begun to outfit their children with computer chips that enable them to be located using the satellite technology of global positioning systems (GPS). These devices, which were developed for locating property in large warehouses, resemble those used on prisoners under house arrest or parolees, except they are ensconced in cheerful pendants or wristwatches that are "child friendly, albeit unremovable without a special device." Known by the brand name "digital angel," this bit of domestic surveillance is available at none other than Wal-Mart for about $35. As the democratization of danger becomes the most compelling feature of the twenty-first century, "chipping" children may soon be as common as the box store.

Then there's the constant assault of articles that detail the violence of urban children's everyday lives. In these, the tropes of innocence and danger oscillate at breathtaking speed. Fully armed children face down savage inequalities in the war at home, while other children—saddled with great adversity—triumph over evil, and manage to care for their siblings, get straight A's, and get into an Ivy League school. Apart from the news, which is ghastly and hideously repetitive, the occasional series "City Kids" titillates the comfortable reader with profiles that alternate between the tropes. One piece described a boy said to have a joined a "wolf pack," and less than two weeks later an outraged reader wrote that this characterization was a "disservice to wolves." Wolves, we are told, "care for each other and do not kill for greed or pleasure." He sternly calls for a dose of hard work and moral values. I note that young wolves still have the opportunity for "normal childhood rambunctiousness," and while thinking of canines wonder whether he is among the dog owners residing in the middle-class Manhattan complex, Tudor City, who opposed a planned renovation of the playground because it would displace the dog run. Then again, he could have been a member of the Urban Canine Conservancy, which formed in the late 1990s and unsuccessfully lobbied the Central Park Conservancy and the New York City Parks Department to open half the lavishly restored Sheep Meadow to dogs. Ruminating on this cud, I realized the city was going to the dogs.

Terror Talk

The terror talk concerning kids has risen to crisis proportions. But it's not really about children. This talk, in fact, mystifies the violence against children as it enacts its own. It works in the same way apocalyptic talk about nature obscures the determinants of environmental problems, and, as I have argued elsewhere (Katz, 1993, 1995), muddies the contours of a viable environmental politics. These discourses—apocalyptic talk about nature and terrorizing talk about kids—are of a piece. In this essay, I want to historicize and offer some ideas about what this talk is about; to connect this argument—which is about global political economy—to present crises affecting urban public space and children's outdoor play; and from there to argue about the public nature of the violence against children and its ties to particular productions of space and nature.

Terrorizing contentions concerning violence against children in the public arena—from abductions and molestations to armed assaults and murders—weigh heavily on the public imagination. According to the sociologist Spencer Cahill (1990), this discourse of threat and violence became commonplace in the United States around 1979. The preoccupation with children's safety was itself part of a larger discourse concerning "the disappearance of childhood" that Cahill notes erupted at the end of the 1970s. The loss of childhood as a hallowed life stage of promise and possibility was signaled and mourned from all quarters. Television programming, clothing styles, rudderless moral guidance, and pervasive apocalyptic doom, among many other things, were offered alternatively as markers of the shift and its cause. The French historian Pierre Ariès (1962) had only recently "found" childhood, and now it was slipping away. What was going on?

Then as now I was dubious that this talk had anything to do with significant increases in violence against children, and indeed have since then learned that the Department of Justice does not keep systematic figures on crimes against persons under twelve years of age.[1] It remains that most of the violence against children is perpetrated by people they know. While youth-against-youth violence has risen in recent years, it seems that measured increases in children's public victimization were not at the root of what I am calling "terror talk." It might be argued that terror talk emerged following an increase in media coverage or the reporting of some particularly gruesome tales. Given that the media are not outside of discourse, and reflect as much as guide dominant preoccupations, pegging the rise of terror talk to its prominence in the media is rather circular. Again, neither people nor pundits were responding to any sort of clear signals that the incidence of crimes against children was increasing substantially. Only its grisly currency was on the rise. But even as the reporting of violence against children became routinized, there was little evidence to suggest that as a society we are really concerned with the problems that face children. How else to explain the level of unencumbered violence against children perpetrated by those with whom they are intimate, the growing number of children living in poverty,[2] or the increasingly misanthropic pubic response to the erosive effects of poverty on children's health and well-being?

In New York City alone, over 50,000 reports of abuse and neglect, encompassing over 80,000 children, were filed every year throughout the 1990s (New York City Administration for Children's Services, 2001). While most reports are unfounded, it is well known that neglect and abuse are always underreported. According to a recent survey by the U.S. Justice Department, for instance, 65 percent of sex offenders in state prisons indicated that their victims were children under eighteen years old. One-third of these children were the offenders' children or stepchildren; of the rest, half were known to the offender. In another vein, the assault on children's welfare brought about by the welfare reform legislation of 1996 and years since is too well known to rehearse here, but suggests that concern for children's welfare is not key in the present political climate.

Perhaps these are simple-minded explanations, but it seemed to me that the emergence and resonance of terror talk concerning children in the late 1970s had much more to do with a broader anxiety about the state of the United States in the world than it did with anything particularly salient in children's everyday lives at that time or since. What then was going on in 1979? Whose childhood, exactly, was disappearing at that time? Five years earlier, the global hegemony of U.S. capital was effectively threatened for the first time since its ascendance during World War II. The nation was reeling from the shock of losing in Vietnam coming fast on the heels of the increase in crude oil prices that was pinned on OPEC (Organization of Petroleum Exporting Countries), but of great benefit to the big oil companies. The "enemies within" had been targeted a few years earlier following the uprisings associated with the civil rights, antiwar, and women's movements. For capitalists and "American dreamers" alike, things by 1979 were looking grim indeed. There was a putative "energy crisis," fuel prices were high, Carter put on a cardigan and gave the "malaise" speech that was said to have handed the election to the Republicans, Iran seized the U.S. Embassy in Teheran and held Americans hostage, and the Sandinistas were victorious in Nicaragua.

These setbacks to the presumptions of U.S. capital and the Pax Americana did not in themselves pose a threat to U.S. children. I would argue, however, that, among other things, they were entwined with and drove the discourse about childhood's disappearance. Taken together, these strikes against the presumed hegemony of the United States in all matters global cast a pall on the so-called American Century. The sense of foreclosure or limits was almost unthinkable in U.S. mythology, and I think was duly sublimated in talk of a vagary of threats to children and childhood itself. The slippage is not hard to imagine. It is almost as if Carter's televised exhortation that the United States face its changed circumstances in the world was imagined as a paternal disquisition to an unruly teen who refuses to grow up. Among the residues of the adolescent's response were Reagan and the rise of disquieting talk about children and childhood. Kids in the United States are still reeling from both.[3]

This interpretation of terror talk merely shows how children, like nature, are a ready canvas on which all manner of social phenomena and anxieties are inscribed, only to be discovered there and used to naturalize one thing or another. I have made this argument to highlight three things. First, I want to dispel the notion that there was any *particular* threat to children that led to the discourse of threat. (This, of course, is not to say that children are not threatened and victimized by terrible violence, only that it hadn't much changed as this talk became resonant.) Second, the discourse helps hide that the private sphere is the locus of the most horrific threats to children, and this serves to sharpen the false dichotomy between the public and private arenas in ways that do not serve children at all. Finally, terror talk has been neatly tied to a set of operations concerning urban public space that have led to marked deteriorations in children's everyday lives. I have attempted to show that the terror talk was the excrescence of a set of political economic displacements, not because I want to psychoanalyze the United States, but because I want to argue that these displacements drive the deteriorations of urban public space that *are* so destructive to children, but which are somehow excused or elided by the terror talk. In other words, this discourse of terror, which is enmeshed with a sharpening uneven development of the landscapes of reproduction, enacts, underwrites, and masks violence against children at the same time as it mystifies the uneven development itself. I want to unpack this relationship with specific reference to U.S. cities and to the production of public space.

The Landscape of Social Reproduction

The last two decades have witnessed a narrowing, deterioration, and deracination of the public spaces of reproduction in the United States. While U.S. eyes were trained on the supplanting of the nation's hegemony abroad, U.S. capital was pulling up stakes from its traditional sites of investment and moving production elsewhere. As the landscape of production shifted from the old industrial centers of the United States, for example, the pattern of investments in the public environment likewise changed. In recent years, the disinvestment in social reproduction has resulted in the serious deterioration of its key sites, including schools, housing, and public open space, as well as health, welfare and child care programs. In the United States since Reagan there has been a well-orchestrated all-out assault on the sense of public responsibility for collective social life witnessed in the "tax rebellions" that have driven drastic reductions in all forms of social welfare, but also propelled the privatization of crucial aspects of the social wage including education, child care, health care, public space, and now social security. This assault is built in part on driving a wedge between processes of production and reproduction: Public responsibility for social reproduction is jettisoned as the workforce is redefined and "globalized," and responsibility for social reproduction is increasingly relegated to the private realm across disparate geographies at all scales. The strategy has been to abdicate all collective responsibility for reproducing the society as a whole. The architects of the vicious programs that are demolishing all semblance of a public civil society were initially surprised at how fast they succeeded and now have become gluttonous with their own success. Even as the repercussions at the state and city scale of dismantling social program after social program are spread to middle- and working-class people and witnessed in the public spaces of everyday life, progressive notions of the social wage, to say nothing of a less retrograde discourse around taxation, remain elusive.

Social reproduction, by which I mean the material social practices that sustain and reproduce a society—its people, its production system, and its cultural forms and practices—at a given level of production, has been a progressive notion in the United States for its entire history. By and large, each generation has seen and participated in an improvement of the means of production and an expanded notion of what was considered necessary to reproduce their social world. Education levels have increased, housing stock has been improved, and the average age of mortality has risen. It seems clear that this movement, which I want to make clear has been achieved through constant struggle and negotiation over these two centuries, is in the throes of being reversed.

Social reproduction is of course spatialized. I have pointed to the depredations suffered in housing stock, schools, and open space in the wake of economic restructuring and the public disinvestments that have accompanied it in the United States, for example. I want to focus here on a little attended, but crucially important, part of social reproduction—children's play, and look at the deterioration of the play environments in urban areas. It is clear that public parks and playgrounds suffer disproportionately in times of fiscal crisis compared with other aspects of urban life. Open space, recreation, and contact with "nature" all seem to be expendable luxuries when compared with schools, clinics, and of course, cops. But are they? The uneven development and care for these spaces in contemporary cities, suggest that the wealthy do not view these spaces as expendable—for themselves—but the private ways by which the privileged increasingly secure their own access to the outdoor environment ensures that safe, attractive outdoor spaces will become a luxury for working class and poor neighborhoods in the city.

In 1991, before the combined conservative weight of Mayor Rudolph Giuliani and Governor George Pataki hit New York City, the Citizens Budget Commission published a report, *Managing the Department of Parks and Recreation in a Time of Fiscal Stress*, that concluded, "The gap between current resources and those needed to have the existing system perform adequately is beyond government's ability to close." By their estimates in 1990, four out of ten parks and playgrounds were in substandard (fair or poor) condition, to say nothing of facilities such as restrooms and drinking fountains, 25 percent of which were not functioning according to them. Recreation services were described as "skeletal" (Citizens Budget Commission, 1991: 32). That was in 1990, and while things got worse through the mid-1990s, by 2000 there was evidence of substantial improvement in the overall condition and cleanliness of the city's parks and playgrounds (89 percent were considered in acceptable condition by the Parks Department's accounting), albeit with predictable geographical disparities in the level and pace of improvement (New York City Department of Parks and Recreation, 2003). But much of this improvement is traceable to private investment through such things as public–private partnerships, self-tithing privatized conservancies, and "adopt a ..." schemes. Indeed in 1995—when conditions in New York City's parks and playgrounds were at their lowest point in recent memory (39 percent were considered in acceptable condition)—"Partnerships for Parks" was launched by the City Parks Foundation and the New York City Department of Parks and Recreation to help address what had become a dire situation. By 2002, the private sector paid about $50 million a year to maintain and restore and support programs in New York City's parks. Volunteer labor contributed another $10 million (Schwartz, 2002). All the while the proportion of public funding and paid staff shrank.

As public investment in public outdoor space is deferred to the vanishing point,[4] social reproduction is hounded into private space or secured in increasingly privatized "public" spaces of everyday life. Central among the recommendations of the Citizens Budget Commission, for example, were "private park conservancies" such as the highly touted Central Park Conservancy. But other private schemes to take care of particular open spaces, even the "flagship" parks in the other boroughs, have been less successful than the magnificently renovated Central Park. Nevertheless, the Parks Department, crumbling under battering waves of budget cuts (by 2001 its full-time staff was a third of what it had been thirty years earlier), followed the lead of the Parks Council and the Citizens Budget Commission, and suggested "park enhancement districts," modeled on the pernicious and ever-proliferating business improvement district, as a new "financing scheme." These callow sentiments were echoed in a disgracefully disingenuous letter to *The New York Times* from Ira Millstein, a senior partner in the Fifth Avenue corporate law offices of Weil, Gotshal and Manges and then chair of the Central Park Conservancy. Millstein, noting how the Conservancy's share of the capital and operational budgets of Central Park had shifted from millions less than the city to millions more in the short time between 1991 and 1994, offered the following "concept for the future": "to *let* all neighborhoods in the city, if they *choose* to do so, to support their local open space with a further revenue stream." *Let* them? If they *choose*? Turning neighborhoods into "park enhancement districts," it seems, would enable each neighborhood to "voluntarily organize itself, decide whether to impose a small surcharge on its local real estate to supplement city support and private philanthropy ... and then use it for its own park, playground or other open space." In neighborhoods where "local real estate" has been largely abandoned by capital and the support of the city and private philanthropy verges on nil, sentiments like Millstein's are a cruel joke. His letter suggested lack of familiarity even with the area that bounds Central Park to the north where Harlem begins.

In central Harlem, where at the same time that Millstein wrote his letter, 457 buildings were ready for demolition, or East Harlem, where 164 buildings were so far beyond repair that they too were ready,[5] and where 35 percent of all households earned less than $10,000 a year and more than half of all children lived below the poverty line, it stretches the imagination—and patience—to think that even a modest tithing scheme would be possible (Citizens' Committee for Children of New York, 1995). This is cynicism at its worst.

Two blocks north of the Park, I spent years working on a participatory design project with two elementary schools and the neighborhood, which had "organized itself" to rebuild the nearly featureless and neglected concrete slabs that were their schoolyards. Along the way there was an international student design competition for the yards with over a hundred entries. Three years after the winning designs were modified and officially approved, the schools were still waiting for the Board of Education to release capital funds they had supposedly put in escrow for the project back in 1988 (Hart et al., 1992). Somehow, Public Schools 185 and 208 lack corporate clout. By late 1997—fully eight years after the schoolyards project began—a scaled-down redesign was completed for one of the yards with money secured by the principal from then City Council representative, Virginia Fields. The other yard, eventually painted brightly and boasting a few rudimentary garden beds, still had the medieval and broken-down play equipment we found there in 1989.

Lack of funds is the perennial excuse, but there is not no money—choices are being made. These choices are visible in the landscape at all scales. One public site of social reproduction that has fared well for instance is prisons. Prison construction and per capita corrections expenditures have routinely outpaced school construction and per capita education spending in the United States since the 1980s as the incarcerated population has grown astronomically. Over 70 percent of the prison space in use in the United States by the mid-1990s, for instance, was built in the previous decade, while only 11 percent of all classroom space in use by that time was built in the 1980s. The production of park space during that period was even more minuscule. And within the arena of public outdoor space—streets, parks, playgrounds, and the like—the choices made have been telling as well. While neighborhood parks withered, for instance, the New York City Parks Department spent $1.3 million to remove and clean four 1,200-pound bronze eagles at the entrance to Prospect Park, the Central Park Conservancy embarked on a project to restore the bridle paths, and the Northeast corner of the park was slated for a $5.9-million improvement to make "a dusty circle" an "impressive entrance."

The costs of these choices to city children—which are not unrelated to the rise in "terror talk" concerning children—are quite high. I have written elsewhere about the social costs of children's declining opportunities for safe outdoor play (Katz 1993b, 2002). Children in the city have all but lost the opportunity for autonomous outdoor play. Until at least twelve years of age, most children in New York are either supervised by a caregiver, part of an organized group, or kept at home. There are obvious class implications to these problems. Children who do not have a parent at home or a paid caregiver often have little choice but to stay home alone after school each day. The practices are also gendered. It is well documented that girls are restricted far more than boys, and that when they are allowed to go outdoors unsupervised, girls' range is far smaller than boys, even boys several years younger than themselves. This holds for urban, suburban, and rural areas (e.g., Tindal, 1971; Hart, 1979; Matthews, 1986). Parents say they are protecting children from abduction, molestation, and attack. Yet, as with the discourse concerning women's safety in the public environment, these productions of space seem to be much more about social control than the protection of girls (Valentine, 1989; Pain, 1991). Indeed, according to the Children's Defense Fund (personal communication, 1994), boys suffer more public injury—from both physical and social sources—than girls. Yet this reality does not provoke parents to restrict their sons' movements in the public environment, although there are indications that this is changing as well (Hart, 1979, 1986). For girls, the mere fear of social danger is enough to keep them indoors. And fear has reached suffocating levels.

Among the consequences of children's restricted access to the public environment are a loss of opportunity for gross motor development that comes from active physical play in open spaces; lost opportunities for developing spatial skills and geographical knowledge, both of which are linked to other forms of reasoning and a range of careers such as those associated with architecture, surveying, and math; and the lost opportunity for children to build an autonomous culture. Many social skills are learned and internalized among children playing on their own. The cost of the steady erosion of children's chances to build their own cultures has as yet to be determined.

These are just some of the palpable consequences of the uneven sociospatial relations and rundown public spaces associated with capital disinvestment and naturalized by the terror talk I pointed to earlier. What kind of geographical imaginations are possible in a population growing up under these conditions? What are the political costs of coming of age in a disintegrating public environment, where the only viable correctives are privately ensured? What kind of citizens—to use a favorite word of the right—will be reproduced in an increasingly divided and publicly unaccountable privatized world that is characterized for children by restricted play environments such as those in middle-class housing developments, constant tending by hired child minders and others, structured programs that charge fees to participate, private play corrals such as those at fast food restaurants, and ubiquitous monitoring and surveillance? Children appear to be getting used to having their activities constantly monitored and surveilled. The terror talk has gotten to them as well. California teens reported to Shirl Buss, a planner and environmental social scientist, that they preferred to hang out in malls because that is where they felt safe.

The real terror is not the melodrama of abduction, which however horrific is exceedingly rare; rather, it is the steady erosion of the environment of everyday life and the privatization of all strategies for dealing with it. These strategies exacerbate the problem along the lines of class, race, and gender in utterly unsurprising ways. When a mundane thing like children's play is fetishized, the promises of social reproduction are dim at best.

If, on the one hand, I've suggested that the terror talk arose, at least in part, in response to the wake-up call for the U.S. bourgeoisie brought about by the debacle in Vietnam; the 1973 oil shocks; and the civil rights, women's, and antiwar movements; and suggested that it smuggled in and helped to mask a particularly pernicious privatization of public landscapes of social reproduction, I also want to look at some of the broader relationships of power that this talk—terror talk—authorizes. And here I want to suggest that, the modern "passion for safety," as one *New York Times* article labeled it, is a disciplining strategy for children and women, among others. The "modern passion for safety" has effectively deracinated most play environments in New York: The last monkey bars have been removed from the city's playgrounds, "tag" has been banned from recess at many schools, and one of the only adventure playgrounds that survived the overhauls provoked by the combination of fearful parents and the litigious sirens of New York City's planning and parks departments was kept locked so that it can only be used by children in school with their teachers' supervision. This playground was in a neighborhood (the prosperous Upper West Side) that has 881 children per park acre. Despite these restrictions and the nostalgic longing of some neighborhood residents characterized as "sixties parents," the adventure playground was slated for overhaul, its destiny to be shaped by boldly colored plastic and benign neglect.

The "modern passion for safety," which resonates with and against the terror talk about young people, disciplines children, literally by keeping them indoors when unsupervised, and figuratively by keeping them surveilled when outside. It disciplines women by suggesting—slyly and otherwise—that unattended children are at risk; the sub- (or not so "sub") text of worry narratives about children's vulnerability blames mothers for leaving their children to the care of others. As Linda Gordon's (1988) work on nineteenth-century movements against cruelty to children suggests, the discourse of "protecting" children as women's work was an effective ideological strategy for rejuvenating the family and creating the separation between the (male) public sphere and the (female) private sphere. It is instructive to read these nineteenth-century texts on the inappropriateness of children's unsupervised play and its constitution as an "immigrant" practice to be undone by the reformists. The same message floats our way in so many contemporary bottles.

The unease with a nonwhite planet, with women working outside the home (unless they are welfare recipients in which case their mothering activities are constituted as lazy moochery), and with the confusing manifestations of "globalization" come home, have produced a fearsome, vengeful, and increasingly privileged ruling class. It has two faces but one heart. One of its faces is witnessed in the abandonment, criminalization, and incarceration of large segments of the youthful population, particularly young men of color, with little promise of meaningful work in the quickly restructuring "global" economy. The public disinvestment in social reproduction (except for incarceration) and the vile hysteria that accompanies it are the natural manifestations of a capitalist class enacting its privilege with the kind of impunity one associates with the unrestrained early years of industrialization. Indeed, even *The New Yorker* ran an article a few years back touting Marx as the "next" trendy author. The article suggests that Marx's most dire predictions about the rapacious nature of capitalism have come to full fruition in the last twenty years. Such analyses portend an even rougher road ahead.

But there is another face to this process. One I've suggested can be read in the landscape. That is privatization, which is effectively reordering the nature and spaces of social reproduction. Here things are more ambiguous. The Central Park Conservancy, which has effectively taken over the operations for capital projects in Central Park, is a case in point. The public landscape it has produced is beautiful, accessible, graceful, educational, recreational—everything that Frederick Law Olmsted envisioned for this oasis from the urban pressures of industrialization. The Central Park Conservancy has spent more than $300 million on Central Park since its founding in 1980 and pays more than 85 percent of the Park's annual operating budget. During the same time, the New York City Parks Department budget has been whittled down to almost nothing, hovering at around 0.5 percent of total municipal spending for years now. The Central Park Conservancy and other Park Enhancement Districts have in many ways enabled this erosion, because they take care of the visible public landscape in prominent locations such as Central Park, Prospect Park in Brooklyn, and Midtown Manhattan's Bryant Park.

This practice drains not only money but clout from less visible landscapes while creating the sensation for more privileged segments of society that things are good. Few wealthy people or tourists ever see the travesty of Marcus Garvey Park—a would-be Gramercy Park in Harlem (but with a better view)—that until recently suffered the effects of a lack of investment. Not maintained, full of litter, with dangerously broken stairs, walls, and pavements, it languished for decades without intervention—public or private. The largesse of the Central Park Conservancy stops short of parks like Marcus Garvey Park in poor areas, even when they abut the Park. There is seemingly no money to fix up and maintain playgrounds and park in poor and "out of the way" neighborhoods. As the gentrification of Harlem has heated up, the situation has begun to change there too. In 2003, a public–private partnership, the Marcus Garvey Park Alliance, was established and began woefully overdue improvements on the park, a potential jewel. While the task at hand was enormous, their budget was quite lean.

One of the most pressing controversies of neoliberalism is that privatization reinforces uneven relations of power and privilege. Privatization is one of the key reasons that parks in poor and less visible areas languish unimproved. Wealthy New Yorkers increasingly pay to produce landscapes of social reproduction for themselves, improving the spaces within their gaze, but leaving others out. Some of this largesse spills over of course, and is part of a time-honored, if contradictory reformist and charitable impulse that does much good. Indeed the northern part of Central Park, which borders Harlem, has now been gloriously renovated. On visits there I have seen children fishing in the Harlem Meer, a buzzing and attractive playground, and lots of people from the neighborhood and elsewhere enjoying the soft edges of the green spaces and pond. There is a stunning environmental educational center with views that would make Olmsted proud and that attracts lots of visitors. While it had taken them more than fifteen years to get to it, the Central Park Conservancy ultimately did a magnificent job with the seemingly intractable northern reaches of the Park. Likewise, as the case of Marcus Garvey Park suggests, partnerships have been formed to tend parks in poorer and less publicly visible parts of the city, although these partnerships are underfunded across the board.

As the formation of these partnerships—and the City Parks Foundation through which many of them have come to exist—suggest, some wealthy donors at least have started to fund improvements and renovations in less visible parks and neighborhood playgrounds. The cleanliness and condition of most neighborhood parks and playgrounds have improved in the years since the low point around 1995 when I first wrote about these issues. Pleasantly surprised with the improvements I discovered in the public environment of New York during the boom years of the late 1990s, I started to think that maybe I had been wrong about the ripple effects of privatization.

Prodded to make sense of the changes, I dug a little deeper and found out that increased maintenance, repair, and cleaning work in the parks were being done by WEP workers (Work Experience Program). About 5,000 uncompensated WEP (or "workfare") workers have replaced more than half that number of salaried employees in the parks, whose jobs have been lost since the early 1970s (Cohen, 1999). At the same time, it is estimated that a core group of between 5,000 to 10,000 volunteers contributes the equivalent of about $10 million of labor annually (Schwartz, 2002). Meanwhile, in the late 1990s, the Parks Department became a bit more savvy and efficient in using its capital budget, and so was able to spend some unspent dollars from previous years. It was not clear how long this source of funds would last, but thanks in part to the use of WEP workers, capital expenditures have exceeded those for operating costs in recent years. Finally, the Department of Parks and Recreation hired a marketing director to guide their selling of virtually everything and anything to pay for their operations. Privatization in this form results in basketball backboards covered in advertising copy, public spaces rented out (sometimes for months) to various private interests from BMW to theater groups, and promotional practices of all sorts, even when they result in closing these public spaces for extended periods of time, such as the international fashion extravaganza, "7th on Sixth," which closes midtown's Bryant Park for about two weeks a year. Like many strapped public institutions and agencies, the Parks Department contemplated issuing a credit card, considered a host of exclusive concessions for all manner of products and services, and was willing to hawk space for various sponsors and supporters.

All of this creative financing is called for because so little public funding is available. But they stop at nothing. Park spaces that are shared with public schools and little leagues are nevertheless considered fair game for advertising. And in the long run, it is not hard to imagine corporate underwriters starting to determine the conditions in which their products are advertised, and therefore limiting the range of activities supported in public parks and open spaces. Where will the boundaries between public and private be drawn then? Whose parks are they? The struggles are already between variously constituted "privates" rather than publics. For instance, wealthy Fifth Avenue residents turned against their class ally—the Central Park Conservancy—because they posted twenty-three discrete placards acknowledging the sponsors of information kiosks. These notations, in two-inch letters, perturbed the residents' sensibilities. Their spokesperson, who referred to them as "major people," mongered fear of the slippery slope with the intimation that, where today it says New York Times Foundation, tomorrow it might say McDonald's or Burger King.

Where, then, do we draw the line on privatization? It starts innocently enough—"adopt a bench," sponsor a playground, pay for tulip bulbs in the conservatory garden—but the trajectory from advertising on back-boards to privately bankrolling the United Nations is all too smooth, and its long-term consequences have not been carefully addressed. Those interested in the maintenance and expansion of the social wage and all that it entails should question this process "at the backboards" as it were. The geography of privatization is uneven. It has allowed public treasuries to be stripped of much needed funds that in theory at least are subject to more democratic means of accountability. Privatization furthers a project of consumership much more so than citizenship. And each of these issues is compelling in the ways that it alters the grounds of social reproduction, the public spaces of our everyday lives.

One of the founders of Central Park Conservancy, Richard Gilder, who gave $17 million to the park in 1995 alone, suggested in a letter to *The New York Times* that the Central Park Conservancy was "a reaffirmation of social democracy." Not five months earlier he was calling shrilly for the Central Park Conservancy to be able to hold all the revenues collected by the Park and for the City to turn all of the Park's operations over to them, because "it should be beyond dispute, the Conservancy does a better job of running Central Park than the Parks Department can."[6] Why this is so, is apparently beyond question. Yet, if this is a "reaffirmation of social democracy"—rather than aristocratic privilege—we had all better look out. It is the politics of public space to turn that privilege on its head.

Notes

1. I should note that the Justice Department is so keenly statistical that they may have figures on how many people were sneezing when they were assaulted. However, to the extent that nonfatal crimes against children are systematically recorded—and they are not in most states—they are considered child abuse and documented by the National Committee to Prevent Child Abuse.

2. According to a recent report by the National Center for Children in Poverty (2005), 11 million children in the United States live in poverty; that is, 17% of all children.

3. In another vein, the anthropologist Marilyn Ivy (1993: 247) makes an interesting connection between the present U.S. obsession with missing and abused children and various therapies aimed at the "missing child within." She pointedly notes that each of these missing child discourses indicates a displacement from the possibilities of politics to the realm of the private.

4. By 2004, less than 0.5% of the New York City budget was allocated to park operations (Schwartz, 2004).

5. The excess represented by these figures is clear when they are compared with the citywide average at that time of forty-eight buildings ready for demolition per community district.

6. In a later article published in *City Journal*, put out by the right-wing Manhattan Institute, Gilder offered some details of these better management practices. At their heart were the conservancy's ability to get around a "seniority based" unionized labor force, to fire people and flexibly assign them. He indicates with no small measure of pride that while unionized employees of the parks department looked on, CPC employees fished "scores" of mysteriously dead fish from Rowboat Lake. The city workers had insisted—correctly Gilder acknowledged—that such tasks were not in their contract. No doubt the willingness of CPC workers to engage in such fishing expeditions was a result of the conservancy's success in instilling "a real sense of pride" in them (Gilder, 1997).

References

Ariès, Philippe. 1962. *Centuries of Childhood: A Social History of Family Life*. Translated by Robert Baldick. New York: Vintage Books.

Cahill, Spencer E. 1990. "Childhood and Public Life: Reaffirming Biographical Divisions." *Social Problems* 37, no. 3: 390–402.

Citizens Budget Commission. 1991. *Managing the Department of Parks and Recreation in a Time of Fiscal Stress, vol. 58*. New York: Citizens Budget Commission.

Citizens' Committee for Children of New York. 1995. *Keeping Track of New York's Children*. New York: Citizens' Committee for Children of New York.

Cohen, Steven. 1999. "Managing workfare: The case of the work experience program in the New York City Parks Department. New York: Columbia University School of International and Public Affairs, March, 1999. Available at *http://www.columbia.edu/~sc32/wep.html*.

Gilder, Richard. 1997. "Set the Parks Free." *City Journal* 7, no. 1.

Gordon, Linda. 1988. *Heroes of Their Own Lives: The Politics and History of Family Violence, Boston 1880–1960*. New York: Viking.

Hart, Roger. 1979. *Children's Experience of Place*. New York: Irvington.

Hart, Roger. 1986. *The Changing City of Childhood: Implications for Play and Learning*. Catherine Malony Memorial Lecture. New York: City College Workshop Center.

Hart, Roger, Cindi Katz, Selim Iltus, and Maria Rosa Mora. 1992. "International Student Design Competition of Two Elementary Schoolyards." *Children's Environments* 9, no. 2: 65–82.

Ivy, Marilyn. 1993. "Have You Seen Me? Recovering the Inner Child in Late Twentieth-Century America." *Social Text* 37: 227–252.

Katz, Cindi. 1993a. "Reflections While Reading *City of Quartz* by Mike Davis." *Antipode* 25, no. 2: 159–163.

Katz, Cindi. 1993b. "Growing Girls/Closing Circles: Limits on the Spaces of Knowing in Rural Sudan and US Cities." In *Full Circles: Geographies of Women over the Life Course*, edited by Cindi Katz and Janice Monk, 88–106. London and New York: Routledge.

Katz, Cindi. 1995. "Under the Falling Sky: Apocalyptic Environmentalism and the Production of Nature." In *Marxism in the Postmodern Age*, edited by Antonio Callari, Stephen Cullenberg, and Carole Biewener, 276–282. New York: Guilford Press.

Katz, Cindi. 1998. "Disintegrating Developments: Global Economic Restructuring and the Eroding Ecologies of Youth." In *Cool Places: Geographies of Youth Cultures*, edited by Tracey Skelton and Gill Valentine, 130–144. London and New York: Routledge.

Katz, Cindi. 2002. "Stuck in Place: Children and the Globalization of Social Reproduction." In *Geographies of Global Change*, edited by R.J. Johnston, Peter J. Taylor, and Michael J. Watts, 248–260. Oxford, UK: Blackwell Publishing.

Matthews, M.H. 1987. "Gender, Home Range, and Environmental Cognition." *Transactions of the Institute of British Geographers* 12, no. 1: 43–56.

National Center for Children in Poverty. 2005. *Basic Facts About Low-Income Children in the United States*. Available at: *www.nccp.org/media/lic05-text.pdf*.

New York City Administration for Children's Services. 2001. *Progress on ACS Reform Initiatives, Status Report 3*. Available at: *www.nyc.gov/html/acs/pdf/status_report3.pdf*.

New York City Department of Parks and Recreation. 2003. *Park Inspection Program Ratings*. Available at: *www.nycgovparks.org/sub_about/cap/statistics.html*.

Pain, Rachel. 1991. "Space, Sexual Violence and Social Control: Integrating Geographical and Feminist Analyses of Women's Fear of Crime." *Progress in Human Geography* 15, no. 4: 415–431.

Schwartz, Anne. 2002. "Budget Cuts and the Parks." *Gotham Gazette.com* available at: *www.gothamgazette.com/article/parks/20021101/14/608*.

Schwartz, Anne. 2004. "City Parks and the Proposed Budget." *Gotham Gazette.com* available at: *www.gothamgazette.com/article/parks/20040520/14/985*.

Tindal, Margaret A. 1971. *The Home Range of Black Elementary School Children: An Exploratory Study in the Measurement and Comparison of Home Range*. Place Perception Research Report 8. Worcester, MA: Graduate School of Geography, Clark University.

Valentine, Gill. 1989. "The Geography of Women's Fear." *Area* 21, no. 4: 385–390.

CHAPTER 7

Geography of Fear: Crime and the Transformation of Public Space in Post-apartheid South Africa

ASHLEY DAWSON

Contemporary public space is being eroded dramatically. This undermining of the public realm is given perhaps its most graphic representation in Mike Davis's diagram of the "ecology of fear," in which urban space is broken down into an ethnically segregated series of concentric rings (Davis, 1998: 365). According to Davis, cities like Los Angeles are coming to resemble the Manichean racial cantonments of colonial and apartheid urban spaces. The gravity of this situation in the United States, with its gated racial enclaves and private security forces, is certainly worth underlining and challenging. However, this decay of the public realm is not an issue in global cities of the developed world alone. According to the United Nations' "State of the Cities Report 2001," cities in the developed world are fast disappearing from the list of the world's largest urban sites (United Nations, 2002). By 2010 for example, Lagos is projected to become the third largest city in the world, after Tokyo and Mumbai, while Milan, Essen, and London will disappear from the thirty largest cities list, and New York, Osaka, and Paris will slip further down the list. These predictions suggest the inadequacy of recent attempts to theorize globalization by focusing on cities in the developed world. Analysts such as

Saskia Sassen (1991) have successfully illuminated the increasingly pivotal role of global cities in the North in the transformation of current political, economic, and social structures. Cities are, now more than ever before, nexuses of exchange, gathering goods, information, and population from their vast hinterlands and exchanging them with other such cosmopolitan entrepots. Yet the powerful global cities of the developed world are only one part, and an increasingly anomalous one at that, of the story of the urban realm and public space.

Today, in fact, we're faced not simply with the decline of public space but with an unfolding global ecological crisis of unprecedented and potentially catastrophic scale. Cities, the cradles of human civilization, lie at the core of this crisis. For the first time in human history, the majority of humanity lives in cities. By 2025, this urbanized segment is expected to comprise at least 60% of the human race. Contemporary cities are the primary sites for humanity's consumption of natural resources and pollution of the environment. The cities of the developed world are currently responsible for the lion's share of such consumption and pollution. However, the model of the consumerist city—which finds its paradigmatic expression in the zoned, gated, and sprawling cities of North America—is currently being exported to the growing megacities of the global South. The implications of the proliferation of this unsustainable urban model are dire.

Discussions of public space take on a totally different tenor when situated in cities of the South such as Mumbai, where 5 million people currently live in peripheral shantytowns with little access to even the most basic necessities of life. The increasing spatial apartheid and social polarization of urban zones in the developed world pales in comparison with the forms of exclusion and deprivation that structure global cities of the south like Lagos, Manila, and Mexico City. The vast majority of humanity's urbanization during this century will take place in such sites. These cities are, by definition, those least able to cope with spiraling pressures on resources; they are, consequently, also the sites of the greatest environmental and social degradation. These problems will only worsen in the future, as such megacities attract increasing numbers of political, economic, and environmental refugees from their hinterlands. The megacities of the South demonstrate that we can no longer afford to ignore the inextricable connection between environmental sustainability, economic development, and political stability.

The cities of South Africa on which this article focuses are particularly apposite instances to discuss in order to refocus attention on urban conditions in the global South. These cities are the most developed ones on the planet's most underdeveloped continent. Since South Africa is the economic dynamo of the sub-Saharan region, the fate of its urban areas will have a disproportionately strong impact on the other nations of Africa. In addition, South Africa is a particularly useful case study since it has historically offered so many parallels to a developed society such as that of the United States. Both nations were established as white settler societies. Like the United States, South Africa has a long history of controlling the movement of its racialized populations in order to facilitate effective labor exploitation and political control. Despite the purported exceptionalism of the United States, its urban realm has been shaped by strategies of racial containment and exclusion that mirror those deployed in South Africa to a significant extent (Massey, 1993: 2). Finally, just as in the American case, South Africa is faced with a situation in which formal ideologies of apartheid have been abolished, to be replaced by the informal practices of apartheid meted out by a grossly unbalanced class system. In both countries, the discourse of criminality is one of the primary means through which contemporary urban space and society are apprehended and structured. Unlike the United States, however, the numerical minority of whites in South Africa has ensured the extremity of social conditions. To a certain extent, Americans can look at South Africa and see the underlying currents of their own society in a particularly stark light.

With the end of apartheid, however, the hope has been that South Africa can transcend this role as dystopian twin of the United States. The new nation has a far more progressive constitution than that of the United States, and it remains imbued with a strong element of hope generated by its political transition. However, as South Africa grapples with the difficult residues of apartheid as well as the political limitations imposed by the global hegemony of neoliberal doctrine, it runs the risk of following the U.S lead by establishing a carceral (i.e., prison-based) economy to control the economically and socially marginalized segments of its population. While the spatial legacy of apartheid has fostered strong forces leading in this direction, there are also resilient social groups working to establish alternative possibilities for the nation. Nowhere is this more evident than in discourses concerning crime and youth identities. In the following article, I will survey the spatial logic of apartheid and discuss the geography of fear that this legacy has helped to instill in contemporary South Africans before turning to an analysis of discourses concerning criminality in the post-apartheid nation.

The Spatial Legacy of Apartheid

"Influx control" was a cornerstone of South African social policy long before the official implementation of apartheid in 1948. Indeed, control of the nonwhite population's spatial mobility was predicated on an ideological edifice that dates from the colonial era. To understand this is to see South Africa's history as continuous with the broader social forms engineered by colonial power. This is a crucial step if we are to connect urban conditions in post-apartheid South Africa to those that pertain in postcolonial nations throughout sub-Saharan Africa. While the specificity of South African history needs to be respected, analysis of continuities with colonial and postcolonial experiences elsewhere has become increasingly important following the demise of apartheid. The contradictions faced during the post-apartheid era are embedded in the spatial form created by apartheid-era policies of social engineering. Like the colonial legacy faced by other postcolonial nations, these problems must be addressed if South Africa is to establish a stable and just social order.

Throughout colonial Africa, an absolute, racially based dichotomy was established that relegated Africans to the realm of tradition, while preserving the spaces of modernity for the white settler population (Bester, 2001: 219). As Mahmood Mamdani (1996: 18) has underlined, this dichotomy of modernity and tradition was used to define the prerequisites of citizenship. A bifurcated state form developed throughout Africa in which the "native" population was ruled through indirect means, their day to day affairs consigned to the autocratic power of "customary" tribal chieftains. Although Africans were constitutionally excluded from urban civil society within this bifurcated state form, an elaborate institutional apparatus had to be developed in order to maintain this isolation. As Gwendolyn Wright (2001: 226) puts it, in such conditions of racialized modernity, "maps of exclusion substituted for real urbanism."

In South Africa, for example, blacks were seen, in opposition to the white population, as an essentially pre-urban group. Throughout the twentieth century, white social critics and bureaucrats worried about the deleterious impact of African urbanization. Migration to the city was viewed as tantamount to the loss of tribal "tradition," contributing to the alleged heightened vulnerability of Africans to corruption and delinquency. The colonial-era policy of creating "native reserves," where the pristine, pre-contact "tribal" identity of the nation's African population would be preserved, was a cornerstone of this ideology, one that was subsequently developed by the apartheid regime through its establishment of the scattered and desolate ethnic "homelands."

Yet the policy of enforcing the rural character of the nation's black population rested on a central contradiction: this population was an essential source of labor for an increasingly industrialized and urban economy. As Mamdani (1996: 6) argues, "the problem with territorial segregation was that it rendered racial domination unstable: the more the economy developed, the more it came to depend on urbanized natives. As that happened, the beneficiaries of rule appeared as an alien minority." This contradiction manifested itself well before the formal implementation of apartheid. South Africa's 1913 Land Act, for example, may be seen as an attempt on the part of the government to dispossess the independent African peasantry and to capture their labor for the booming mining industry (Mabin, 1992: 16). This primitive accumulation meant that rural households had less autonomy from the capitalist system of waged labor, and were under increasing pressure to export significant amounts of labor to other markets in urban areas (Mabin, 1992: 16). Such increasing urbanization put the lie to the dogma of Africans' purportedly pre-modern identities. The government responded to this impasse by adopting a pass system, implemented with the Natives (Urban Areas) Act of 1923. The pass system was designed to control migratory flows of African laborers captured by the capitalist economy. As would be true during the late apartheid era, this policy of "influx control" did not succeed in controlling workers' migration to urban areas. As a result, massive overcrowding resulted in urban areas such as Sophiatown and Alexandra, often leading to land invasions by squatters.

The National Party's answer to these growing contradictions after its successful bid for power in 1948 was to reinforce the state's repressive apparatus while also constructing massive urban townships such as Soweto to house the burgeoning urban black population. In addition, the party established a series of ethnic "homelands" that supported the time-worn ideology of Africans' tribal identities, while also displacing the costs of social reproduction to these barren rural hinterlands. Johannesburg, the quintessential South African city, is a perfect example of the rationally planned, modernist city produced by the apartheid regime's policy of social and spatial engineering. Forced removals of blacks from the city's business core after 1948 resulted in the virtually perfect realization of the Manichean spatial form that Frantz Fanon (1963: 38–40) describes as characteristic of the colonial city. This compartmentalized space required the full panoply of the modern state for its administration and maintenance. The classic tools of modernist social engineering, including urban planning, public administration, and criminal justice, were all deployed in South Africa in order to ensure the maintenance of differential structures of citizenship through rigidly segregated spatial form (Robinson, 1992: 294). By the early 1970s, over a million people had been removed by force from South Africa's cities (Bester, 2001: 219). Just as was true in the "homelands," the townships were planned in a manner intended to reinforce perceived ethnic differences among Africans, with order being maintained through putatively autonomous tribal authorities (Robinson, 1992: 297).

This bifurcated social structure could not be maintained in the long run. As the rural economies of the homelands stagnated during the economic slowdown of the early 1970s, permanent migration to cities intensified and conditions in the townships worsened. The wave of strikes that rekindled overt resistance to apartheid during this period was directly related to the state's refusal to house those it saw as "illegal" urban residents (Mabin, 1992: 18). Faced with the mobilization of the urban-based mass democratic movement during the 1980s, the regime issued a landmark "White Paper on Urbanization" in 1986 that rescinded the decades-old policy of attempting to stem black urbanization using the dehumanizing pass system (Mabin, 1998). In its place, the government proposed the creation of autonomous satellite towns spread around major cities. This, it was hoped, would facilitate black urbanization while preserving white segregation and security. Although this move to foster "orderly urbanization" had an impact on South Africa's cities, it was also an incontrovertible acknowledgment of the regime's inability to control the forces of popular resistance in metropolitan areas. By the late 1980s, the core sections of many cities had become "grey areas," zones of ethnically mixed settlement from which white capital and residents were fleeing en masse. Similarly, government attempts to uproot massive squatter camps had, in significant instances such as Cape Town's Crossroads community, proven unsuccessful. Finally, the mobilization of powerful township civic organizations around issues such as rent and transport led to the demand for "one city" rather than the fragmented, isolated, and economically autonomous urban enclosures created by apartheid (Robinson, 1992: 209). The spiraling contradictions of apartheid urban policy were, then, pivotal to the regime's eventual abdication of power in 1990. If the urban crisis was at the center of apartheid's collapse, the resolution of this crisis is central to the viability of the post-apartheid social order (Robinson, 1992: 205).

A Dream Deferred: Post-apartheid Reconstruction and Urban Form

Johannesburg is the most economically developed city in sub-Saharan Africa. Like many postcolonial cities in sub-Saharan Africa, this city of nearly 5 million inhabitants has inherited the polarized zoning patterns of the colonial/apartheid era. Johannesburg is bifurcated neatly in two. To the north of the central business district lie sprawling, lush white residential suburbs like Sandton. To the south, overcrowded, sterile dormitory suburbs such as Soweto house the majority of the city's residents. In the critical perspective of a recent World Bank report, the pattern of sprawling suburbanization produced by apartheid social engineering is highly inefficient in economic terms. It is also extremely costly environmentally, since such decentralized urban form militates against the provision of affordable and effective systems of public transportation (Beatley, 2000: 4). In addition, such polarized urban space is also unsustainable in social terms. Despite the official end of apartheid, these two racialized segments of the city exist in increasing isolation, suspicion, and hostility. As Lindsay Bremner (1998) argues, the chances that residents of such a divided city will develop a sense of mutual obligation and the public spaces that can sustain such civic engagement are increasingly bleak.

By contrast with the outlying municipal zones, Johannesburg's central business district is currently a kind of no-man's land. Property remains for the most part in the hands of the old white monopolies such as mining houses and banks. The streets and other public spaces of the city, however, are the domain of an increasingly multinational African population. After over a century in which nonwhites were excluded systematically from urban space, the significance of this transformation cannot be exaggerated. A dynamic informal sector runs riot in these polyglot spaces, mocking the severe modernist planning of the apartheid urban realm. It is in these illicit spaces that a genuinely novel urban order is emerging in post-apartheid South Africa. Yet, as Bremner (1998) puts it, this "city of necessity" is "traversed by the city of crime and speculation." The breakdown in mechanisms of formal governance has, in other words, also created severe problems for the inhabitants of the so-called "grey areas." As is true of other African cities, this breakdown is making life increasingly unsafe for many residents. In addition, the internationalization of the inner city precipitated by migrants from throughout southern Africa as well as from the Francophone countries to the north has resulted in dramatically escalating incidences of xenophobia (Simone, 1998). Foreign Africans are increasingly being blamed for problems such as the overcrowded informal sector, the growth of the drug trade, and the physical decline of the inner city. Such hostilities are likely to increase if the state cannot preserve civil order. The legacy of uneven development that characterized the apartheid order is thus likely to impact urban spaces adversely for generations to come.

It is extremely expensive to be poor in South Africa today. The sprawling form of the nation's cities ensures that residents of distant townships have to make long and costly commutes to reach their workplaces. While certain areas of cities such as Johannesburg rival the most opulent and hyperconsumptionist cities of the developed world, the areas where the poor majority live continue on the whole to lack even the most basic forms of infrastructure. During the late apartheid years and the early years of the transition to democracy, a strong movement arose to challenge these conditions. Marrying the popular base of the civic movement with the intellectual capital of radical segments of the academic community, this movement called for the restructuring of South Africa's cities (Mabin, 1998). The new paradigm was backed by groups like SANCO, a coalition representing the national civic movement. Metropolitan areas were to be reintegrated and growth was to be concentrated, making cities more economically efficient and more accessible to the poor (Watson, 2002: 1). This model is in line with the "dense city" paradigm proposed by progressive urbanists such as Richard Rogers (1997: 33), who calls for the creation of ecologically and socially sustainable cities for the burgeoning urban segment of humanity. This new blueprint for urban development was perhaps best expressed in the African National Congress's (ANC) Development Facilitation Act of 1995 (DFA) and, more broadly speaking, in the party's Reconstruction and Development Plan (RDP). The RDP, however, was articulated in the context of a negotiated political transition in which the ANC had to contend with representatives of the old regime while also keeping its left wing content. As critics such as Patrick Bond (2000: 195) have argued, the upshot was that the populist movement became a neoliberal government, and consequently failed to transform the economic fundamentals established by the apartheid regime. Similarly, ambitious plans to foster dense city cores ran afoul of economic and technological trends that exacerbated the drift towards multi-nucleated metropolitan physical structures (Bloch, 1996: 65). In conjunction with the spatial legacy of apartheid and the growing NIMBY-ism of the wealthy, preponderantly white residents of the new South Africa, these conditions effectively delegitimized efforts at citywide planning among both affluent and poor constituents (Dewar, 1992). Similarly, the demands of groups like SANCO for a more equitable provision of basic services to all citizens of municipal areas also fell by the wayside. Indeed, the office of the RDP was quietly abolished shortly after the ANC assumed power following the first democratic elections in 1994. In its place, the government announced a policy with the suspicious acronym of GEAR, a strategy for economic empowerment that mouthed the rhetoric of community involvement while ignoring the structural barriers that militated against economic bootstrapping (Mabin, 1998).

Conditions in South Africa have demonstrated that neoliberalism may succeed in delivering services more efficiently to the affluent, but that it seriously exacerbates problems associated with poverty, crime, and the environment (Swilling, 1998). Since 1994, the modernist framework for sweeping, utopian change has been largely bypassed and consequently discredited in contemporary South Africa, leaving little alternative to models of "participatory governance" articulated in the preceding period of transition. Such calls hinge on models of small-scale, self-generated transformation facilitated by local and central government intervention (Dewar, 1992: 247). In the best of instances, this sort of model may initiate a far more responsive and engaging form of democracy. In addition, as Mark Swilling (1998) suggests, South Africa possesses a strong tradition of independent urban social movements that have attempted to initiate such forms of participatory governance during the transition period. However, such community-driven development strategies may ultimately exacerbate polarizing social conditions. Like the land invasions that brought down formal apartheid while helping cement the spatial logic of segregation, this model may simply contain rather than answer the demands of the economically disenfranchised majority for substantial social transformation. Poor communities are often far too fragmented and disorganized to participate effectively in the individualistic, choice-driven mode of communication central to the ethos of participatory government. In the absence of a viable and well-funded model for community-driven urban planning and reconstruction, social conditions in South Africa's cities have become increasingly violent.

Geography of Fear: Law and Order in the New South Africa

Commentators on crime in South Africa are often quick to point out that the extremely high levels of crime that have been making headlines since the late 1990s have been a fact of life for the majority of the nation for the last several decades. Criminality was, however, essentially hidden from affluent whites by a police force whose two prime functions for most of the twentieth century were the enforcement of influx control laws and the quashing of political opposition. After formal apartheid was dismantled in the early 1990s, however, white South Africans no longer were protected by the rigid segregation and political oppression that had previously shielded them. By the mid-1990s, the recorded murder rate in South Africa was over four times that of the United States, a highly violent society by international standards (Marsh, 1999: 181). However, as Bremner (1998) has pointed out, the geography of crime in contemporary South Africa reflects two overwhelming social factors of the new nation: poverty and vulnerability. While statistics are often difficult to trust given the fact that the majority of violent crime takes place within domestic settings between people who know one another, black South Africans are twenty times more at risk from homicide than whites (Louw, 1997: 12). Yet it is crimes against affluent whites that have attracted the most attention because of the disproportionate influence of those they affect.

With an annual growth rate of approximately 20 percent since the early 1980s, security has been one of South Africa's leading new industries

(Bremner, 1998). The continuity in these statistics across the late- and post-apartheid eras suggests the extent to which South African society is saturated not simply with violence, but with the pervasive fear of violence. In fact, with the demise of formal apartheid and its official racist lexicon, the discourses of crime and security have become the primary conceptual frame through which the economically hegemonic white minority represents national culture. As is true in other countries like the United States, such representations of criminality often serve as a coded form of racial discourse. The culture of excess that the apartheid economy allowed white South Africans to consolidate has now become an Achilles heel. The massive houses, sweeping lawns, and azure swimming pools of affluent suburbs are a plum ripe for the picking in post-apartheid South Africa. Faced with the erosion of their high standard of living, white South Africans have increasingly come to see the proliferation of crime as an index of the ANC government's corruption. If, as the reasoning goes, the new government is unable to maintain law and order in the suburbs, then it cannot be fit to run the country in general. Without law and order, the nation's economy will necessarily stagnate. While there may be some truth to such assertions, the upshot of such discourse has been a dramatic escalation of the forms of spatial fragmentation and dislocation endemic to apartheid society. White South Africa, in other words, is just as gripped by a bunker mentality today as it was during the worst days of apartheid.

The privatization of public space is one of the primary modes in which this fragmenting effect has taken place. Private security forces now outnumber the public forces of law and order in South Africa by a factor of two to one (Bremner, 1998). With names like "Stallion" and "Terminator," these private security forces advertise the massive force they deploy in their reactive policing strategies. "Armed response" is a common warning motto one sees hung next to the "beware the dog" signs in the affluent suburbs of South African cities. There are practical reasons for such signs: unless they subscribe to private security forces, homeowners in wealthy neighborhoods often cannot get insurance coverage (Emmet, 2000: 30). Such market forces end up intensifying the spatial legacy of apartheid discussed above. As Bremner (1998) notes, many of the new private security forces are run and staffed by disaffected former members of the apartheid-era "defense" forces, and, ironically, by demobilized cadres of the ANC liberation army. The reaction of these private security firms to the growth of crime during the post-apartheid era has been to adopt explicitly militarized strategies of control. The armored vehicles and military assault weapons deployed by these security companies underline their unmistakably paramilitary character. Since there are few effective democratic constraints on the force exercised by such companies, affluent white suburbs are increasingly becoming a free-fire zone in which anyone who appears suspicious may be the target of homicidal violence. Criminals are answering this escalation of force in kind. In a country awash with military hardware left over from the thirty years of liberation struggles in the region, weapons are all too easy to procure. The result is a vicious circle of violence, a distorted version of the bloody stalemate between liberation forces and the apartheid regime that occurred during the late 1980s (Emmet, 2000: 30).

Linked to the growing use of private paramilitary forces is the increasing privatization of public space in suburbs. Streets are being blocked off and entire neighborhoods are seceding from the urban grid to form gated communities. Unlike the gated communities in the United States, South Africa's upscale protected neighborhoods are guarded by booms designed to resist attack by military assault vehicles. The image of the laager, the defensive circle of wagons created by the Afrikaner pioneers or Voortrekkers as they pushed into the African interior centuries ago, is an apt symbol for such gated communities. Entrance to these closed communities is heavily policed, with identity documents required for all those who wish to gain admission. In effect, a privatized version of the pass system is once again being established in South Africa. While that system sought to operate on a national level, however, controlling the movements of blacks alone, the new pass control regime segments space for all citizens. Urban space is broken up into a series of discrete enclaves, with harrowing corridors of transit lying between. This is neither economically nor politically viable in the long term. The vital characteristics of successful urban cultures throughout the ages, including cosmopolitanism, interaction, and equality, are all eradicated by the new privatized laager system.

Unlike their affluent co-nationals, South Africa's poor majority cannot afford the reactive paramilitary police forces that maintain the illusion of security in the suburbs. Consequently, at the same time as white neighborhoods are hiving themselves off from the public realm, black neighborhoods are forced to rely on the overburdened and underfunded public forces of law and order. Despite the evident political will within the government to grapple with the problem of the culture of violence inherited from the anti-apartheid struggle, there has been very limited success in mitigating the forms of criminality and vulnerability to which the majority of the population is susceptible. There are a number of reasons for this. First, after years of functioning simply as the repressive arm of the state, police forces are struggling with limited success to retool themselves into a viable peacekeeping force. As Jonny Steinberg (2001: 9) has argued, the main national threat that the ANC anticipated after coming to power in 1994 was a white backlash against democracy rather than the rise of criminality. As a result, South Africa retains a transitional police force that is caught between the old order and the new. In addition, most poor communities lack the kind of stability and cohesion required to deploy the neighborhood watches and security programs that typify affluent suburbs (Louw, 1997: 17). Finally, most of the violent crimes that occur in such neighborhoods take place between family members or people who know one another. South African police remain ill-equipped to deal with such culturally embedded crimes.

This latter problem suggests a strong gendered factor that seldom appears in dominant accounts of criminality in contemporary South Africa. Indeed, over 80 percent of the murders in the country are connected to a pervasive culture of domestic violence (Louw, 1997: 13). Moreover, South Africa has the highest recorded rate of rape in the world. This high incidence of violence against women has been related to the historical and contemporary displacement of black men in South Africa, as compensation to the many humiliations of being black is sought in the domestic arena, where women and children are still largely seen as men's property (Louw, 1997: 13). The underacknowledged character of such domestic violence is an indictment of the underlying tenets of the criminal justice system, which still largely seeks to punish violence against property rather than against human beings.

A corollary aspect of criminality in contemporary South Africa that is inadequately addressed emerges when the intergenerational character of criminality is considered. In a startling account, Antony Altbeker (2001: 90) describes the split reactions to the recent funeral of a young gangster in a township. The gangster's parents and their generation are struck dumb as they solemnly mourn the loss of this favored son. In contrast, their son's debauched cohort arrives at the funeral in flashy BMWs and fires automatic weapons into the air in hedonistic celebration of their dead colleague's violent path to the good life. Altbeker's description of this gangster's funeral suggests that post-apartheid South Africa is now reaping the bloody rewards of its policy of social fragmentation. Apartheid consciously engineered the fragmentation of black communities by systematically splitting apart families through the policies of ethnic homelands and influx control. The resulting destabilization of community life is an important factor in contemporary crime. In such a context, Graeme Simpson's (2001) account of the continuities in South African history is highly important. According to Simpson (2001: 115), "amidst all the formal change which has taken place in South Africa, the experiences of marginalization, impoverishment, and relative deprivation, which lay at the heart of the youth-based violent political resistance to apartheid during the 1980s, have not only been sustained, but continue to underpin much of the criminal violence which dominates the social and political landscape of the post-apartheid era." Rejecting the terms of debate concerning youth gang activity as either antisocial banditry or socially functional resistance, Simpson (2001: 118) argues that, depending on the social context, the resiliency of youth cultures can take the form of either political resistance or criminal activity. The line between the two is far harder to draw than is suggested by recent accounts of the shift from political activity to criminality among South African youth. If young people turn to criminality as a means of gaining status and material affluence in a social context that systematically continues to deny them both, criminality cannot be apprehended or addressed simply through the forms of draconian protection being pioneered by the affluent citizens of South Africa. The roots of the problem lie far deeper.

Policing the Transition

In May 1996, the recently elected ANC government announced its National Crime Prevention Strategy (NCPS). This document was a product of a series of momentous shifts within the party that began before it gained power in the nation's first democratic election. During the late 1980s, the forces of the ANC and the apartheid regime were locked in a bloody spiral of violence that threatened to destroy the country. Miraculously, both sides were able to see the folly of this situation, and in 1990 overt negotiations towards a political transition began. Attempts to eradicate the political violence that had plagued South African society figured prominently in the liberation movement's evolving plans during this period (Emmet, 2000: 40). While, for its part, the state lifted bans on organizations such as the ANC, the liberation movement abjured armed struggle as part of the negotiated settlement. By 1994, the ANC's Reconstruction and Development Plan included provisions that unequivocally defined violence as a mental health problem. Victims of apartheid-era political violence were seen as needing comprehensive care predicated on individual reconstitution and empowerment. Since the publication of this document, there has been an increasing appreciation in South Africa of the need to engage with violence and crime using a public health perspective (Butchart and Emmet, 1992: 3). Within such a perspective, violence is seen as an underacknowledged epidemic that is predicted to incapacitate just as many people worldwide as all communicable diseases by 2020 (Butchart and Emmet, 1992: 8).

Central to the public health perspective on crime is the acknowledgement that health services rather than the criminal justice system are the most significant contact point between victims of violence and the authorities. This perception is no doubt related to the disrepute in which apartheid-era police forces were held because of their belligerence toward the liberation movement. The public health model is also, however, motivated by a focus on the predominantly domestic setting within which most violence in a society like South Africa occurs. Consequently, instead of simply attempting to accost the perpetrators of violence, the new public health model focuses on the victims of violence, attempting to develop preventive strategies to forestall future episodes of victimization. According to Butchart and Emmet (1992: 19), typical strategies for preventing the recurrence of violence include gun control, alcohol regulation, environmental modification, the provision of safe houses, the development of alternatives to gang membership for youths, and violence postvention facilities. In addition, departing from the traditional focus of the criminal justice system on the criminal alone, the public health model views crime holistically, analyzing the broad social factors that either contribute to or erode community cohesion. The government's emphasis on this model of prevention must be seen within the broader attempt by the liberation movement to reconstruct South African society in order to foster a culture of human rights and solidarity using forums such as the Truth and Reconciliation Commission.

Insights derived from the public health model concerning the preventive strategies needed to cope with social violence were embedded in the ANC's NCPS. The NCPS contains four fundamental pillars: reform and streamlining of the criminal justice process; strengthening of community values through education; crime reduction through environmental design; and fresh efforts to cope with the increasing profile of transnational crime (Marsh, 1999: 5). Efforts at prevention are designed to include not simply governmental workers but also transnational and local nongovernmental organizations and members of affected communities. One prominent example of such multipronged initiatives is the *Soul City* program (Rocha-Silva, 2000: 93). Perhaps best known through its televised dramatic serial format, *Soul City* is a media-focused program initiated by the Institute of Urban Primary Health Care, based in the township of Alexandra's Health Centre. The television serial uses an "edutainment" format that mixes soap opera–style drama with messages designed to facilitate prevention of crime- and violence-related injury, as well as other public health crises such as HIV/AIDS. In addition to its televised format, *Soul City* also uses other media, including newspapers, radio, and novellas to disseminate its messages. Individual episodes are designed through an extensive community-based research program designed to develop appropriate measures for coping with health care crises and to monitor the impact of the serial among target groups.

Initiatives such as *Soul City* and the related serial *Yizo Yizo* dramatize the sensitivity and potential impact of the public health care model in dealing with violence and crime.

Unfortunately, the last three pillars of the NCPS have received relatively little funding as the state has attempted to revamp a criminal justice system mired in apartheid-era bureaucracy. Like the ANC's plans for urban revitalization following the end of apartheid, much progressive rhetoric concerning violence prevention has remained just that. In addition, strategies such as community policing that have proved effective in other contexts such as the cities of North America have had limited success in the highly disorganized conditions of South Africa's poor township communities (Bremner, 1998). The failure to fund and implement measures designed to prevent social violence is likely to have wide-reaching impacts in South Africa since the criminal justice system simply cannot cope with the increasing levels of crime. While affluent white suburbs have turned increasingly towards militarized laagerization, poor communities have in some instances resorted to vigilantism that has dramatically intensified the cycles of violence in such communities. Perhaps the most famous instance of such violence is that occasioned by the formation of People Against Guns and Drugs (PAGAD), an Islamic organization that engaged in running gun battles and episodes of bombings with the infamous gangs of the Cape Flats (Marsh, 1999: 185).

The ANC's neoliberal fiscal policies have helped make it difficult to provide credible alternatives to such vigilante groups. Such policies are, of course, designed to stimulate economic growth, the premise being that crime is rooted in fundamental problems like unemployment and poverty. While this logic is hard to refute in general terms, it elides the public health model's sophisticated appreciation of the social grounding of crime. After all, increasing levels of employment cannot be the sole answer for crime since gangsters can always make far more money and do so with far more macho style than can industrial workers. Solutions to the growth of criminality have to be grounded in a far broader enterprise of rebuilding social connections. As Simpson (2001) has emphasized, the government needs not simply to provide employment and economic development for the poor, but also to mend the social fabric in poor communities in order to offer a stake in society for the marginalized. This will certainly involve channeling the energies of self-defense units such as PAGAD in constructive directions. It will also, however, require the provision of a whole series of alternative outlets for youth. Prominent steps in this direction include the shoring up of families, the creation of a culture of learning in schools, the cultivation of alternative positive sexual identities for young men, and the empowerment of women (Simpson, 2001: 128). Underlying such steps must, of course, be the development of viable alternatives to the privatization of space that is currently sweeping South Africa.

Conclusion

In a recent article on what he calls "mass incarceration," Loïc Wacquant (2002: 44) argues that the United States has created a penal state that copes with the lack of marketable cultural capital among African Americans in the post-Fordist economy by placing an increasing proportion of them in prison. There is, he argues, a genealogical link between slavery, Jim Crow–era segregation, the ghetto system of Fordist-era industrial capitalism, and the post-Fordist carceral economy of today (Wacquant, 2002: 41). This carceral economy has effectively revived the disenfranchisement that condemned African Americans to "social death" prior to the civil rights movement. Prison inmates in many states in the United States are routinely stripped not just of cultural capital, but also of social redistribution in the form of public aid and the right to political participation (Wacquant, 2002: 57). Could South Africa, which, as I note above, has long mirrored conditions in North America, follow the lead of the United States toward the creation of a post-liberation model of social disenfranchisement using the discourse of crime? Do significant continuities exist between apartheid and post-apartheid era controls over the black majority population's access to public space? The increasing fragmentation of space and correlated rise of criminality suggests that underlying social structures are pushing South Africa in precisely the direction described by Wacquant (2002) in his analysis of the United States.

One substantial distinction between the United States and South Africa offers hope that this trend is not, however, an inevitable one. Unlike the United States, South Africa's marginalized black population is not an ethnic minority. The recently enfranchised black majority in South Africa continues to view crime not in the bourgeois sense of individual malfeasance, but in terms of the lack of broad forms of social equity (Bremner, 1998). Despite the fact that it is precisely this community that is most frequently victimized by social violence and crime, the social analysis of crime based on enduring forms of class- and race-based inequality embraced by the majority of South Africa's poor holds out hope for corresponding socially based preventive measures. The alternative to such measures is truly bleak. South African organizations have articulated many far-sighted policies during the period of transition, including the progressive principles of urban redevelopment and violence prevention embodied in the RDP and legislated in the Development Facilitation Act and the National Crime Prevention Strategy.

Unless such policies are effectively implemented, the spiral of violence and counterviolence embedded in the last century's legacy of spatial apartheid will only deepen. South Africa cannot afford such an intensification of the geography of fear.

These problems—which typify conditions in many megacities around the world—will not simply disappear with economic development. Too often such development favors the few who already benefit from access to social and economic resources. Yet, as Michael Sorkin (2001: viii) noted recently, the contemporary architectural avant-garde in the developed world has adopted an attitude of total indifference toward the vexing problems of ecological and social sustainability posed by urban growth. It is far more difficult to evade such problems in contemporary megacities such as Cairo, Shanghai, São Paulo, and Johannesburg, where pressures on resources and infrastructure have reached unprecedented levels. As the preceding discussion of South Africa's urban history has made clear, cities in the underdeveloped world typically are heirs of colonial planning policies that purposely set out to fragment urban space. The apartheid city is perhaps the paradigmatic realization of such policies of racial segregation. This legacy has meant that the vast majority of those living in postcolonial cities tend to occupy the blank zones created by colonial urban planning practices. The denizens of such cities either live in vast squatter camps on the urban periphery or, in even more extreme cases, occupy interstitial spaces in the city center such as abandoned lots and sidewalks. Arjun Appadurai (2000: 644) has linked this economy of scarcity in urban housing to the increasing instability of citizenship and the rise of ethnic chauvinist movements in places such as Mumbai.

In South African cities like Johannesburg and Cape Town, apartheid urban planning practices that targeted the nonwhite majority created a rigid modernist grid of bungalows deprived of both private and public amenities such as sanitation and open space. South Africa's recent attempts to cope with accelerating crime rates have focused attention on the role played by such barren spaces in perpetuating forms of communal fragmentation and isolation. As the RDP acknowledges, a key element in coping with the negative impact of apartheid-era spatial practices will be to provide resources to strengthen indigenous community-building practices. This must include the provision of funding for affordable infrastructure to service such areas. Rogers (1997: 58) notes that the self-organization capacity of even the poorest communities has helped transform illegal squatter settlements around the world into socially cohesive and ecologically sustainable neighborhoods when technical aid and basic infrastructure have been provided. Of course, such provision in many instances will also require major changes in the local state. Without substantial democratization, many poor neighborhoods will remain peripheral in both a physical and a social sense, dangerously accelerating the spiral of alienation and violence bequeathed by colonial and postcolonial social hierarchies.

In addition to such local transformation, the degradation of public space must also be addressed on a broader scale. As Michael Sorkin (2001: 53) argues, the only way to stem the massive growth of the underdeveloped world's mega-cities is to "redirect investment to divert the metastasis of opportunity that accelerates the desire to come" to such cities in the first place. This will involve sustained policies of decentralization on a national scale, including the creation of peripheral cities that offer amenities and opportunities sufficient to counteract the lure of the megacity. Unfortunately, the South African case makes it clear that the resources to implement such policies are increasingly scarce in the current conditions of neoliberal hegemony among both global and national governmental institutions. The urgent social and ecological problems apparent in the global cities of the South are therefore also ineluctably tied to issues of social justice on a global scale. Stemming the decline and degradation of public space must be a vital component in any movement for global social justice. It is hard to see how the social and environmental crises brewing in the South's megacities will be headed off unless the deep inequalities that divide humanity today are transformed.

References

Altbeker, Antony. "Who Are We Burying? The Death of a Soweto Gangster." In *Crime Wave: The South African Underworld and Its Foes*, edited by Jonny Steinberg, 88–94. Johannesburg: Witwatersrand University Press, 2001.

Appadurai, Arjun. "Spectral Housing and Urban Cleansing: Notes on Millennial Mumbai." *Public Culture* 12, no. 3(2000): 627–651.

Beatley, Timothy. *Green Urbanism: Learning from European Cities*. Washington, D.C.: Island Press, 2000.

Bester, Rory. "City and Citizenship." In *The Short Century: Independence and Liberation Movements in Africa, 1945–1994*, edited by Okwui Enwezor, Okwui, 219–224. New York: Prestel, 2001.

Bloch, Robin. "Reconstructing South Africa's Cities." In *Local Places in the Age of the Global City*, edited by Roger Keil, Gerda Wekerle, and V.J. Bell, 59–65. New York: Black Rose.

Bond, Patrick. *Elite Transition: From Apartheid to Neoliberalism in South Africa*. London: Pluto, 2000.

Bremner, Lindsay. "Crime and the Emerging Landscape of Post-Apartheid Johannesburg." In *Blank—: Architecture, Apartheid and After*, edited by Hilton Judin and Ivan Vladislavic. Rotterdam: NAi; New York: Distributor, D.A.P. (Distributed Art Publishers), 1998.

Butchart, Alex and Tony Emmet. "Crime, Violence, and Public Health." In *Behind the Mask: Getting to Grips with Crime and Violence in South Africa*. Pretoria: Human Sciences Research Council, 2000.

Davis, Mike. *Ecology of Fear: Los Angeles and the Imagination of Disaster*. New York: Henry Holt, 1998.

Dewar, David. "A Manifesto for Change." In *The Apartheid City and Beyond: Urbanization and Social Change in South Africa*, edited by David M. Smith, 244–248. New York: Routledge, 1992.

Dewar, David. "Settlements, Change, and Planning in South Africa Since 1994." In *Blank—: Architecture, Apartheid and After*, edited by Hilton Judin and Ivan Vladislavic. Rotterdam: Nai; New York: Distributor, D.A.P. (Distributed Art Publishers), 1998.

Emmet, Tony and Alex Butchart, eds. *Behind the Mask: Getting to Grips with Crime and Violence in South Africa*. Pretoria: HSRC (Human Sciences Research Council), 2000.

Enwezor, Okwui, ed. *The Short Century: Independence and Liberation Movements in Africa, 1945–1994*. New York: Prestel, 2001.

Fanon, Frantz. *The Wretched of the Earth*. New York: Grove, 1963.

Judin, Hilton and Ivan Vladislavic, eds. *Blank—: Architecture, Apartheid and After*. Rotterdam: Nai; New York: Distributor, D.A.P. (Distributed Art Publishers), 1998.

Louw, Antoinette and Mark Shaw. *Stolen Opportunities: The Impact of Crime on South Africa's Poor*. N.p.: Institute for Security Studies, 1997.

Mabin, Alan. "Dispossession, Exploitation, and Struggle: An Historical Overview of South African Urbanization." In *The Apartheid City and Beyond: Urbanization and Social Change in South Africa*, edited by David M. Smith, 15–22. New York: Routledge, 1992.

Mabin, Alan. "Reconstruction and the Making of Urban Planning in 20th Century South Africa." In *Blank—: Architecture, Apartheid and After*, edited by Hilton Judin and Ivan Vladislavic. Rotterdam: NAi; New York: Distributor, D.A.P. (Distributed Art Publishers), 1998.

Mamdani, Mahmood. *Citizen and Subject: Contemporary Africa and the Legacy of Late Colonialism*. Princeton, N.J.: Princeton University Press, 1996.

Marsh, Rob. *With Criminal Intent: The Changing Face of Crime in South Africa*. Kenilworth, South Africa: Ampersand Press, 1999.

Massey, Douglas S. *American Apartheid: Segregation and the Making of the Underclass*. Cambridge, Mass.: Harvard University Press, 1993.

Robinson, Jennifer. "Power, Space, and the City: Historical Reflections on Apartheid and Post-Apartheid Urban Orders." In *The Apartheid City and Beyond: Urbanization and Social Change in South Africa*, edited by David M. Smith, 292–300. New York: Routledge, 1992.

Robinson, Jennifer. *The Power of Apartheid: State, Power, and Space in South African Cities*. Boston: Butterworth-Heinemann, 1996.

Rocha-Silva, Lee and Graeme Hendricks. "Soul City." In *Behind the Mask: Getting to Grips with Crime and Violence in South Africa*, edited by Tony Emmet and Alex Butchart, 93–108. Pretoria: HSRC (Human Science Research Council), 2000.

Rogers, Richard. *Cities for a Small Planet*. Boulder, Colo.: Westview Press, 1997.

Sassen, Saskia. *The Global City: New York, London, Tokyo*. Princeton, N.J.: Princeton University Press, 1991.

Simone, AbdouMaliq. "Globalization and the Identity of African Urban Practices." In *Blank—: Architecture, Apartheid and After*, edited by Hilton Judin and Ivan Vladislavic. Rotterdam: Nai; New York: Distributor, D.A.P. (Distributed Art Publishers), 1998.

Simpson, Graeme. "Shock Troops and Bandits: Youth, Crime and Politics." In *Crime Wave: The South African Underworld and Its Foes*, edited by Jonny Steinberg, 115–128. Johannesburg: Witwatersrand University Press, 2001.

Smith, David M., ed. *The Apartheid City and Beyond: Urbanization and Social Change in South Africa*. New York: Routledge, 1992.

Smith, René. "Yizo Yizo: This Is It? Representations and Receptions of Violence and Gender Relations." Ph.D. diss. University of Natal, Durban, 2000.

Sorkin, Michael. *Some Assembly Required*. Minneapolis, Minn.: University of Minnesota Press, 2001.

Steinberg, Jonny, ed. *Crime Wave: The South African Underworld and Its Foes*. Johannesburg: Witwatersrand University Press, 2001.

Steinberg, Jonny, ed. "Introduction: Behind the Crime Wave." In *Crime Wave: The South African Underworld and Its Foes*, edited by Jonny Steinberg, 2–12. Johannesburg: Witwatersrand University Press, 2001.

Swilling, Mark. "Rival Futures: Struggle Visions, Post-Apartheid Choices." In *Blank—: Architecture, Apartheid and After*, edited by Hilton Judin and Ivan Vladislavic. Rotterdam: NAI; New York: Distributor, D.A.P. (Distributed Art Publishers), 1998.

United Nations. "State of the Cities Report 2001." July 1, 2002. Available at: *www.un.org/habitat/index.html*.

Wacquant, Loïc. "From Slavery to Mass Incarceration: Rethinking the 'Race Question' in the U.S."
    New Left Review 13 (January/February 2002): 41–60.
Watson, Vanessa. *Change and Continuity in Spatial Planning*. New York: Routledge, 2002.
Wright, Gwendolyn. "The Ambiguous Modernisms of African Cities." In *The Short Century: Independence and Liberation Movements in Africa, 1945–1994*, edited by Okwui Enwezor, Okwui, 225–229. New York: Prestel, 2001.

CHAPTER 8

Clean and Safe? Property Redevelopment, Public Space, and Homelessness in Downtown San Diego

DON MITCHELL AND LYNN A. STAEHELI

The whole homeless population continues to frustrate us and we're not unique in this. It's a problem in most major cities.
—Dave Allsbrook, Centre City Development Corporation, interview, 1/24/01

I think the problem is that homeless people make housed people uncomfortable seeing them. What I resent is the principal motivation [in] making homeless invisible instead of creating services and resources that are needed to get them off the streets.
—Rosemary Johnston, Program Director, Interfaith Shelter Network, interview, 1/23/01

Interviewer: *How would you characterize the downtown redevelopment?*
Respondent: *I think it is exciting. I moved downtown. There's so much going on downtown. I think it's exciting. I think you have to begin to look at new approaches. Public spaces should be privately owned, not publicly owned.*

Interviewer: Why?

Respondent: Because private people can enforce the rules. Cities can't. Everything becomes an entitlement. So if you build a beautiful park and the homeless move in you can't move them out.

—Father Joe Carroll, President, St. Vincent de Paul Villages, interview, 1/26/01

The politics of public space can be addressed from any number of angles. Research in geography and other fields has explored the processes of exclusion—by race, gender, class, sexuality, age, and disability—by which public space's "publicness" is defined and contested (e.g., Fraser, 1990; Young, 1991; Imre, 1996; Ruddick, 1996; Smith, 1996; Staeheli, 1996; Domosh, 1998; Gleeson, 1998; McCann, 1999; Low, 2000). Other work has examined the role of law in structuring and delimiting public spaces, exploring the dialectical relationship between political violence and the more structured violence of the law (Blomley, 1994a, 1998, 2000a; Mitchell, 1996, 1997). Still other work has examined the ways that public spaces become staging grounds for political movements—movements of labor, women's rights, sexual liberation, or racial equity (Bell et al., 1994; Bell and Valentine, 1995; Adams, 1996; D'Arcus, 2001; Mitchell, 2002). In partial contrast, scholars have explored the ways that public spaces are ceremonial staging grounds for the state to display itself to its citizens or subjects (Hershkovitz, 1993; Atkinson and Cosgrove, 1998). Finally, if public space is taken to be a space of sociality, as a gathering place, research has shown how this sociality is limited by the politics of power (Mitchell, 1995; Low, 2000; Staeheli and Mitchell, 2004) a politics that sometimes resolves itself into questions of design (Hopkins, 1990; Boyer, 1992; Crawford, 1992; Crilley, 1993; Goss, 1993, 1996).

Research that has focused on what makes public space *public* has been animated by questions of access and exclusion, law and custom, power and protest. It has been concerned with showing who is pushed out, or who cannot get in at all. This issue has been of particular importance in what can be called the "end of public space" literature (Davis, 1990; Sorkin, 1992; Mitchell, 1995). As cities have redeveloped, public space has become a key battleground—a battleground over the homeless and the poor and over the rights of developers, corporations, and those who seek to make over the city in an image attractive to tourists, middle- and upper-class residents, and suburbanites. This work, and the political and economic practices that it critiques, as well as some of those groups who contest redevelopment on the ground, insistently raises the question that Lefebvre (1996) clearly enunciated back in 1968: Who has the right to the city?

In this chapter, focusing on public space, property redevelopment, and homelessness in San Diego, we seek to provide a case study that explores the complexity of that question. San Diego's redevelopment cannot be understood outside an examination of the role that homelessness has played in it. For proponents of downtown redevelopment, one of the crucial issues has always been—and remains—the homeless and other street people (Mike Stepner, interview, 1/23/01; Leslie Wade, interview, 1/25/01; Fred Baranowski, interview, 1/26/01). They are seen as the primary impediment to redevelopment and its success. In order for redevelopment to succeed, the city had to find ways to remove—or at least to manage (Dave Allsbrook, interview, 1/24/01; Baranowski, interview, 1/25/01)—the homeless population. Yet at the same time, redevelopment itself exacerbates and *causes* both invisible and visible homelessness as single-room occupancy hotels are destroyed, rents rise, shelters are relocated, and services (like public toilets) closed down (Miller, 1985; Allsbrook, interview, 1/24/01; social service provider, interview, 1/24/01; Father Joe Carroll, interview, 1/26/01). This contradiction—that redevelopment both exacerbates and is hindered by homelessness in downtown—has led to a contentious politics of property and public space, a politics that raises in stark terms the question of who really has a right to the city.

To see exactly how the geography of homelessness has both shaped and been shaped by the transformation of downtown San Diego, it is critical to understand the relationship between *property* and public space in redevelopment. For, we will argue in this chapter, it is in *that* relationship that the fate of the homeless—and hence, as its proponents claim, redevelopment—is determined. The next section therefore seeks to stake out a set of claims about why the politics of public space, and its relationship to homelessness under conditions of redevelopment, should be understood as a politics of property—or at least of changing property regimes. In these changing regimes, we will suggest that a new definition of what the public is—a new determination of who has the right to the city—is being worked out. By drawing on a series of interviews conducted with redevelopment officials, civic boosters, and social service providers in January 2001, we will then explore, in the second section of the paper, the quite complex details of this restructuring of property and the right to the city in San Diego.

Redevelopment, Property, and Public Space

Redevelopment in San Diego

Considered on its own terms, the redevelopment of downtown San Diego has been a spectacular success.[1] Its degree of success can be glimpsed in this recollection of a downtown worker connected to the Horton Plaza Mall development, which opened in 1985 and is considered the cornerstone of redevelopment in San Diego, "I was [working] at University Towne Center [in La Jolla, north of downtown] ... when Horton was being developed. And there was no reason to come downtown ... unless you got called for jury duty.... [I]t was all x-rated movie houses, sailors, homeless people. It was no place you'd want to be at night" (downtown worker, interview, 1/24/01). Bill Keller, a storeowner with a business across the street from Horton Plaza concurs: "Downtown was perceived as a dangerous place with nowhere to park" (Keller, interview, 1/26/01).

But now all this has changed. Keller was one of the original tenants in Horton Plaza and later served the president of the Gaslamp Quarter Association, a business group dedicated to the preservation and redevelopment of downtown San Diego's historic and entertainment district. He now sounds almost incredulous when he describes the "intense activity" along the sidewalks of Fifth Avenue—the heart of the Gaslamp—on a Friday or Saturday night. With thousands of people out bar hopping, strolling, and sitting in sidewalk cafes, "it's just buzzing, it's just amazing" (Keller, interview, 1/26/01; Mitch Mitchell, interview, 1/26/01).[2] Horton Plaza Mall is now one of the leading tourist destinations in San Diego (along with the Zoo and Marine World), and the nearby Gaslamp Quarter is filled with people taking a break from the new Convention Center (itself a key component of downtown redevelopment), and with college students and other young people who find it the best place in the city to party.[3] In the words of the downtown worker quoted above, with the Mall's opening, "all of a sudden, in 1985, you had people gathering together in a downtown environment that people thought would never be successful. But it worked."

Mitch Mitchell, vice president for public policy at the San Diego Chamber of Commerce, thinks San Diego is the "crown jewel" of redevelopment around the country, and to support his argument points to a boom in downtown residential construction, the development of a new—and quite fancy—downtown supermarket, and the fact that property redevelopment, including both gentrification-type upgrading, and large redevelopment authority–led projects, has not been confined to a single district but is expanding through the whole of the downtown area. For Mitchell, the success of redevelopment is directly linked to the city's ability to create "a vision" for the whole of downtown, and to undertake redevelopment in phases, not just piecemeal (see also Acuna, 1990; Stepner, interview, 1/23/01; Allsbrook, interview, 1/25/01; Mitchell, interview, 1/26/01). The latest phase of redevelopment has now extended into the old warehouse and social services district east of Downtown, an event marked, perhaps inevitably, by the elimination of its historic name, Center City East, and its rebirth as "East Village." Indeed, "East Village" is now the site of intensive redevelopment pressure as a large "ballpark district" centered on the Padres' new baseball stadium has been created at its southwest edge.

San Diego's current phase of redevelopment can be traced to the early 1970s when the city focused redevelopment efforts away from areas north of Broadway (the skyscraper core) to the south to the area around the old Horton Plaza Park and then down along Fifth Avenue (the Gaslamp Quarter) which still possessed a wealth of old buildings, many of them architecturally significant, and which had already long been an entertainment district, even if, as the Chamber of Commerce's vice president put it, it "was a seedy environment directed towards the military personnel that were docking here for a day or a week or whatever" (Mitchell, Interview, 1/26/01).[4] Indeed, Horton Plaza Park itself was a long-time gathering point for the homeless, the elderly poor, and other marginalized people. With its underground public toilets, benches, and proximity to the bus station, Rescue Mission, inexpensive bars, and so forth, the park served as a gathering place, something of a social center, and the location of essential services (Cooley, 1985; *Los Angeles Times*, 1985; Cornell, interview, 1/23/01; Stepner, interview, 1/23/01; social service provider, interview, 1/24/01). Fourth and Fifth Avenues, indeed much of the south of Broadway area, contained a large number of inexpensive lodgings. Besides shelters like the Rescue Mission, numerous single-room occupancy hotels and cheap bars crowded the area.

Horton Plaza Mall was built at the edge of the historic center of the city, Horton Plaza. Seeking to design a festival marketplace, the architect Jon Jerde sought to recreate the feel of a confined European street, with its "exuberant sense of public life," while also drawing on "an abstraction of indigenous architectural language" so as to reflect something of "San Diego's rich history".[5] As its developer, Earnest Hahn, declared on opening day, "It's not a shopping center. It's a street, it's a happening, it's a festival marketplace" (Harris, 1985: 2.1). But it was a happening that turned its back on the city: three sides consisted of blank facades or large parking garages, and the fourth, fronting Horton Plaza Park, sought to draw people out of that park and into the precincts of the shopping center. The "center was built like a fort with very little interface to the area around it," according to a source involved with its development, a strategy that allowed suburban and tourist visitors to "feel safe. Security was very heavily emphasized at this particular center" (downtown worker, interview, 1/24/01).

For Bill Keller, one of the early merchants in the mall, who later became important in the preservation and gentrification of the nearby

Gaslamp Quarter, the construction of Horton Plaza as a privately owned and controlled "public" space was critical to the success of downtown redevelopment: "I think Horton Plaza created the first public space in downtown for people from the suburbs to … begin the process of coming back into the neighborhood" (Keller, interview, 1/26/01). At the same time, this merchant claims that "people don't use" Horton Plaza Park, the city-owned park in front of the mall. Yet while the park may be neglected, some fifteen years after Horton Plaza opened, according to Keller, "the public space that is interesting in San Diego is really the sidewalks." That is, the privatized public space of the Horton Plaza Mall has made the revitalization of the publicly owned public spaces of the sidewalks possible. Yet to simply call the Mall "privatized" and the sidewalks "public" misses the point of how the very meaning—and the very regulation—of property has changed during the course of redevelopment in San Diego. It also misses the degree to which homelessness—and the regulation and exclusion of homeless people—has been both a key force behind this change, and a result of it.

Property Rights, Property Regimes, and Public Space

If, as we indicate above, the politics of public space has numerous facets, it is nonetheless curious that geographers and others have spent only a small amount of energy exploring public space as a form of property, that itself exists within a regime of property relations, especially as they are defined by rights.[6] It is true that much of the work on public space over the past decade derives from a set of influential arguments (especially Davis, 1990; Sorkin, 1992) concerning the "end of public space." These arguments looked critically at the privatization of public space—its enclosure in malls and festival marketplaces—and at its severe regulation in what Smith (1996) called the "revanchist" city. This work has been productively linked to issues of gentrification and redevelopment, and to the construction of the "neoliberal city" (Smith, 1996; MacLeod, 2002). But "privatization" has been understood in largely metaphorical terms—as a stand-in for a more general process of exclusion or a limiting of access—without a concomitant examination of the nature of property itself. A more through look at public space under redevelopment in terms of property is warranted.

Nicholas Blomley (2004), geography's preeminent theorist of property, points out that "urban spaces and their property regimes—for all sorts of reasons—tend to appear 'settled'. Property—like space—appears as an apolitical and unproblematic backdrop to political life." But, as Macpherson (1978) points out, property rights can be defined as a *right to exclude* (see Blomley, 2000b). Perhaps more accurately, property is defined *as property* by a set of specific rules and practices that determine how exclusion may be affected. Ownership entails the monopoly right of use; property laws set the limits of that right, records who owns that right, and specifies how that right may be enforced. Even though this right to exclude has to be set against its corollary, the right *not* to be excluded (Macpherson, 1978; Blomley, 2004), it is nonetheless the case that specific relations of exclusion necessarily define property. Even public property is defined by the right to exclude—and by the monopoly right of use. The difference is that this right is held by the state, and the monopoly is often (though not always) defined as "the people." But to say that much is only to invite the questions: Just who are "the people"—and who are they not (Marston, 1990)?

For Blomley (2000a: 88), the property right to exclude necessarily implies a violent act:

> Expulsion … entails a right. The powers of the state can be invoked to assist in that expulsion. Police can be called to physically remove a trespasser; injunctions prepared, criminal sanctions sought. As such, expulsion is a violent act. Violence can be explicitly deployed or (more usually) implied. But such violence has state sanction and is thus legitimate.

The critical questions, then, concern the *conditions* under which such violence is implied or enacted, in whose name violence is implied or enacted, the rules by which exclusions are limited or sanctioned, and, finally, the reasons that exclusion—and the violence it entails—is advanced.

Under capitalism, private property implies a further set of relations. As a fungible, delineated *thing*, its use value is, to a large extent, equivalent with its exchange value. The purpose of owning property is to have it increase in value. But since landed property can only exist in relation to other properties—it cannot be separated from neighboring properties—every owner of property has an economic interest in every other owner's property. The right to use and the right to exclusion, therefore, is limited by exactly those same rights held by others. Property thus exists in a *regime* of practices, laws, and meanings that formally and informally determine the exact nature of a property right. In a city, private property—and the values it contains—is necessarily determined in part, by the practices, laws, and meanings that determine the use of public property.

These are critical issues in connection to redevelopment for a number of reasons. First, in San Diego, as is typical in American cities, redevelopment has been advanced as a means of increasing the value of private property, and therefore making it attractive to inward investment and a net benefit to current owners.[7] Indeed, since San Diego's redevelopment arm, the Centre City Development Corporation (CCDC) operates through property tax-increment financing, its very *raison d'etre* is to increase property values (Allsbrook, interview, 1/24/01). With its powers of condemnation and taxation, and particularly with its power to promote or block the issuance of the Conditional Use Permits that allow particular kinds of businesses and services to operate or not (Cornell, interview, 1/23/01; social service provider, interview, 1/24/01; Carroll, interview, 1/25/01), CCDC, a semipublic entity, possesses certain rights to exclude—to exclude people and uses, even from privately owned property. But it can only legitimately do so if it is serving the interests of private property as a whole.[8]

Second, redevelopment in cities like San Diego, as an incremental, expanding process, relies on a particular dialectic of public and private property. Public property is critical to redevelopment in several ways. Public and semipublic developments—like convention centers or ballparks—are often crucial lynchpins in the redevelopment process. This is certainly the case in San Diego where the convention center has long been seen as the basis of downtown's growth and success (Acuna, 1988; Hamilton, 1994; Showley, 1994; Keller, interview, 1/26/01), and where a new San Diego Padres baseball stadium has become the center of an expansive new area of intensive redevelopment in San Diego's "East Village".[9] In addition, public *spaces*—like sidewalks, parks, city streets, and plazas—are frequently cornerstones of redevelopment efforts. Publicly funded beautification of public spaces is used to jumpstart private property redevelopment, in part because improvements in public space have relational benefit to the value of surrounding private property. In this sense, private property development *relies* on public property redevelopment.

Yet at the same time, the redevelopment of private property frequently displaces poor and very poor populations. This has been the case in San Diego (Allsbook, interview, 1/24/01; social service provider, interview, 1/24/01; Carroll, interview, 1/26/01).[10] As poor people have been forced out of cheap lodgings, and as cheap bars, card shops, pool rooms, theaters, and social service agencies, where many poor downtown residents spend their days, were forced out of the area by redevelopment (see Schacter, 1985; Schwartz, 1985; Serrano, 1988), the street presence of homelessness has grown. Many homeless have resorted to public space—Horton Plaza Park, sidewalks in front of newly opened bars and restaurants in the Gaslamp, or the spacious lawns outside the Convention Center—thereby threatening the very increases in value that would prove redevelopment's success. Homelessness in public space—on public property—was both a result of redevelopment, and, many feared, threatened its demise (Acuna, 1989; Baranowski, interview, 1/25/01). Considerable effort has been expended (as we will see) in figuring out how to regulate the homeless on public property, or how to expel them altogether. It raised the question of just how much they could be excluded from property that presumably belongs to all the public. What new property rules were required? To what extent could public property be privatized—privatized either in the sense that rules of exclusion similar to private property could be enacted, or that private interests could control access to public space?

Those questions, in turn, raise a third important issue related to property and redevelopment. Private property owners, working as individuals, have a presumptive right of exclusion.[11] The law scholar Jeremy Waldron (1991) has argued that in the American city the only place homeless people can *be*, without being at the sufferance of another, is on public property.[12] Everywhere else they must have *a priori* permission to be.[13] This holds true even in shelters and transitional housing where the controlling agencies reserve the right to expel those who do not follow the agencies' rules. Waldron (1991) thus argued that in a "libertarian paradise" in which all property is governed by private property rules, homeless people would simply have no place to be, no place where they could live. Even if we don't follow Waldron to the dystopian extreme he so compellingly outlines, it remains the case that public property is the only place that homeless people—who otherwise have no place over which they have private property rights—can live or act autonomously.[14] The nature of the laws that govern public space, therefore, also determines the sorts of autonomy homeless people may possess, even as these laws establish the rules by which people may be invited into or excluded from public space.

When, therefore, the maintenance and policing of public space is handed over to business and property owners organized into a Business Improvement District—as, we will see, is the case in San Diego—the means by which public space is regulated, and hence the relationships that constitute it as property, are transformed. A helpful way to understand the nature of this transformation is to see it as part of the transformation of the property *regime* operative in the contemporary city. Drawing on an argument by Krueckeberg (1995), Blomley (2004: XV) argues that "urban land … needs to be recognized as land over which a legal regime of real property is operative." The term "regime" implies a relatively settled, fairly consistent, set of practices, ideologies, and social relations. A regime can be—at least metaphorically—mapped. Its contours can be drawn. Or to abandon the metaphor, certain relatively settled relations and rules are *institutionalized*. Roles—of owners and users, of police and transgressors—are (again relatively) clear.

But this is not to say that property regimes do not vary over space and time. Indeed, as with regimes of accumulation or social reproduction (Boyer, 1990; Katz, 2001), property regimes are, in fact, dynamic and contested. They are, for that reason, both a shaper, and an outcome, of the exercise of power. When regimes are undergoing transformation—which is the case in San Diego (although certainly not uniquely there)—relations become unstable and are, at least to some degree, deinstitutionalized. They are up for grabs. Property becomes a site of social contestation. Since property regimes are necessarily relational, however, it is important to remember that they must necessarily exist beyond, and encapsulate, the specific relations and rights of property governing any specific parcel at any given time. Yet it is only by focusing on specific parcels, and specific times, that property regime changes can be mapped.

Or, perhaps, such mapping can only be accomplished by focusing on who is being excluded from public and private property—and how.

From Public Space to Pseudo-Private Property

In these terms, the politics of public space can be usefully understood as a politics of property. Public space is, however, much more than property. As we have already noted, it is also a site of politics of various sorts. In contemporary American cities, and in terms of property redevelopment, however, it is perhaps most importantly a problematic site of sociability. Public investment in inner cities has increasingly focused on creating signature festival spaces—baseball stadiums, aquariums, redeveloped city squares and parks, urban marketplaces, historic streetscapes—that draw visitors and residents into the city to meet, mingle, and spend (Jameson, 1985; Zukin, 1991, 1995; Sorkin, 1992; Kearns and Philo, 1993; Knox, 1993; Lees, 2001). Considerable investment has been made in remaking downtown sites of *spectacle* (Harvey, 1989a). Public space is seen, in this light, as the marker of urbanity. Lively streets, lively cafes, lively spaces for gathering: these are what mark a city *as* a city.

Rapid suburbanization and white flight, stepped up disinvestment in inner cities,[15] the transformation of labor markets, the ravages of bulldozer redevelopment, and the decline of housing quality in the postwar period have contributed to what has been widely perceived as the decline—and maybe even the death—of American downtowns. The reconfiguration of public spaces—reclaiming them from malignant uses, in the language of the urban right (Magnet, 2000)—has therefore become a central focus of urban redevelopment in the hopes of reversing the decline. But to reclaim such spaces, it is almost universally held, they have to be made "safe," they have to be made alluring to exactly those—the white upper and middle classes—who have fled the city for the suburbs. Spectacle, in other words, needs to be carefully controlled. Such control—developed over years of experiment and still not entirely complete—has entailed rewriting the rules of public property, transforming the laws that govern it, and more and more frequently handing its regulation over to private entities (Zukin, 1995). It has also entailed a literal privatization of public space, a moving of the spaces of sociability onto private property, that is, recreating the suburban mall downtown. For critics like Darrell Crilley (1993), such a privatization creates "pseudo-public space," no longer really public in the sense of open access for all. But as Goss (1996) has shown, the production of pseudo-public spaces is not always regressive. It can open up opportunities for different kinds of sociability and it can invite in those—like women or gays—who may be excluded from the public spaces through the exercise of violence (not the sort of violence discussed above, but the more "private" violence of assault) (see Pain, 1991, 1997, 2000; Lees, 1998, 2001).

Public space in this sense, is made possible by private property—or, at minimum by the creation of a new *kind* of property relation, one in which private interests can enforce exclusions in publicly accessible spaces. But that is only one means of securing "public" space. Against Crilley's pseudo-public spaces, we can now also place *pseudo-private* spaces. These are spaces that are formally owned by the state, by the public, but that are subject to control and regulation by private interests. Examples include public sidewalks patrolled by business improvement district-hired security forces, or parks governed by conservatories or other private organizations. Such pseudo-private spaces, we will suggest in the remainder of this paper, have become necessary to the redevelopment of downtown under a system that makes *accumulation*—the increase of value—the primary reason for maintaining or improving the public spaces of the city, and in which sociability and spectacle are merely the means toward that primary goal. Under these conditions, the production and presence of homeless people in pseudo-private spaces becomes doubly problematic. Homeless peoples' very right to the city is thrown into question, since as we have noted, they simply have no claim on, and are not protected by, private property, and now have a decreasing claim on public spaces that are reconstructed as pseudo private.

Such a claim needs to be established and supported empirically, and so we now turn to a closer look at redevelopment in San Diego, and particularly at its Business Improvement District–led program for regulating and maintaining the public spaces of the downtown called "Clean and Safe."

Clean and Safe: Changing Relations of Property and Public Space in San Diego

Horton Plaza and Horton Plaza Park. Horton Plaza Park in many senses—physical, social, political—is the center of contemporary redevelopment efforts in San Diego. Even as redevelopment has spread south through Gaslamp, west to the waterfront, north onto Cortez Hill, and east into the East Village, even as the new Padres baseball stadium has become the focal point for redevelopment hopes and energies, Horton Plaza Park remains central to all discussions of the successes and failures of redevelopment in San Diego. Deeded to the city in 1894 by San Diego pioneer Alonzo Horton, who stipulated that it forever remain a park, the half-block Horton Plaza was the center of the city.[16] By the 1960s, however, Horton Plaza Park had become a gathering place for the poor and homeless, and by the 1970s was largely avoided by middle-class workers and visitors in the downtown area. When redevelopment was first being contemplated, its status as a *public* park posed a particular problem for the redevelopment planned around it. Planners—and the Hahn Corporation, the developer eventually selected to build the Horton Plaza shopping center—felt that the park's very publicness, and its association with the underside of the city, would threaten the success of the mall in particular and redevelopment more generally. As Mike Stepner, the former City Architect recalls, "The initial [redevelopment] plan ... call[ed] for a lot of public space" because as redevelopment was getting underway, "there wasn't [much] public space in downtown" (Stepner, interview, 1/23/01). Besides Horton Park, there was only Pantoja Park just to the west (called Condo Park by many because it is now the center of a significant cluster of townhouses and apartments that give the park a feel of being the private preserve of the homeowners).[17] But public space was quickly seen as a problem, rather than a good. "When downtown redevelopment started," both public parks "were really ... homeless havens" (Stepner, interview, 1/23/01). If the restrooms below Horton Park had been important to shoppers downtown when there were still department stores there—Mike Stepner's wife remembers taking her children into them to change diapers—by the time redevelopment got underway, the restrooms had "become real hell holes" (Jones, 1985; Stepner, interview, 1/23/01), inhabited by the homeless and drug users. More generally, redevelopment planners argued that the park would need, at the least, a significant face-lift, and new rules would have to be established limiting its use. Given this, and despite Alonzo Horton's stipulation, a portion of the Horton Park was ceded to the Hahn Corporation in exchange for its agreement to rehabilitate the park (using CCDC funds). There was a protracted discussion, in fact, about deeding the entire park to Hahn: "The privatizing of that public square was a real issue" (Stepner, interview, 1/23/01).

As part of the rehabilitation, the restrooms—at the time the last remaining public ones downtown—were filled in. The park was relandscaped, historic-style benches (with arm rests that prevented people from lying on them) were installed, and the fountain was reconditioned. But "the homeless issue did not go away" (downtown worker, interview, 1/24/01). It is worth examining, for a moment, therefore, the discourse surrounding the redevelopment of the park, first in 1985 and then again when it was further redeveloped in 1991. Before the Horton Plaza toilets were removed, the landscape architect Lawrence Halperin led an evening tour through them. In the words of one CCDC official, "It was interesting. People were sleeping in the restrooms. The place was in disrepair. Five of the toilets had no doors on the stalls, and one man was permanently perched on the latrine. Permanently—because people in other tours mentioned him too" (quoted in Jones, 1985: 2.3). The toilets, and the man permanently lodged in them, served as something of a synecdoche for all that was perceived to be wrong with the park. Filling in the underground toilets and redeveloping the surface of the park—it was hoped—would dislodge the homeless and make the park more available to the rest of the public.

CCDC devoted $775,000 to the redevelopment of the park in advance of the Horton Plaza opening. Lawns were resodded; the bus stop (which "provided not only an audience for the many would-be preachers who wailed about sin and hellfire, but also targets for the pickpockets and panhandlers" [Cooley, 1985: 2.1]) was moved a block away; the fountain was reconditioned; and both uniformed and undercover police increased their presence in the park. The early results seemed favorable. A police captain reported a few weeks after the Mall's opening, "We think we have played a role. I also think it's the 'middle class Americans' who have infiltrated the area and have changed the atmosphere" (quoted in Cooley, 1985). A CCDC spokeswoman was pleased: "It almost has a European flavor. It's a great spot to sit and people-watch" (Cooley, 1985). But neither the CCDC spokeswoman nor the police captain was quite sure what had become of the homeless and elderly who had formerly used the park: "Quite frankly," said the police captain, "the transients have simply become less visible. I think there has been a dispersion of the transient population. Maybe they went to other areas of the city" (Cooley, 1985).[18]

Wherever they may have gone in the first weeks of the mall's opening, they soon returned: the man, at least figuratively, was back on his latrine.[19] By 1989, "tiny Horton Plaza Park" was once again "home to the homeless, the alcoholic, the misplaced, the recently released, the open-air preachers," and merchants in the mall were becoming increasingly vocal in their complaints. A *Los Angeles Times* architecture critic, drawing on the work of William Whyte (1988), lamented that "Horton Plaza Park is today a desolate place," suggesting that the plantings were used mostly as "urinals in what you might call the wee wee hours," and noting that although Hahn had sponsored a noon-time concert series in the park at the time of Horton Plaza's opening, he had since moved all concerts and pushcarts into the space of the mall itself (Sutro, 1989: 5.1). A "Horton Plaza Activities Committee," composed of local "business-types" sought to reinstitute entertainment in the park during the summer (Sutro, 1989). Instead, just before Christmas, 1989, the city removed the park benches closest to the entrance of the Robinson's department store, the only large store that opened onto the park. The city stated as its goal in the bench removal a desire "to 'normalize' the park, to get the transients to move and make the park more acceptable to legitimate shoppers, tourists and passers-by," in the words of a Parks and Recreation manager (Perry, 1989: 2.1). The city promised to replace the benches the following June.

Despite the promise, the city council voted in June 1990 to remove *all* benches from the park, and to tear up the lawns and replace them with prickly plants and flowers (Horstman, 1990; Johnson, 1990).[20] The goal, in the words of City Architect Mike Stepner's report to the city council was "to return the space to full public usage by all segments of the community" and to "dilute the influence of the so-called undesirables." Council member Bob Filner argued that the plan was "an attempt to save the park" (quoted in Johnson 1990: B2). Practices of exclusion, to put it in the terms laid out above, were being transformed through design—or at least that was the attempt. The expectation was, once again, that the benches, and perhaps even the lawns, would be replaced a year later, after the "undesirables" had been chased out. The cost of park redevelopment would this time be paid by neighboring businesses. The city and business interests, in fact, had spent almost two years negotiating over park redesign and who would pay for it (Johnson 1990). The *Los Angeles Times* (July 8, 1990: B.2) complained in an editorial that the redesign "smacks of a classic attempt to sweep these people"—whom the *Times* described as "the homeless and others who use the park peacefully"—out of view of the tourists rather than deal with "the more fundamental task of housing the thousands who live on San Diego streets." On June 20, 1991, the city finally followed through on its plan to re-landscape the park, sending bulldozers in at 5 a.m. in order to "restore the dignity" of the park, in the words of both John Roberts, the managing director of the U.S. Grant Hotel across the street, and Ron Oliver, president of the Central City Association (both quoted in Granberry, 1991: B.1). "The problem is the vagrants," Oliver added (Granberry, 1991: B.1).

Or as one informant connected to Horton Plaza recently put it, "[U]ntil downtown can really come to grips with … ["the issues of vagrancy"], I think it's very difficult for the retail component to interface with the park and the [bus stop]" (downtown worker, interview, 1/24/01). Dave Allsbrook of the CCDC recalls the 1985 design of the park was the result of "a fairly elaborate public process," but that the 1990 make-over that replaced the benches and grass was the result of business and development lobby pressure: "Hahn, the owners of the Horton Plaza, were very concerned" because the dividing line between the public park and the mall's property was invisible on the landscape. Eventually, "the Central City Association [the business wing of the Downtown Partnership] weighed in on the issue and ultimately the park was reconfigured" (Allsbrook, interview, 1/24/01). The redevelopment of the park was undertaken precisely to ensure and protect the interests of nearby property owners.

Nor does it seem that the timing of the redevelopment was accidental. The city first voted to make changes to the park as the Centre City Planning Committee (CCPC)—directed by Horton Plaza developer Earnest Hahn himself—was finalizing its redevelopment master plan. During debate over the plan, one of the CCPC members, Louis Wolfsheimer, a San Diego Port Commissioner,[21] "launched a tirade against the 'crazies' who populate downtown" at one the CCPC meetings in early November 1989 (Acuna, 1989: B.2). According to the *Los Angeles Times* (1990),

> Wolfsheimer is not the first person to complain about what many perceive as downtown's most glaring weakness. For several years, business owners, shopkeepers, office workers, downtown civic groups and others have warned that the area's future as a residential neighborhood and as the region's cultural focal point is jeopardized by the onslaught of peripatetic petty criminals, panhandlers, the mentally disturbed, drug users and dealers.

Downtown San Diego's redevelopment was on "a collision course," with street people (*Los Angeles Times*, 1990). For his part, Wolfsheimer was careful to separate what he called the "crazies" from "the homeless or transients who live downtown," a distinction that became increasingly important in the discourse about street people and redevelopment downtown at the end of the 1980s. For on that distinction hinged a set of policies and practices geared towards, on the one hand, *regulating* the "crazies" and on the other hand, *managing* the others. And in the interaction of both, new relations of property began to develop.

Managing Homelessness

Redevelopment was having the effect of both increasing homelessness and making it more visible (Miller, 1985; Frammolino, 1985; Schwartz, 1985; Schraeger, 1994).[22] This visibility, in turn, led to increased spending of redevelopment funds on low-income housing and social services.[23] Indeed, the visibility of homeless people seemed to drive much social service development (and business community support for it). According to a knowledgeable social service provider, Rachel's Center, a drop-in center for women in East Village, "grew out of the redevelopment of Horton Plaza because it displaced so many people. And women homeless who were formerly invisible were now very visible, and there was no place for women to go to the bathroom, to just have a safe place just to sit and spend the day" (social service provider, interview, 1/24/01).[24] When one of the authors noted to this social service provider that what "is really striking to me walking around [the city] is there's no place to sit," the provider responded: "It's deliberate. It's an absolutely deliberate thing. It's a city of contrasts in a sense of how can the citizens be so generous as to support projects like St. Vincent's, Catholic Charities, Rachel's, ... Salvation Army, and the works that we do, and yet have such a mean spirit legislatively towards the poor" (interview, 1/24/01).[25]

This legislative "mean spirit"—and simultaneous generosity—manifested itself in a number of ways in the 1980s and 1990s. For example, just before Horton Plaza opened, Ernest Hahn donated a million dollars to James Rouse's Enterprise Foundation to be used to build low-income housing downtown and in Barrio Logan, just to the southeast (Enge, 1985). In 1987, following a multimillion-dollar gift from Joan Kroc (widow of the founder of McDonald's), St. Vincent de Paul opened the first of its shelters and service facilities on its campus in East Village; other huge gifts, including one from a prominent real estate developer Pail Mirabile followed.[26] Other services—the Rescue Mission, Rachel's Center for women, the Neil Good Day Center, and the Salvation Army—were similarly heavily supported. At the same time, CCDC and the city only reluctantly supported the expansion of social services and the construction of low-income housing. Father Joe of St. Vincent de Paul complains that every time he tries to expand—"People don't realize agencies like ours are big players downtown ... [P]eople do not realize that [we] really are in effect a developer ... [one of] the top five percent of employers of downtown," he says—CCDC raises objections and the city makes the acquisition of a conditional use permit (CUP) nearly impossible (Carroll, interview, 1/25/01).

Nearly every social service provider we talked with raised the issue of CUPs (e.g., Cornell, interview, 1/23/01; social service provider, interview, 1/24/01; Carroll, interview, 1/25/01).[27] Every provider of social services in

San Diego must obtain a CUP, and CUPs have become a key battleground in redevelopment. Conditional Use Permits—also issued for trash dumps, adult bookstores, rock-crushing facilities, dance clubs, and the like—set the ground rules for the operation of a facility. All social service facilities in San Diego must have a CUP (issued by the city) in order to operate. In early redevelopment efforts, the city encouraged the movement of services—along with adult bookstores, peep shows, and so forth—out of the Gaslamp area by refusing to renew CUPs. The permitting process became a forum for those opposed to the siting or expansion of social services, and throughout the early 1990s, the city regularly delayed or denied permits. But advocates for the homeless also used this process against the city to force it to approve shelter and transitional housing. After losing the landmark *Hoffmaster v. San Diego* case that required the city to approve sites for low-income and shelter housing, the city stalled by refusing CUPs. The lawyers who had argued *Hoffmaster* convinced the judge who decided the case to mandate the approval of all CUPs for transitional and emergency shelters unless the city published a list of acceptable sites for such housing (Cohelan, interview, 1/23/01). The city eventually did so, but it still frequently blocks the issuing of CUPs. During 2001, for example, a facility was attempting to get its CUP modified so that it could serve as a nighttime drop-in center. Some of the local businesses objected and tried to block the expanded CUP. The dynamic is interesting: The center gets "great donations from businesses that are located blocks away, that are on the nineteenth floor on B Street." But the "relationship between the agency and the businesses" on the same block as the facility "is not very good, because these people feel that their business is threatened" (social service provider, interview, 1/24/01). Businesses located near homeless service providers fear the effects of street people hanging out near their businesses (Carroll, interview, 1/25/01), and often fight against the issuance or expansion of CUPs.

At its starkest, the CUP process means that social service providers "have no right to exist, absolutely no right to exist. None whatsoever.... I have to get a CUP for everything I do....... The little guys can't do it. And we need little guys at the shelters along with the big guys. It takes $100,000 to do a CUP process. So you end up [with] churches open[ing] up a shelter illegally and we get these long drawn-out battles in court..." (Carroll, interview, 1/25/01; see also Johnston, interview, 1/23/01). The property rights of social service providers, in other words, are highly constrained, largely because of the feared effect that approval will have on the values of other property. "Conditional Use Permits," says a social service provider, "are probably the biggest albatross on social service's back that exists" (interview, 1/24/01). While much of downtown is being made over for the benefit of private property owners, private social services—which are also property owners (indeed St. Vincent de Paul is one of the largest landowners and developers in the city)—find themselves the center of contention and ever greater public scrutiny.

Regulating Homelessness

If CUPs represent one angle on the "legislative mean-spiritedness" that the social service provider identifies, another can be seen in the ongoing debates over what to do about street people—homeless, panhandlers, idlers of various sorts—who still remain on the streets of the Gaslamp, around Horton Plaza, or along the walkways that connect the Convention Center to the rest of downtown. But the story here, in fact, is rather complex and contradictory. Or as the *Los Angeles Times* put it, "Like other big cities, San Diego has alternated between the carrot and the stick for the homeless and panhandlers" (Perry, 1993: A.3). For a century, California had a law that simply banned panhandling. In 1991, however, the California Supreme Court struck down the law, asserting that panhandling was a protected form of speech and so could not be banned on public property. Cities around the state responded in a number of ways. San Francisco was one of the first to pass an anti*aggressive* panhandling law that sought to control certain types of behavior associated with begging (but not begging itself). San Diego, by contrast, at first relied on stepped-up enforcement of municipal codes that made it a misdemeanor to block a sidewalk, regulated public drinking, prohibited jaywalking, and the like (King, 1993; Perry, 1993). Since misdemeanors have to be witnessed in order to be cited, the San Diego Police Department produced and distributed "A Citizen's Guide to the Control of Transient-Related Crime" (no date), which outlined the proper procedure for making citizen's arrests and gave a list of applicable state and local laws.[28]

San Diego announced this "old-fashioned crackdown" by claiming it was going after "panhasslers" and citing them on any legitimate basis it could find (King, 1993: A1).[29] A reporter for the *San Francisco Chronicle* seemed to find this initiative preferable to San Francisco's new antiaggressive panhandling law (approved by voters in November 1992), because it avoided "an ethical debate," and seemed to escape the notice of homeless advocates (who in any event were less organized than those in San Francisco) (King, 1993: A1). The crackdown was supported by some prominent social service providers—like Father Joe Carroll—who opposed panhandling, but who also felt that it was impossible to outlaw it entirely. Aggressive panhandling, as defined in San Francisco, Father Joe sardonically noted, "sounds like my insurance agent" (King, 1993: A1).

Nonetheless, San Diego Mayor Susan Golding began pushing for an aggressive panhandling law in August 1993. The law was passed in

October that year. The law made it illegal for "any person on the streets, sidewalks, or other, public places open to the public, whether publicly or privately owned, to aggressively coerce, threaten, hound, harass, or intimidate another person for soliciting money or goods" (Municipal Code, Chapter 5, Article 2, §52.4001). Together with the aggressive policing of San Diego's streets on other counts, the law earned San Diego the distinction of being named among the five top cities with the "meanest streets" in America, as designated by the National Law Center for Homelessness and Poverty (1996; Vobejda and Havemann, 1996). But it is, in fact, not clear that the law had much of an effect on regulating homeless people in the public spaces of San Diego. When asked in 2001 about the importance and efficacy of the law, few of our informants could remember much about it (even though it remains on the books), and some suggested that it is simply not enforced (Binder, interview, 1/25/01).[30] As the president of the Downtown Partnership complained, "the police do not really think it is their job to roust people when they're sleeping in doorways. Even though there's ordinances that speak to that, to the police that's not a biggie when they ought to be solving robberies" (Baranowski, interview, 1/25/01).[31]

The Partnership has therefore promoted a series of other, private means of controlling homeless people on public property (Baranowski, interview, 1/25/01). In the late 1990s, the Partnership, in conjunction with CCDC, contracted with the Alpha Project to have formerly homeless men and women "patrol" the streets of downtown San Diego. The Alpha Project is run by Bob McElroy, who cultivates something of an outsider status among social service providers in San Diego (McElroy, interview, 1/26/01). He says that many of the mainstream service providers, like St. Vincent de Paul and Catholic Charities, enable homelessness rather than work to solve it. Solutions, according to McElroy's brand of conservative Christianity, require something like tough love, direct control over the lives of homeless people, and a program that will "challenge [the homeless] to get off [their] butt[s]" (interview, 1/26/01). This is a philosophy that resonates well with the Downtown Partnership.

In the late 1990s, CCDC and the Partnership hired the Alpha Project to "patrol" Horton Plaza Park and to report "public drunkenness, urination, drug deals" (Allsbrook, interview, 1/24/01; Baranowski, interview, 1/25/01; McElroy, interview, 1/26/01). McElroy described Alpha's mode of operation as follows:

> Police can't do anything about [the homeless]. They have a constitutional right to be there [on the street].... [W]e have a very active ACLU here ... so there was a reluctance for the city to enforce

anything. So they called us. I said … 'we're gonna go out there and offer these people help and we'll store their belongings and we'll give them transportation,' … any thing a person needs, we have resources for. But [we say] 'You also can't stand in front of this business and harass people and run this guy's business into the ground.' And ninety-nine percent of the people say, 'I respect that'…. Others will want to debate and espouse their constitutional rights, at which time we take people out on the traffic medians. If they want to do that, then we espouse our constitutional rights to inform the passing public that we're a social service agency and we offered this person every thing that he's panhandling for, we offered him a job, we give him a home, we've offered him transportation, we've offered him sobriety, so what that does is dry—if people didn't give to panhandlers, there wouldn't be any panhandlers, cor-rect…. So we blow their income and they move. That's how we get people to move. Don't harass nobody, don't pepper spray nobody, don't push nobody around…. Peer to peer. That's why it works (interview, 1/26/01).

McElroy admits that this usually just moves panhandlers from one place to the next—"that's what community policing is all about"—but it does have the effect of cleaning the streets in the targeted area, and then, perhaps, leads to stepped-up enforcement—and community organization—in the area to which the homeless have moved (interview, 1/26/01).[32]

CCDC and the Partnership were pleased with the results of the Alpha intervention (even if not entirely pleased with McElroy's management of it) and by the summer of 2000 had regularized it as the "Clean and Safe" program (Huard, 2000; Millican, 2000). Clean and Safe is the public name of a Property-based Business Improvement District (P-BID) that covers the whole of downtown. The P-BID released the city's Parks and Recreation Department from responsibility for the maintenance of public spaces downtown—street plantings, medians, parks, and so on—and handed it over to a private concern: the Downtown Partnership.[33] Downtown businesses and property owners pay an assessment to the Partnership (which has been designated by the city as the manager of the P-BID) so that all may receive an "enhanced level of services." The P-BID, although regulated by state law, is a private organization, accountable to a privately appointed board of directors. It faces only minimal (largely accounting) oversight from the city.

According to the president of the Downtown Partnership, the impetus behind the P-BID formation was a "general dissatisfaction [over city services], coupled with the rise of the homeless in downtown" (Baranowski, interview, 1/25/01). The P-BID takes responsibility for "general cleanliness [on] a daily basis. Because of the homeless issue, there is constant defecating, urinating, wine bottles, on a daily basis. And if nothing else, if we can stay ahead at ground zero on that, we're doing superbly." The P-BID does "constant maintenance, constant cleanliness, constant power washing because that stuff stinks" (Baranowski, interview, 1/25/01).

Cleaning is thus an important aspect of the P-BID's work. The other is making the streets and public spaces "safe" for residents, downtown employees, and visitors. In response to business and property owners' demand for more direct efforts at removing the homeless from the streets and parks, this second facet of the program is the employment of "Community Ambassadors" to patrol downtown. The Partnership officially describes the Ambassador program in the following terms:

> The newest and most exciting component to the [P-BID] district is the public safety program. A team of *Community Ambassadors* on both foot and bicycles act as goodwill ambassadors to downtown San Diego. These dedicated men and women are trained to assist local law enforcement identify crime and public safety issues. Equipped with communication devices, Community Ambassadors serve as extra "eyes and ears" in downtown. In addition, our ambassadors are "customer-service friendly," to our visitors. They give directions and offer general assistance to help everyone enjoy the unique qualities of downtown San Diego. Our Ambassadors also:
>
> Deter aggressive panhandling and other nuisance crimes
>
> Work with the Homeless Outreach Team (HOT) to provide social service outreach referrals
>
> Assist with directions and information
>
> Maintain open communication with police to report on-going issues
>
> Add a presence in downtown to prevent vandalism and other undesirable behavior

The president of the Partnership, however, uses slightly different terms to describe the program:

> There are two types of safety ambassadors. And I'd better be careful on this. One group are greeters. They walk around downtown

in pairs and give directions, hand out maps, assist. They're not safety. They're welcome ambassadors, so to speak, and they all wear nice uniforms and caps, and you know, you can tell that's who they are. There's another part [who] are the safety ambassadors that are a little meaner, a little rougher looking, so to speak. They stay out of the public view a little bit more. But they're not leg-breakers. Without being leg-breakers, they're the guys who will get in the face of the homeless people, and I don't want to say verbally abuse them by any means. We don't want to do that. But, you know, you send two girls out who are used to giving directions and smiling at people, they're not the people you want in the face of the homeless. So we've had to, in the last month, hire six additional people who are a little bit on the—I don't want to say rougher looking—but you don't want to mess with them is what it amounts to. So the police have given those people special training in terms of what you can and can't do. And our hope and our fear frankly [is] that they don't take it upon themselves to do things they're not supposed to in terms of keeping downtown safe. They don't get in fights. They're to be our eyes and ears out in the community, and with direct contact with the police department. But again that's a real fine line that we can't afford to cross (Baranowski, interview, 1/25/01).

It is also a line, apparently, that the designers of the Clean and Safe program had to be convinced to draw.

When it was being debated, homeless advocates and social service workers called dozens of shelters around the country to gauge the effects of similar programs elsewhere,

and we got an earful. And we found out in some cities, the ACLU had sued because the Clean and Safe ambassadors were harassing homeless people and depriving them of their rights, and of course none of this was shared in the initial unveiling of this vision. So, we went back to the committee with this information and we were hardly greeted warmly. The Downtown Partnership staff was very upset that we had uncovered this information and [that we had] got letters of support (Johnston, interview, 1/23/01).

Eventually, Clean and Safe agreed that Ambassadors would have to take a training program led by ACLU and volunteer lawyers, "and I haven't really heard a lot of complaints from the homeless population about it" (Johnston, interview, 1/23/01).[34]

And the program is very popular among business owners in the area, even if there are tensions over which parts of downtown are getting the most attention (downtown worker, interview, 1/24/01; Wade, interview, 1/25/01; Keller, interview, 1/26/01).[35] One of its main benefits, according to the Chamber of Commerce's Mitchell is that "they've sent a message which is that the business owners want to be sure the customers are safe and be sure the areas clean" (interview, 1/26/01). For many, its value is precisely in the privatization of services (Zinner, interview, 1/24/01; Carroll, interview, 1/25/01).

But for others, that is also exactly its cost: "The beauty of downtowns in my opinion is that downtowns, any downtown, accepts what's there. If you are a little bit eccentric, and a little bit crazy, people accept it. They don't single you out as they would in a suburb or a small little shopping center. You recognize it. You expect it in an urban area" (social service provider, interview, 1/24/01). While arguing that public spaces ought to be privatized, Father Joe Carroll (interview, 1/25/01) also asserts that CCDC (along the other redevelopment players) "has a purification mentality" that is seeking to create a city only for the "upper middle and upper class." Rosemary Johnstown (interview, 1/23/01) of the Interfaith Shelter Network puts the point this way: "There were all these kudos about these BIDs in other areas of the country. You know they're called 'Clean and Safe.' And I had problems with ... that name because it seems to me that the homeless population as a whole represents a greater threat to our complacency than to our safety."[36]

The homeless—and the Clean and Safe–type programs that they have called up when they have stood in the way of redevelopment—also thus seem to herald a new property regime in downtown areas. Private entities are given control over public property. The traditional, at least partially democratic, regulation of public property is replaced with a privatized set of rules of exclusion, and a form of violence—perhaps potential—that while retaining state sanction, is nonetheless left in the hands of private individuals. As the president of the Downtown Partnership was so careful not to make explicit, downtown's new private ambassadors have a very set idea of who belongs, and who does not belong, in the public spaces of the city. Something like Jeremy Waldron's (1991) libertarian paradise is one step closer to being achieved. Formally public property is turned into pseudo-private space.

This new property regime changes the nature of public space downtown. Father Joe, who bemoans the "purification" of downtown, sums up the contradictions that lie at the heart of this transformation succinctly:

Horton Plaza [Park] is owned by the city. Their solution was to make it unfriendly. But if they gave it to Horton Plaza [shopping center], they could maintain it and keep people off. All of a sudden nobody has benches now. Nobody has the privileges of what the Park used to offer. The city's solution is to make it so unfriendly no one will use it (interview, 1/25/01).

Perhaps Clean and Safe can be seen as a compromise, an innovation that does not fully privatize public *space*, leaving it to the whims of, say, a single corporation. But it is a compromise accomplished by changing how public *property* is regulated—and by whom.

This result is, perhaps, even more important than if Horton Plaza Park and similar spaces had been fully privatized. For it transforms the very nature of what is *public*. It transforms the meaning and practices—the regime—of property such that the very expectation that there is a public *good* is undermined. In this sense, what is at work is exactly the neoliberalization of the city: liberalization because it is based on a presumptive equality of ownership and ownership rights, a world in which relations of exchange predominate; neo because it does not eliminate the public entirely so much as change its meaning, and change who has control over it. In this transformation, the homeless become pariah, at once a symbol of all that is wrong with the public sphere and an ongoing hindrance to redevelopment and the good it brings in the form of increased property values. By turning over responsibility for maintaining and regulating public property to a private organization, the homeless find they have been even further stripped of any right to the city.

Conclusion

On a late Thursday night in January 2001, Fifth Avenue in San Diego absolutely bustles. Car horns blare; groups of twenty- to thirty-year-olds cruise from bar to bar; late-serving restaurants do a large business; and even in the winter, conventioneers from the North and East fill the outdoor tables that spill out of the eateries. Music escapes the dance clubs. Earlier in the evening, the restaurants—many of them specializing in the highly designed, and remarkably expensive, foods that are the hallmark of contemporary American urban cuisine—are full. Even down at the foot of Fifth, near where a hole in the ground marks the spot where the new baseball stadium will be built, if all the lawsuits can ever be worked out, the street bustles. Here things seem a little seedier and parking lots more frequently break the urban fabric. But this is all still a far cry from what the street, and the district surrounding it, was like only fifteen years earlier.

As Bill Keller notes, the sidewalks of downtown San Diego now are the public spaces of the city. CCDC's Dave Allsbrook agrees: "Down there on Thursday, Friday, Saturday night, it's amazing. It's wall-to-wall people up and down the sidewalks" (interview, 1/24/01). But their publicness is something different than it was before redevelopment took hold. While city police still patrol the streets—we watched one detain a shoe-shiner as the latter was crossing the street outside Croce's restaurant, and make it clear that he did not belong in that part of town—so too do uniformed and other "ambassadors." Neither the police nor the ambassadors seem much interested in moving the revelers along, no matter how much they are in violation of numerous municipal and state codes governing noise, public drunkenness, and the blocking of sidewalks.

In the early morning around sunrise, after the partiers have finally left, several homeless people sit quietly on the curbs that hem in the plantings in Horton Plaza Park. As the city begins to waken, and workers begin to commute downtown, the ambassadors return and "get in the face" of the homeless, encouraging them to move along. They also sweep and power-wash the walkways, getting the public spaces of the city ready for the day, returning the park to what it now is: a pseudo-private space regulated by and for the property and business interests of the city—which is another way of saying that redevelopment has been amazingly effective, and, in fact, the streets, sidewalks, and parks aren't what they used to be. They give a different inflection, now, to the word "public," limiting it to those who can support the value—and the values—now encapsulated in the redeveloped downtown. More and more there is simply not room for the poor and homeless in downtown San Diego.

This does not at all imply that public space is no longer important. Indeed, the city is under court orders to provide winter shelter for the homeless populations that despite and because of redevelopment will not go away. But each year, as the redevelopment frontier advances, it has been harder and harder to find a building in which, or even a lot on which, to even temporarily house some of the more than 7,000 homeless residents of the city. The city's solution has been to buy several "sprung structures"—giant tents—and to place them right in the middle of a couple of out-of-the way streets (not far from the sprawling St. Vincent de Paul campus). Because the city still owns the streets, it can get away with placing the shelters there. All the rest of the property is simply too valuable (Cornell, interview, 1/23/01; Binder, interview, 1/25/01). So, after a fashion, public space *remains* the space where homeless people can be, despite all the changes that redevelopment has wrought.

Notes

1. San Diego's redevelopment can be understood as a single case of the wider "entrepreneurial" redevelopment of American and European cities, as well as the now twenty-five years of research on urban growth machines. See, among others, Molotch (1976); Logan and Molotch (1987); Cox and Mair (1988); Stone (1989); Harvey (1989a, 1989b); Kearns and Philo (1993); Staeheli and Clarke (1995); Clarke and Gaile (1998); Hall and Hubbard (1998); Jones and Wilson (1999).
2. If the merchant is incredulous about the level of activity, he is also an astute and humorous observer of the changes he has seen around his store (which in fact shares a wall with the last-remaining adult bookstore in downtown): "In its earlier incarnation, [the Gaslamp] had the Stingaree (the red light district) and it was all about sex then. And it is all about sex now. I think this is where people come when they're looking for love, whether [for] one night or an eternal relationship."
3. The relationship between success of Horton Plaza and the Convention Center is close. As news articles from the late 1980s make plain, there was much concern before the Convention Center was built about whether Horton Plaza could be successful. See, for example, Acuna (1988).
4. Early efforts to redevelop Broadway, Horton Plaza, and the Gaslamp Quarter hinged on the relocation of the Rescue Mission, the closing of numerous massage parlors, topless bars, single-room occupancy hotels, and card shops (see Schacter, 1985; Schwartz, 1985; Serrano, 1988). That is, redevelopment proceeded through a sanitization of urban space. And as redevelopment continued, the *cordon sanitaire* extended outward (see Frammolino, 1986).
5. See *www.jerde.com/projectsframe.html*. Jerde is perhaps best known in the United States for his designs for the 1984 Los Angeles Olympics and for his development of Universal Studio's CityWalk in Los Angeles. For brief critical reviews of Jerde's Mall architecture, which see it as a failure of public space, see Betsky (1991) and Ouroussoff (2000).
6. There is of course a substantial literature in geography on the role of property in capitalism. See Smith (1979, 1990); Walker (1981); Harvey (1982, 1989b). The geography of rights has been recently explored by Blomley (1994a, 1994b) and Mitchell (2003). Even so, these two discourses have rarely been brought together, prompting Blomley (2000b: 651) to complain that "geographic writing on property rights and property more generally is surprisingly undeveloped."
7. Blomley (1998) explores some of the implications understanding development as a narrative (and hence a practice) of "upgrading" property, a narrative that entails the establishment of "good" and "bad" property. Blomley shows that activists often operationalize normative judgments about property in order to rally opposition to gentrifiers. Without discounting the importance of that, the San Diego case shows that normative judgments about good and bad property have been essential in closing, gentrifying, or demolishing housing, services, and establishments (like cheap liquor stores, adult bookstores, and strip clubs) that either served low-income populations in downtown or had long been ghettoized there.
8. While eminent domain law, of course, says that condemnation can only be in the "public interest," CCDC's tax-increment financing effectively limits that public interest to interests congruent with those of private property owners.
9. The property rules associated with the ballpark are complex. Despite massive amounts of public money spent on the project (the financing of the ballpark is the subject of a series of lawsuits that has delayed its construction for more than two years), the baseball stadium itself is owned by the baseball team. Some of the surrounding grounds remain in city possession, including an area beyond centerfield that has become a public park. The park, with its view of the playing field, however, is closed during games.
10. A report commissioned by the city council in 1984 explicitly made this point (see Miller, 1985), as did a report by the city's Housing Commission. This second report found that single-room occupancy hotel rooms declined by 1,247 units to 3,333, or 26% of the total, between 1976 and 1984 (Schwartz, 1985: B.1; Frammolino, 1985). The Housing Commission expected that the number of rooms would fall by another thousand by 1988 (Fammolino 1985). Meanwhile, rents in single-room occupancy hotels increased by 80% between 1980 and 1985 (Schreager, 1994: 41). All agreed that the destruction of these rooms, and their increasing costs, were contributing to the growth of homelessness (Frammolino, 1985).

11. This right is, in fact, limited, at least in publicly access private property by civil rights laws and the like. Even so, certain otherwise legal *activities*—such as political rallies, begging, or picketing—can be barred outright in a way that they cannot on public property. During the 1980s, protesters sought to perform a series of skits in the Horton Plaza mall protesting U.S. involvement in El Salvador. The shopping center management barred them, leading to a series of court cases, eventually appealed to the state Supreme Court. The Court refused to hear the case, letting stand a verdict upholding the center's right of exclusion (even though the California constitution had previously been found to protect the right of activists to circulate petitions in privately owned shopping centers) (Hager, 1986, 1987).

12. In geography, this argument has proven influential in the work of Blomley (1994 b), Mitchell (1997, 2003), and Collins and Blomley (2003).

13. Property law grants renters or other leaseholders, unlike the homeless, exclusive rights of access and exclusion, even, to some extent, over their landlords. They are, in Waldron's terms, covered by a private property rule. Homeless people are not.

14. The law and economics scholar Ellickson (1996) recognizes this, if in a backhanded way, in his review article laying out the case for greater regulation of the public spaces in which homeless people hang out.

15. The best study of this is Sugrue's (1996) analysis of postwar disinvestment in Detroit.

16. For ninety years, "Horton Plaza" referred to the public park on Broadway between Third and Fourth Avenues. With the development of the mall, the name Horton Plaza was legally transferred to the Hahn Corporation (which then vigorously protected its rights to that name as a trademark). The public park is now legally called Horton Park (but is usually referred to as Horton Plaza Park).

17. See Granberry (1991). Former City Attorney John Witt similarly views Pantoja Park as the preserve of nearby homeowners: "Pantoja Park is open space for those residential units that are on either side of it down there. It's been a park for longer than that, but I think the folks who live there kind of consider it their turf, although a lot of office workers use it" (Interview, 1/24/01).

18. On opening night at the mall, however, one could buy *images* of the homeless. At one gallery, $250 would purchase a framed lithograph called "America's Finest City" (then San Diego's motto) depicting "a gritty urban tableau: vagrants, bag ladies, Hare Krishnas, police and pedestrians milling about the park amid overflowing garbage cans, pathetic palms. And a run-down commercial district with cinema marquees advertising such films as 'Naked Stewardesses" and 'Kung Fu Exorcist'" (Harris, 1985: 2.1).

19. If not literally: When replacement restrooms finally opened several blocks north at 3rd and C in mid-1987, they were staffed by an attendant in a booth who would buzz users through the always-locked doors on an as-needed basis and ensure that they left promptly (Lemke,1987: 2.3).

20. Steve Flusty (2001) describes similar processes in Los Angeles.

21. The Port Commission provided the land that the Convention Center was built on, and is a major player in downtown redevelopment (Acuna, 1988).

22. San Diego's history of single-room occupancy hotel destruction, a central cause of the growth of homelessness together with the geography of the growth of its social service networks is complex and important, but cannot be treated here.

23. This too is a complex and contradictory story, involving a series of lawsuits that sought to require the city to spend its legally mandated low- and moderate-income housing set-aside funds. It deserves its own separate analysis.

24. Another provider indicates that Dave Allsbrook of CCDC "is a big supporter of Rachel's," and in his position as chief planner for CCDC has not been one "more interested in the bottom line than anything else" (Cornell, interview, 1/23/01).

25. The interview continues: Interviewer: "Is there any place to gather?" Respondent: "For the poor?" Interviewer: "Um-hum." Respondent: "Not that I am aware of" (interview, 1/24/01).

26. A history of the St. Vincent de Paul Village can be found at: *www.svdpv.org/*. The issue of visibility was clearly an impetus to the development of St. Vincent de Paul Village. Before the Village, "a homeless shelter you could use just night-time, six at night to six in the morning, and I asked a dumb question. I said 'why don't they stay during the daytime?' 'It costs more money.' OK. So my job—it seemed a simple solution. I didn't think it was complicated at all. 'Cause I said, 'what do they do all day?' 'They walk around the business

district. In fact, they create a problem.' And I said, 'Why don't we just keep them in there,' and then of course we found out they needed to be educated, they needed medical care.... So we decided to put everything in what I call the one-stop shopping center" (Carroll, interview, 1/25/01).

27. By contrast, a promoter of redevelopment in East Village complains that St. Vincent de Paul and other agencies do not need CUPs for the low-income housing it builds, only for its shelters and soup kitchens (Wade, interview, 1/25/01).

28. The most interesting thing about this document is, given its focus on public drunkenness, disorderly behavior, and consuming alcohol in public places, how well it fits the behavior of the sort of bar-hopping revelers that made downtown redevelopment appear so successful. Perhaps what sets such revelers that off from other street people is that the former rarely get charged with "molesting a trash can." Among the crimes increasingly policed during this crackdown was one of "tampering with or removal of city refuse"—that is, rummaging in trashcans for recyclables. One public defender notes that homeless people in San Diego would wrack up numerous charges for "molesting a trash can" (among other petty crimes), which, with failure to pay fines or appear in court quickly transformed into outstanding warrant felonies, criminalized an otherwise mostly peaceful class (Steve Binder, interview, 1/25/01).

29. According to Steve Binder, a public defender, the high point for police citation of homeless people for misdemeanor crimes came in 1991 with some 8,700. Two years later—when San Diego engaged in its "old-fashioned crackdown," there were only 118 citations (the papers report 42 citations in the first days of the crackdown). If Binder is correct in his numbers, the result can probably be explained by a much more aggressive approach to the homeless both outside the immediate downtown and overnight when they might lodge in doorways (and be cited for that) (Binder, interview, 1/25/01).

30. Even so, outstanding misdemeanor warrants remain one of the most important issues facing homeless people in San Diego (Binder, interview, 1/25/01). In response, social service providers and members of the city's legal establishment—prosecutors, defenders, and judges—have created the innovative Homeless Court that seeks to dismiss outstanding warrants in exchange for "time served" in rehabilitation, counseling, or job programs.

31. By contrast, Steve Binder, the public defender and one of the founders of the Homeless Court, reports that the biggest obstacle to getting people off the streets and into shelter, transitional housing, or various treatment programs, is the sheer weight of outstanding warrants for petty crimes like illegal lodging, trash can molesting, aggressive begging, public drunkenness, and the like (interview, 1/25/01). And Father Joe Carroll sees quality of life as predominantly a policing issue: "They'll say to me, you let the homeless hang out across the street from your property. Well, it ain't my property [that they are hanging out on]. I can't tell someone to get off somebody else's property. That's a police job. And I'll support the police doing it."

32. Baranowski confirms this effect: "The Port [of San Diego] is complaining to us now because they are saying 'because you are rousting your homeless from your areas, they're coming across Harbor Drive onto our areas. Stop.' ... Little Italy, or Hillcrest, they complain to us because they're saying 'you're doing a darn good job of rousting your homeless'" (interview, 1/25/01).

33. "On June 30th the City maintained it. On July 1st, they gave us the keys and said, good luck guys" (Baranowski, interview, 1/25/01). On BIDs generally, see Zukin (1995).

34. For his part, public defender Steve Binder calls Clean and Safe "a misallocation of resources" because "it belies the fact that [homeless] need services, not law enforcement or a gentle prod to get out of town" (interview, 1/25/01).

35. Keller suggests that the Gaslamp Quarter Association did not see the "safe elements" as "critical." Its interest was more in the cleaning and maintenance activities (Interview, 1/26/01).

36. The Clean and Safe Program has been supplemented by police-led Homeless Outreach Teams (HOTs), comprised of community police officers, social service workers, and mental health experts that patrol downtown. The HOTs are universally lauded for their work and for their effectiveness. They are, of course, considerably more expensive than Clean and Safe Ambassadors, and they rely on public money for continuity (Cornell, interview, 1/23/01; Zinner, interview, 1/24/01).

References

Acuna, A. 1988. "Convention Center is Raising Hopes for Downtown Vitality." *Los Angeles Times* (San Diego Edition), June 26, p. 2.1.

Acuna, A. 1989. "Port Commissioner Assails Presence of 'Crazies' Downtown." *Los Angeles Times* (San Diego Edition), 3 November 3, p. B.2.

Acuna, A. 1990. "Redevelopment Looks at All of Downtown." *Los Angeles Times* (San Diego Edition), October 1, p. B.1.

Adams, P. 1996. "Protest and the Scale Politics of Telecommunications." *Political Geography* 15, 419–442.

Atkinson, D. and Cosgrove, D. 1998. "Urban Rhetoric and Embodied Identities: City, Nation, and Empire at Vittorio Emanuel Monument in Rome, 1870–1945." *Annals of the Association of American Geographers* 88, 28–49.

Bell, D., Binnie, J., Cream, J. and Valentine, G. 1994. "All Hyped Up and No Place to Go." *Gender, Place and Culture* 1, 31–47.

Bell, D. and Valentine, G., eds. 1995. *Mapping Desire: Geographies of Sexualities.* London: Routledge.

Betsky, A. 1991. "Westside Pavilion: Old-Style Mall Turned into an Assault on the Senses." *Los Angeles Times* (Home Edition), November 21, p. J.2.

Blomley, N. 1994a. *Law, Space, and the Geography of Power.* New York: Guilford.

Blomley, N. 1994b. "Mobility, Empowerment, and the Rights Revolution." *Political Geography* 13: 407–422.

Blomley, N. 1998. "Landscapes of Property." *Law and Society Review* 32, 567–612.

Blomley, N. 2000a. "'Acts,' 'Deeds,' and the Violences of Property." *Historical Geography* 28, 86–107.

Blomley, N. 2000b. "Property Rights." In R. Johnston, et al., *The Dictionary of Human Geography, 4th ed.* Oxford, UK: Blackwell, 651.

Blomley, N. 2004. *Unsettling the City: Urban Land and the Politics of Property.* New York: Routledge.

Boyer, B. 1990. *The Regulation School: A Critical Introduction.* New York: Columbia University Press.

Boyer, M.C. 1992. "Cities for Sale: Merchandizing History at South Street Seaport." In *Variations on a Theme Park: The New American City and the End of Public Space,* edited by M. Sorkin, 181–204. New York: Hill and Wang.

Clarke, S. and Gaile, G. 1998. *The Work of Cities.* Minneapolis: University of Minnesota Press.

Collins, D. and Blomley, N. 2003. "Private Needs and Public Space: Politics, Poverty and Anti-Panhandling By-Laws in Canadian Cities." In *New Perspectives on the Public/Private Divide,* edited by the Law Commission of Canada. Vancouver: University of British Columbia Press.

Cooley, K. 1985. "Bums Out, Shoppers In: Downtown's Horton Plaza Park Gets a Shiny New Face." *Los Angeles Times* (San Diego Edition), September 6, p. 2.1.

Cox, K. and Mair, A. 1988. "Locality and Community in the Politics of Local Economic Development." *Annals of the Association of American Geographers* 78, 307–325.

Crawford, M. 1992. "The World in a Shopping Mall." In *Variations on a Theme Park: The New American City and the End of Public Space,* edited by M. Sorkin, 3–30. New York: Hill and Wang.

Crilley, D. 1993. "Megastructures and Urban Change: Aesthetics, Ideology and Design." In *The Restless Urban Landscape,* edited by P. Knox, ed., 126–164. Englewood Cliffs, NJ: Prentice Hall.

D'Arcus, B. 2001. "Marginal Protest and Central Authority: The Scalar Politics of the Wounded Knee Occupation." PhD diss., Syracuse University.

Davis, M. 1990. *City of Quartz: Excavating the Future in Los Angeles.* London: Verso.

Domosh, M. 1998. "'Those Gorgeous Incongruities': Polite Politics and Public Space on the Streets of Nineteenth Century New York City." *Annals of the Association of American Geographers* 88: 209–226.

Ellickson, R. 1996. "Controlling Chronic Misconduct in City Spaces: Of Panhandlers, Skid Rows, and Public Space Zoning." *Yale Law Journal* 105: 1165–1248.

Enge, M. 1985. "Hahn Puts Up $1 Million to House San Diego's Poor." *Los Angeles Times* (San Diego Edition), June 11, p. 2.3.

Flusty, S. 2001. "The Banality of Interdiction: Surveillance, Control and the Displacement of Diversity." *International Journal of Urban and Regional Research* 25, 658–664.

Frammolino, R. 1985. "Residential Hotels Win Panel's Favor." *Los Angeles Times* (San Diego Edition), November 21, p. 2.1.

Frammolino, R. 1986. "Council Passes Strict Zoning, Building Rules for Eastern Downtown." *Los Angeles Times* (San Diego Edition), September 24, p. 2.3.

Fraser, N. 1990. "Rethinking the Public Sphere: A Contribution to Actually Existing Democracy." *Social Text* 25/26, 56–79.

Gleeson, B. 1998. *Geographies of Disability.* London: Routledge.

Goss, J. 1993. "The 'Magic of the Mall': An Analysis of Form, Function, and Meaning in the Contemporary Retail Built Environment." *Annals of the Association of American Geographers* 83, 18–47.

Goss, J. 1996. "Once-Upon-a-Time in the Commodity World: An Unofficial Guide to Mall of America." *Annals of the Association of American Geographers* 89, 45–75.

Granberry, M. 1991. "Face-Lift Crew Deposes Park Vagrants." *Los Angeles Times* (San Diego Edition), June 21, p. B.1.

Hager, P. 1986. "Justices to Consider Mall Ban on Political Skits." *Los Angeles Times* (Home Edition), October 25, p. 1.28.

Hager, P. 1987. "High Court Won't Hear Free-Speech Case Involving Protest Play at Mall." *Los Angeles Times* (Home Edition), May 2, p. 1.32.

Hall, T. and Hubbard, P., eds. 1998. *The Entrepreneurial City: Geographies of Politics, Regime, and Representation.* London: Wiley.

Hamilton, P. 1994. "The Metamorphosis of Downtown San Diego: How Centre City Development Corporation has Guided Downtown from a Quiet, Office Only Area into a Vibrant Urban Center." *Urban Land* 53 (4), 32–38.

Harris, S. 1985. "Far From the Dusty Lot and Dilapidated Downtown of Only 3 Years Ago…: Horton Becomes a Happening on Opening Day." *Los Angeles Times* (San Diego Edition), August 10, p. 2.1.

Harvey, D. (1982) 1999. *The Limits to Capital.* London: Verso.

Harvey, D. 1989a. *The Condition of Postmodernity.* Oxford, UK: Blackwell.

Harvey, D. 1989b. *The Urban Experience.* Oxford, UK: Blackwell.

Hershkovitz, L. 1993. "Tiananmen Square and the Politics of Place." *Political Geography* 12, 395–420.

Hopkins, J. 1990. "West Edmonton Mall: Landscapes of Myth and Elsewhereness." *Canadian Geographer* 30, 2–17.

Horstman, B. 1990. "City OKs Removal of Grass, Benches at Horton Plaza." *Los Angeles Times* (San Diego Edition), October 9, p. B.3.

Huard, R. 2000. "Council Backs Private Patrols Downtown: City Labor Union Raises Objection." *San Diego Union-Tribune*, February 2, p. B.3.

Imre, R. 1996. *Disability and the City: International Perspectives.* London: Paul Chapman.

Jameson, F. 1985. "Postmodernism, or the Cultural Logic of Late Capitalism." *New Left Review* 146, 53–92.

Johnson, G. 1990. "City Yanks Benches from Under Undesirables Downtown: Council Adopts Plan to Replace Grass with Flowers, Remove Benches in an Effort to Roust Criminals and Drunks at Horton Plaza." *Los Angeles Times* (San Diego Edition), July 3, p. B.2.

Jonas, A. and Wilson, D., eds. 1999. *The Urban Growth Machine: Critical Perspectives, Two Decades Later.* Albany, NY: State University of New York Press.

Jones, L. 1985. "Lack of Toilets Downtown a Problem: Council Gets Lesson on Restrooms." *Los Angeles Times* (San Diego Edition), March 14, p. 2.3.

Katz, C. 2001. "Hiding the Target: Social Reproduction in the Privatized Urban Environment." In *Postmodern Geography: Theory and Praxis, edited by C. Minca, 94–110.* Oxford. UK: Blackwell.

Kearns, G. and Philo, C., eds. 1993. *Selling the City: The City as Cultural Capital, Past and Present.* Oxford, UK: Pergamon.

King, J. 1993. "Old-Fashioned Crackdown: San Diego Goes After 'Panhasslers'." *San Francisco Chronicle*, January 16, p. A.1.

Knox, P., ed. 1993. *The Restless Urban Landscape.* Englewood Cliffs, NJ: Prentice Hall.

Krueckeberg, D. 1995. "The Difficult Character of Property: To Whom Do Things Belong?" *Journal of the American Planning Association* 61, 301–309.

Lees, L. 1998. "Urban Renaissance and the Street: Spaces of Control and Contestation." In *Images of the Street: Planning, Identity, and Control in Public Space,* edited by N. Fyfe, 236–253. London: Routledge.

Lees, L. 2001. "Towards a Critical Geography of Architecture: The Case of an Ersatz Colosseum." *Ecumene* 8, 51–86.

Lefebvre, H. 1996. *Writings on Cities.* E. Kofman and E. Lebas, trans. and eds. Oxford, UK: Blackwell.

Los Angeles Times. 1985. "Horton Plaza Exudes Life" [Editorial]. *Los Angeles Times* (San Diego Edition), August 18, p. 2.2.

Los Angeles Times. 1990. "The Homeless Lose More Ground: Actions by Council, Shelter Agency Leave Indigent in the Cold" [Editorial]. *Los Angeles Times* (San Diego Edition), July 8, p. B.2.

Lemke, C. 1987. "Monitor to Assure Security: Public Restrooms Will Open Soon Downtown." *Los Angeles Times* (San Diego Edition), April 23, p. 2.3.

Logan, J. and Molotch, H. 1987. *Urban Fortunes: The Political Economy of Place.* Berkeley, CA: University of California Press.

Low, S. 2000. *On the Plaza: The Politics of Public Space and Culture.* Austin, TX: University of Texas Press.

McCann, E. 1999. "Race, Protest and Place: Contextualizing Lefebvre in the US City." *Antipode* 31, 163–184.

MacLeod, G. 2002. "From Urban Entrepreneurialism to a 'Revanchist City'? On the Spatial Injustices of Glasgow's Renaissance." *Antipode* 34: 602–624.

Macpherson, C. 1978. *Property: Mainstream and Critical Positions.* Toronto: University of Toronto Press.

Magnet, M., ed. 2000. *The Millennial City: A New Urban Paradigm for 21st-Century America.* Chicago: Ivan R. Dee.

Marston, S. 1990. "Who Are 'The People'? Gender, Citizenship, and the Making of the American Nation." *Environment and Planning D: Society and Space* 8, 449–458.

Miller, M. 1985. "Homeless Get Help—But It's Too Little." *Los Angeles Times* (San Diego Edition), February 11, p. 2.1.

Millican, A. 2000. "'Ambassadors' to Work for a Clean, Safe Downtown." *San Diego Union-Tribune,* July 28, p. B.2.

Mitchell, D. 1995. "The End of Public Space? People's Park, Definitions of the Public, and Democracy." *Annals of the Association of American Geographers* 85, 108–133.

Mitchell, D. 1996. "Political Violence, Order, and the Legal Construction of Public Space: Power and the Public Forum Doctrine." *Urban Geography* 17, 158–178.

Mitchell, D. 1997. "The Annihilation of Space By Law: The Roots and Implications of Anti-Homeless Laws in the United States." *Antipode* 29, 303–335.

Mitchell, D. 2002. "Controlling Space, Controlling Scale: Migrant Labor, Free Speech, and the Regional Development in the American West in the Early 20th Century." *Journal of Historical Geography,* 28, 63–84.

Mitchell, D. 2003. *The Right to the City: Social Justice and the Fight for Public Space.* New York: Guilford.

Molotch, H. 1976. "The City as Growth Machine." *American Journal of Sociology* 82, 309–332.

National Law Center on Homelessness and Poverty (NLCHP). 1996. *Mean Sweeps: A Report on Anti-Homeless Laws, Litigation, and Alternatives in 50 United States Cities.* Washington, DC: NLCHP.

Ouroussoff, N. 2000. "Architecture: Fantasies of a City High on a Hill; Commentary: The Expansion of Citywalk Embraces the Myth of Mall Culture that Shies Away from the Grittier Realities of Urban Life." *Los Angeles Times* (San Diego Edition), April 9, Calendar 4.

Pain, R. 1991. "Space, Sexual Violence, and Social Control: Integrating Geographical and Feminist Analyses of Women's Fear of Crime." *Progress in Human Geography* 15, 317–394.

Pain, R. 1997. "Social Geographies of Women's Fear of Crime." *Transactions of the Institute of British Geographers* 22, 231–244.

Pain, R. 2000. "Place, Social Relations and the Fear of Crime: A Review." *Progress in Human Geography* 24, 365–387.

Perry, A. 1989. "San Diego At Large: Shop Till You Drop, But Don't Expect a Bench." *Los Angeles Times* (San Diego Edition), January 13, p. 2.1.
Perry, T. 1993. "No Alms for the 'Panhasslers': Cities: San Diego Cracks Down on Aggressive Beggars Who Block Paths and Use Threatening Language…" *Los Angeles Times* (San Diego Edition), January 12, p. A.3.
Ruddick, S. 1996. *Young and Homeless in Hollywood.* New York: Routledge.
San Diego Police Department. N.d. *A Citizen's Guide to the Control of Transient-Related Crime.* PD-932-CR. San Diego: San Diego Police Department.
Schacter, J. 1985. "Gaslamp Card Room Face Switch in City's Efforts to Oust Them." *Los Angeles Times* (San Diego Edition), August 20, p. 2.2.
Schraeger, S. 1994. "A Low-Rent Housing Alternative." *Urban Land* 53(4), 40–43.
Schwartz, R. 1985. "Downtown Hotel Residents Losing Their Meager Homes." *Los Angeles Times* (San Diego Edition), September 13, p. 2.1.
Serrano, R. 1988. "Downtown's Troublesome Pocket of Crime: Pimps, Panderers and Pushers Makes This Stretch of 7th Avenue Home Turf." *Los Angeles Times* (San Diego Edition), August 22, p. 2.1.
Showley, R. 1994. "Coming of Age: San Diego's Development Markets." *Urban Land* 53, no. 4, 21–30, 80–81.
Smith, N. 1979. "Toward a Theory of Gentrification: A Back to the City Movement by Capital Not People." *Journal of the American Planning Association* 45, 538–548.
Smith N. 1990. *Uneven Development: Nature, Capital, and the Production of Space, 2d ed.* Oxford, UK: Blackwell.
Smith N. 1996. *The New Urban Frontier: Gentrification and the Revanchist City.* New York: Routledge.
Sorkin, M., ed. 1992. *Variations on a Theme Park: The New American City and the End of Public Space.* New York: Hill and Wang.
Staeheli, L. 1996. "Publicity, Privacy, and Women's Political Action." *Environment and Planning D: Society and Space* 14, 601–619.
Staeheli, L. and Clark, S. 1995. "Gender, Place and Citizenship." In *Gender in Urban Research,* edited by J. Garber and R. Turner, 3–23. Beverly Hills, CA: Sage.
Staeheli, L. and Mitchell, D. 2004. "Spaces of Public and Private." In *Spaces of Democracy,* edited by M. Low and C. Barnett, 147–160. London: Sage.
Stone, C. 1989. *Regime Politics: Governing Atlanta, 1946–1988.* Lawrence, KS: University of Kansas Press.
Sugrue, T. 1996. *The Origins of the Urban Crisis: Race and Inequality in Postwar Detroit.* Princeton, NJ: Princeton University Press.
Sutro, D. 1989. "Architecture: Urban Space Message for San Diego." *Los Angeles Times* (San Diego Edition), March 22, p. 5.1.
Vobejda, B. and Havemann, J. 1996. "Large U.S. Cities Target Homeless, Advocates Say." *Washington Post,* December 12, p. A.23.
Waldron, J. 1991. "Homelessness and the Issue of Freedom." *UCLA Law Review* 39, 295–324.
Walker, R. 1981. "A Theory of Suburbanization: Capitalism and the Construction of Urban Space in the United States." In *Urbanization and Urban Planning in Capitalist Society,* edited by M. Dear and A. Scott, 383–429. London: Methuen.
Whyte, W. 1988. *City: Rediscovering the Center.* New York: Doubleday.
Young, I. 1991. *Justice and the Politics of Difference.* Princeton, NJ: Princeton University Press.
Zukin, S. 1991. *Landscapes of Power: From Detroit to Disney World.* Berkeley, CA: University of California Press.
Zukin, S. 1995. *The Cultures of Cities.* Oxford, UK: Blackwell.

Interviews

Transcripts of Interviews (for those not retaining confidentiality) are held by both authors and may be viewed upon request.
Allsbrook, Dave, Centre City Development Corporation, 1/24/01
Baranowski, Fred, President, Downtown San Diego Partnership, 1/25/01
Binder, Steve, Public Defender and Founder of "Homeless Court," 1/25/01

Carroll, Father Joe, Executive Director, St. Vincent de Paul, 1/25/01
Cohelan, Tim, Public Interest Lawyer, 1/23/01
Cornell, Marilyn, Homeless Advocate, 1/23/01
Downtown Worker, Anonymous, 1/24/01
Johnston, Rosemary, Interfaith Shelter Network, 1/23/01
Keller, Bill, President Gaslamp Quarter Association and Business Owner, 1/26/01
McElroy, Bob, Executive Director, Alpha Project, 1/26/01
Mitchell, Mitch, Vice President for Public Policy, San Diego Chamber of Commerce, 1/26/01
Social Service Provider, Anonymous, 1/24/01
Stepner, Mike, Planner and Former City Architect, 1/23/01
Wade, Leslie, East Village Association, 1/25/01
Witt, John, Former City Attorney, 1/24/01
Zinner, Jeff, Centre City Development Corporation, 1/24/01

Index

E

Edge-cities, 43–44
Edge nodes, 36, 43–44
Ely, R., 57
Embourgeoisement, process of, *see*
  Public space, in Second
  Empire Paris
Emmet, T., 132, 133, 135, 136
Enclosure, *see* Gated communities, zoning,
  taxes, and incorporation of
Energy consumption, 43
England, 50, 52
Enlightenment, 2
Entrepreneurs, expectations of, 53
Environmentalists, 45, 58, 59
Epstein, R., 69
Essen, 123
Ewen, E., 38
"The Eyes of the Poor" (Baudelaire),
  18–19

F

Facilitation Act of 1995 (DFA), 130
Fair housing legislation, 45
The Fall of Public Man (Sennett), 22
Fanon, F., 127
Federal Housing Administration (FHA),
  35, 36, 37, 38, 39, 58
Federal tax policies, 44; *see also* Private,
  urban-scale construction
Filner, B., 156
Fischler, M. S., 86
Florida, 86
Fort Worth, TX, 49
Foucault, M., 6, 86
Foundation for Research on Economics
  and the Environment (FREE), 67,
  68, 69
Fournel, V., 29
Frammolino, R., 158
France, 24
Frank, T., 15
Frantz, K., 84, 85
Fraser, N., 4, 144
Fraser Institute, 68
Friedman, M., 62

G

Gaines, J., 94, 95
Garnett, W., 40
Garreau, J., 43
Gated communities, zoning, taxes, and
  incorporation of
  conclusion, 99–100
  defining gated community, 84–85
  enthonographic cases/settings, 88–91
  enthonographic methodology/analysis,
    92–99
  history of the gated community, 85–86
  introduction, 9–10, 81–84
  rise of gated communities, 86–88
Geography, defining, 6–7
Ghettoization, *see* Political economy, of
  public space
Ghraib, A., 13
Gilder, R., 120
Giuliani, R., 2, 20, 112
Gleeson, B., 144
Global positioning systems (GPS), 107
Golding, S., 160
Gordon, L., 116
Goss, J., 144
Gottlieb, A., 68
Granberry, M., 156
Gray, J., 59
Great Depression, 37, 46
Greater Metropolitan Region (Los
  Angeles), CA, 88, 89, 93–94, 99
Greenbelt Towns, 37
Greendale, WI, 41
Greenham Common, 61

H

Habermas, J., 4, 6
Hahn, E., 147, 157, 158
Halper, E., 100
Halperin, L., 155
Hamilton, P., 150
Hanchett, T., 44
Hardin, G., 9, 64, 65, 67, 68, 70, 73
Harlem, NY, 113
Harlem River Houses for African
  Americans, 37